THIS BOOK IS A SPECIAL GIFT

TO:

_____

FROM:

_____

DATE:

_____

MESSAGE:

_____

_____

THE VOICE

366 DEVOTIONS TO LEAD YOU ON YOUR WAY

BEHIND YOU

"THIS IS THE WAY; WALK IN IT." ISAIAH 30:21

Solly Ozrovech

CHRISTIAN ART PUBLISHERS

Originally published by Christian Publishing
Company under the title *Die stem agter jou*

© 2002

English edition © 2002
CHRISTIAN ART PUBLISHERS
P O Box 1599, Vereeniging, 1930

First edition 2002

Translated by Louise Emerton
Cover designed by Christian Art Publishers

Set in 12 on 14 pt Weidemann Book by Christian Art Publishers

Printed in Singapore

ISBN 1-86852-904-5

02 03 04 05 06 07 08 09 10 11 – 10 9 8 7 6 5 4 3 2 1

RIBUTE

With *A Voice Behind You*, Christian Art Publishers celebrates Solly Ozrovech's 75th birthday, and pays tribute to a remarkable and popular writer.

Solly Ozrovech's devotion to the Creator runs like a golden thread through his life. Since his conversion at the age of sixteen, he has been a powerful instrument in the hands of the Lord. After working as a full time minister for forty years, he dedicated himself to writing. His inspirational books have had an unequalled impact on the Christian book market. His books enrich millions of readers both locally and internationally, encouraging them to develop a more intimate relationship with their Savior.

During his almost 15 year association with CAP, approximately 60 books have emerged from this gifted writer's pen, contributing uniquely to the extension of God's Kingdom.

May this book in particular be a guide to readers, blessing each one and inspiring spiritual growth so that the precious love of our Creator God can impact more lives.

Together with Solly Ozrovech, we say: *Soli Deo Gloria!*

– Chris Johnsen –
Publisher

OREWORD

The child of God walks along an unknown path to eternity. And many fear this unfamiliar road. They are like children lost in a dark, fearful forest. They quiver at strange noises amongst the shadowy trees; they fear monsters lurking in the shadows ready to attack unsuspecting travelers; they are afraid to go back ... and they are uncertain about the road ahead; the paths to the right and left are filled with imaginary terrors, and so they end up walking in circles.

But the child of God is not a traveler to nowhere; not a wanderer without direction; not a seeker who never finds; not children of the wind – but children of the Almighty God! We are faced with choices every day: forward or back; left or right? What should we do? Who will advise us? How reassuring then to hear a confident, loving voice whispering over your shoulder: "THIS IS THE WAY, WALK IN IT."

At times in our lives the voices of people can no longer reach us. We cannot hear them and we cannot listen because our need is too great; our sorrow is too unbearable; our illness too life-threatening; our children have strayed too far; our marriage is in troubled waters. But God's voice can always reach us with His guidance, comfort, healing and reconciliation. Wherever we find ourselves in despair and doubt, in every crisis, God's voice will reach us. What depth and range are to be found in His voice! In this book we hear God's greatest declaration of love: He gives us His Son, the Living Christ: He is the WAY, the TRUTH and the LIFE! May you be bountifully touched by His Holy Spirit and hear His Voice clearly as you read this book.

DEDICATION

With grateful memories to Dr. Gawie Hugo; a family doctor who saw his duty as a calling.

To his wife, Rita: may God's voice comfort you and may His grace touch your life in many ways each day.

January

The LORD replied, "My Presence will go with you, and I will give you rest."

Then Moses said to Him, "If Your Presence does not go with us, do not send us up from here."

~ Exodus 33:14-15 ~

Prayer

Holy God and our heavenly Father in Jesus Christ: "If Your presence does not go with us!" The mere thought is frightening. We need You so much on this pilgrimage into the unknown.

If Your Presence does not go with us, we will be "alone" and at the mercy of the unknown in our time of need, conflict, failure and disappointments; in our family life; in life and in death!

Without You there is no future: no Light on our way, no Promised Land waiting for us, no future and no Eternity!

Go with us, Lord, because without You we do not want to risk the unknown. Without Your love and mercy we cannot survive. Without Salvation in Jesus Christ we cannot be Your children. Without Your Holy Spirit we have no Guide on our path through life.

Lord our God and Father, please accompany us every step of the way into the uncharted future of a new year. As You have been with us in the past, please be with us once again in the future.

Let Your peace be with us.

Let Your love enfold us through Christ.

Let Your Holy Spirit be our daily Guide.

Let the joy of salvation through Your Son, our Savior, fill our hearts.

May the Holy Spirit inspire us at all times.

We plead with You Lord: *"If Your Presence does not go with us, do not send us up from here."* We ask this in the Name that is exalted above all others, in the Name of our Savior, Jesus Christ.

Amen

A New Year; A new way; the same God!

I will instruct you and teach you in the way you should go; I will counsel you and watch over you.

~ PSALM 32:8 ~

The prospect of a new year could be both disquieting and exciting. It could be exciting because it could be a year filled with new possibilities and opportunities and, at the same time, disquieting if you face the unknown future with anxiety, wondering whether the problems and disasters of the past will repeat themselves.

When we reflect on the future, it is a rather common mistake to allow the events of the past to cloud our vision. International crises, financial setbacks, droughts, floods, as well as personal problems and disappointments tend to dictate our pattern of thought when we ponder the possible consequences for us.

Today, more so than ever before, the moment has come to place your unwavering trust in the omniscience of God. He truly cares about you and He loves you profoundly: *But because of his great love for us, God, who is rich in mercy, made us alive with Christ ...* (Eph. 2:4). Everyone has a need for love: true, profound and sincere love. Various personal and social factors indicate that mankind lost this love due to the Fall. It is small wonder then that there are so many instances of suicide, divorce, family conflict, stresses and strains, and even war. Therefore, you will have to rediscover, without delay, the fact that in this loveless world there is still Somebody who has a special interest in you: a God in heaven who is Love and who loves you tenderly.

Believe in the promises of Jesus and approach the new year in the presence of the living Christ. He will guide you through the labyrinth of life because He knows what is best for you. Your duty lies in obeying Him. Then your anxiety will be replaced with self-awareness born of the love of God!

You are truly a God of Love! Thank You for sending Your only Son to bring about my salvation too. Amen.

Psalm 32:1-11

THE DISCIPLINE OF PRAYER

Do not be anxious about anything, but in everything, by prayer and petition, with thanksgiving, present your requests to God.

~ PHILIPPIANS 4:6 ~

O f all the Christian disciplines, prayer is probably the one most commonly practised and, often, the least understood. So many people regard prayer as a life jacket only to be used in the most desperate of circumstances. Yet again, others regard it as a method of telling God what they really want, including asking for His blessing for a decision already taken. With such attitudes it is easy to understand why so many people believe that their prayers go unanswered.

A relationship of prayer is a process that is established and strengthened over many years. Only then will your prayer life become meaningful and fulfilling. You have to develop an affinity for the living Christ by constantly acknowledging His holy presence in your everyday life. It is a process of growing closer to Christ through Bible study and meditation in the quiet presence of the peace of God.

Prayer is not only talking to God, but also listening to Him. If we listen with our souls and our minds, God will talk to us through the Holy Spirit and reveal His plan for our lives. Prayer that results in obedience to His will, transforms the act of praying into a pulsating and dynamic force in our spiritual life.

Do not forget to thank and praise God throughout the year for the privilege of prayer. Cast all your cares, fears, problems and requests upon Him knowing that He grants you what is best for you. Ask Him for grace to handle every situation to the best of your ability. Then wait patiently on the Lord and be sensitive to the whisperings of the Holy Spirit. He will lead you on the path of peace – peace that transcends all understanding. As His will unfolds itself and you obey it, the way forward will become clear.

Lord, I wish to glorify You forever, through Christ, as my Father. Through the guidance of the Holy Spirit, help me to obey You in prayer as well. Amen.

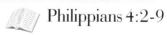 Philippians 4:2-9

ℒOVE IS THE MOST EXCELLENT WAY

And now I will show you the most excellent way.

~ 1 Corinthians 13:1 ~

I n order to tread the path into a new year successfully, we must ensure that the road of our choice is the most excellent way. This we can only achieve with the help of the Holy Spirit. The divergent doctrines we hear concerning Jesus Christ, are confusing for many people whose intentions are sincere. What should one believe about Jesus Christ when His followers are divided into a thousand splinter groups that are often antagonistic towards one another?

Our religion is not a system of theories about Jesus Christ. It is Christ. In the maze of conflicting Christian viewpoints there are certain guidelines that rise above all differences and create understanding and goodwill. The greatest of these is love. Jesus was the embodiment of God's perfect Love. He calls on us to walk the path of love: *"I am the Way"* (cf. Jn. 14:6). No compromise can be tolerated. If we wish to follow the most excellent way, we must follow the way of His love.

A response to the challenge of Christian love calls for deep devotion. Even when you have given everything, you still want to give more. It is then that you open your life to the influence of the Holy Spirit. That which you cannot achieve by own effort and strength, God will achieve through you. Should you wish to love as Christ did, you must allow Him to live in your heart and mind, revealing His love through you.

What does it mean to believe in the love of Christ? To be able to recite a confession by heart? To belong to a specific church? No, it is to have a wonderful, mighty and loving Master whom we love and trust completely, whom we will follow devotedly and who enables us to increasingly become that which God meant us to be. That is the life to which Christ is calling you this year and, even if His standard is high, it is not impossible, because His Holy Spirit residing in us makes the impossible possible – to choose the best: to choose Love!

Lord, reveal Your love in my life so that I may love my neighbor. Help me to aspire to this commandment of Yours. Amen.

 1 Corinthians 13:13

WORD OF LIFE: GOD'S WORD

I want you to know, brothers, that the gospel I preached is not something that man made up.

~ GALATIANS 1:11 ~

No right-minded Christian would venture into the new year without being armed with the Word of God. From the beginning of man's existence on earth, he has developed theories on a wide variety of subjects. Some of these are based on his religious convictions or on a philosophical premise; others display the product of man's own brainpower or imagination; and others still are the result of academic research.

A large number of people regard the Bible with scepticism. Others, again, apply scientific principles to analyze the Bible in their quest for evidence that will placate their reason. All of this naturally leads to conflicting views that contribute little more than to confuse and obscure the whole issue of the authority of the Bible. These people render the Word to be as clear as muddy water for the ordinary reader.

Although the Word of God was the subject of fierce criticism through the ages, it has remained steadfast. Theories differed from one another; scientific formulae changed; viewpoints diverged, but the Eternal Word of the Eternal God, based on truth and wisdom from above, remained constant. As the writer of Hymns confesses: ... *Through His Spirit God effects it: words of perfect clarity which lead us to reality* (Hymn 305:1).

The Bible's message has been divinely inspired. The Gospels set a pattern for your daily life that has stood the test of time. Abide by the Bible's teachings steadfastly this year. You will find these to be a source of never-ending inspiration, stability and peace.

Thank You Father, that I may build my life on You, and thank You for the knowledge that You never falter. Strengthen my faith so that I will not doubt. Amen.

Galatians 1:11-24

SEIZE THE DAY!

"... At the time of my favor I heard you, and in the day of salvation I helped you."

~ 2 CORINTHIANS 6:2 ~

When you look back on the life that you have lived, you can, quite easily, point out the highlights of certain special days: when you first fell in love, your first day in a responsible position, and then that cherished moment when you were confronted with the living Christ and you became aware of the wonderful reality of Him. These, and other times, may be classified as "great" moments in your life.

By emphasizing the "great" moments of life, you run the risk of exposing the many things in life that are ordinary and lacking in excitement. How wonderful it would be if every day could be lived on a high spiritual and inspirational level. The truth is that every day could be a "great" day in your life if only you appreciated and exploited the present and passing moment. Every day is a new birth with new prospects and opportunities that fall to you from the loving hand of God so that you can *live*. We must say *Yes!* to life in totality. Jesus says in John 10:10: *"... I have come that they may have life, and have it to the full."* Accept every moment of every day as a gift of grace from the hand of God and utilise it fully. Then every day will be a "great" day.

Cherish you memories, but appreciate the importance and wonderful possibilities of "today". Your attitude towards today will influence all your tomorrows, therefore "today" could be the greatest and most creative moment of your whole life. Do not regard it as less important, but thank God for the opportunities it presents. Today you can draw on the memories of yesteryear; today you can receive forgiveness from God; today you can erase the sins and failures of the past; today you can create the foundations for an even greater tomorrow!

When I am confused and surrounded by darkness, I know that You will deliver me. You are great and good, and do not scorn my feeble prayers. Thank You for your constant presence. Amen.

 2 Corinthians 6:1-10

THE ROAD AHEAD

"Have I not commanded you? Be strong and courageous. Do not be terrified; do not be discouraged, for the LORD your God will be with you wherever you go."

~ JOSHUA 1:9 ~

It is with a heart filled with sincere gratitude towards God that we look back on the road that we have traveled during the past year. It could well be that, for you, it was a year filled with a multitude of problems or bitter sorrow. Give thanks to God that the past is irrevocably behind you. However, meet the future with fervent prayer and in the infinite hope that, by the grace of God, this will be a better year. Karl Barth said that to *hope* is to hear tomorrow's music today.

Although many people try to discover the secrets that the future holds, nobody knows what really is in store for any of us. It is God-given wisdom to stop fretting about the future and what it may hold. Prepare yourself for any eventuality that God may bring on your path.

The Scouts' motto is: "Be prepared!" These words also hold a spiritual depth and quality that few people judge according to merit. To be able to enter the unknown future in hope and trust, a positive and living faith in God is imperative. Such a faith is more than a mere intellectual accord regarding the existence of an Eternal Being. It is a firm conviction that the living Christ is the perfect manifestation of God the Creator, and that He dwells in the hearts and lives of those who love Him.

When Christ lives in your heart and in your thoughts and you are conscious of your oneness with Him, you will be able to face the new year without fear. You will have the quiet reassurance that you will not be confronted by any situation that you and the living Christ within you, will not be able to surmount together.

Lord, I rejoice in the knowledge that You hold my life in Your hands. I trust You with my entire life. Thank You for the inspiration of Your Word. Amen.

Joshua 1:1-9

⊙HE VOICE OF GOD

"Go and lie down, and if he calls you, say, 'Speak, LORD, for your servant is listening.'"

~ I SAMUEL 3:9 ~

When one studies the Scriptures with care, one finds many occasions when people heard the voice of God. It seems as though we, in our time, do not witness such dramatic and holy moments when people hear God's voice coming from the clouds. However, it does not mean that God is no longer talking to us. In fact, there are numerous instances where there is not the slightest doubt that the hand of God has touched the lives of people, consequently changing their lives radically. Through their obedience they were led in a specific direction by God.

If you, in your life, maintain an intimate walk with God and remain sensitive to the whisperings of the Holy Spirit, you will discover that you will soon be in harmony with God's will. This, especially, requires the discipline of prayer and meditation. We must learn to be silent in the holy presence of the Lord. You will then gradually discover that you are becoming increasingly aware of His voice in all situations of your life.

It is precisely then that you must pursue the highest measure of faith. Instead of acting on impulse, you learn to wait for the Lord and for His guidance. It may be revealed to you through intuition, by the circumstances in which you find yourself, or through the guidance and actions of those around you; just like Elijah was mentor to Samuel. But you will know without doubt when God speaks to you. And later, upon looking back down the road, circumstances will confirm this fact. God speaks to man in a thousand voices, if only our soul would listen. He has His own unique way of talking to each individual. We need only learn to be sensitive to the voice of God.

Lord, You are so wonderful, because You cleansed me with Your blood. Thank You that I may live as a saved soul. Amen.

 1 Samuel 3:1-10

𝒫RAY — REGARDLESS …

"When my life was ebbing away, I remembered you, LORD, and my prayer rose to you, to your holy temple."

~ JONAH 2:7 ~

𝓜 any people deny themselves the privilege of the peace of God, simply because they feel too undeserving to talk to God. When in despair, they will not draw near to the throne of mercy because, in the past, they have not spent much time in the presence of the Lord. They thus feel that they are not entitled to draw near to Him in times of distress. Others, yet again, are overwhelmed by feelings of guilt or shame about something that has happened and therefore they hesitate to draw near to God in prayer. Whatever the philosophy behind their thoughts, they deprive themselves of the peace of God, which surpasses all understanding. In this way, they fail to find the way through which the deepest human despair can be softened.

Jesus has promised that He will not cast out anybody who comes to Him. He also emphasized that He had not come to call the righteous, but sinners to salvation. Throughout the Scriptures you can read of His unfathomable mercy and endless love that reach out to all people: the good and the bad, the worthy and the unworthy.

It is never too late for you to turn to Him who answers all prayers and to put your problems before Him. He will always hear your call of despair and embrace you with His love. However unworthy you may feel at this moment, reach out to Him in prayer and He will take you by the hand – and nobody will snatch you from His hand. Regardless of how difficult it may seem, under no circumstances should you deny yourself the mercy of His peace. Through disciplined prayer time, even you will be able to savor His grace. Hem each day with prayer and you may rest assured that it will not fray at the edges.

Father, I want to live my whole life glorifying You. Help me not to lose sight of You when times are difficult. Guide me towards obedience through Your Spirit. Amen.

Jonah 2:1-7

GOD'S PERFECT TIMING

... I am the LORD; in its time I will do this swiftly.

~ ISAIAH 60:22 ~

Never get impatient with God because He does not react to your despair when you desire. It is only when you live in perfect harmony with Him that His perfect timing becomes clear to you. It is wrong to try to subject and hold the omniscient God to your timetable. You look at the circumstances and problems that weigh you down from the perspective of time, while God sees the larger picture from the perspective of eternity. Therefore, remind yourself constantly during the year that lies ahead, that God's timing is always perfect; even though it may not always seem that way to you, and even though you may find it extremely difficult to adjust to this.

Very often we find it difficult to accept God's timing. Sometimes we rush into His presence with an urgent request, commanding Him to act – and to do so immediately before disaster strikes! It is then that you act from your own strength, according to your own discretion and wisdom – and the consequences are usually disastrous. The honest truth is that your timing is not synchronised with God's.

If you want to keep pace with God's timing, you must truly know Him to begin with. The first and most important requirement is to develop a meaningful relationship with God. Naturally, this also applies to your Savior, the Living Christ. When His will becomes of primary importance to you, then only will you become aware of God's perfect timing in your life and you will come to understand it. You will no longer be ruled by panic-stricken thoughts or actions, nor will you be carried away in a fit of anxiety by an emergency situation caused by external circumstances. Then you will know the quiet contentment and peace of mind that are a part of those who have implicit faith in God.

Lord, You are omnipresent. When I lose all hope, You are there. You will even deliver me from death. Thank You that I may know that my life is safe in Your hands. Amen.

Isaiah 60:17-22

GOD'S UNCEASING PRESENCE

"... And surely I am with you always, to the very end of the age."
~ MATTHEW 28:20 ~

The nearness of the living Christ to everybody who is in need of Him, is one of the great and comforting messages of the Gospel. Nevertheless, many people find it difficult to enter His presence. They spend painful hours in prayer to achieve this objective.

The Scriptural truth is that the Master is precisely there where you are. In your honest pursuit to get to know Him better, and through your efforts to break through your doubt and uncertainty to a clearer realization of His presence, He is involving you in a struggle and He wants to say to you, "Stop wrestling with the fear and doubt that are of your own making and come to Me. I will give you tranquillity and peace. I am with you, wherever you find yourself, even in your moments of deepest doubt." It will save you much heartache in the coming year if you take Jesus at His word and put your trust in Him because you believe that He is by your side.

Christian disciples know that in order to accept Christ's merciful and loving invitation, you must divest yourself of all the pet sins that have become part of your lifestyle. Some people want to enjoy the presence of the living Christ, but on their own selfish terms. That can never happen, because in order to experience and enjoy the presence of Christ, you must submit yourself to Christ's conditions.

Accepting the Lord as your Savior and Redeemer is the basis of your spiritual life and your union with Him. Without this foundation for your faith, you can never experience His presence. By embracing the living Christ as your Lord and Master, you also accept the merciful gift of His Holy Spirit into your life. Only then will you become vividly aware that, through His Holy Spirit, Jesus is present within you every moment and that He is always by your side.

> Lord, make my words and deeds of service acceptable to You. Allow Your power to work through me so that I may live for Your greater glory every day of my life. Amen.

Matthew 28:11-20

ℒIVE LIFE TO THE FULL

I know that there is nothing better for men than to be happy and do good while they live.

~ ECCLESIASTES 3:12 ~

𝕴t is not a sin to be happy. Your Heavenly Father gave you a life to be treasured and enjoyed to the full. Should it be filled with the spice of pealing laughter and humor, you are that much richer. True happiness can ease the stresses and strains of life and heal a confused spirit. When you have learnt to laugh at yourself, you are protected from the folly of pride and egoism. It brings your life into balance, with a freedom that you can get from no other source.

Live your life in such a way that it is interspersed with joy and happiness. Life will unfold itself with understanding and friendliness in all its beauty. You have reason for great joy: God loves you, Christ died for you, the Holy Spirit leads you onto joyous paths. If you are able to laugh at yourself, you will make this world a better place, not only for yourself, but also for those around you.

True happiness and joy only befall those who are at peace with themselves. To live with inner peace, you first have to be at peace with God. The sublime peace of God is the main source of true happiness, and it yields those qualities that are indispensable for a rewarding existence. Together with God's peace and the joy that flows from it, you arrive at greater understanding of your fellow man. You are in no hurry to pass judgement and never give in to the temptation of harsh words. You laugh with your fellow man, but never at him.

No man who is truly happy and who takes the best of what life has to offer will speak unfriendly or negative words about his fellow man. Make time to live life to the full and, with help from the Holy Spirit, develop a cheerful and friendly disposition. It always bears honest testimony of true Christlikeness.

Lord, You are present in every stage of my life. You comfort me in sorrow, but You also bless me in abundance. With You by my side, I will not be afraid of anything. Amen.

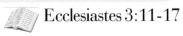 Ecclesiastes 3:11-17

NOURISH YOUR SOUL

... "I am the bread of life. He who comes to me will never go hungry, and he who believes in me will never be thirsty."

~ JOHN 6:35 ~

It is a sorrowful but undeniable fact that through the ages there have been people who have gone hungry. Many have died from starvation. Famine is usually mentioned together with other disasters such as floods, earthquakes, fire, wars and plagues. The consequences of famine can be devastating, resulting in physical and mental disabilities and maladjustment. Many social uprisings and instances of violence can be traced back to the suffering of hungry people.

Any thinking person knows the value of a nutritious and balanced diet. In order to achieve a healthy existence and meet the demands of daily life, food is essential. Neglecting your diet will inevitably result in listlessness, lethargy and a general lack of interest in the daily tasks awaiting you. Life becomes a soul-destroying monotony.

Never lose sight of the fact that your spiritual life also requires nourishment. It is an important and integral part of your existence on earth, as well as in eternity. A life that lacks the invigorating strength of the living Christ will soon lapse into an existence devoid of color and energy. You will stumble through life without course or direction. Therefore, make sure that you maintain a sustained conversation with this Christ, so that you can constantly draw on His strength flowing from His everlasting reserves. In this way you will ensure that your life will be powerfully enriched, because this very Jesus is living inside you through His Holy Spirit. Pray that the Lord will preserve you in the coming year from focusing solely on your physical needs while you have an urgent need for the Bread and Water of life. Jesus said in John 10:10: " ... *I have come that they may have life, and have it to the full.*"

Lord, You are my daily bread and Your truth sets me free. Thank You for presenting us with the Word so that we may get to know You better. Help me to find You therein. Amen.

John 6:30-40

May the God of peace ... equip you with everything good for doing his will.

~ HEBREWS 13:20-21 ~

ᑕhere are certain guidelines that apply to all Christians wishing to find the will of God for their lives. The call to sanctification, to spiritual growth, to love and serve your fellow man, are just a few expressions that apply to all those who love and serve Jesus Christ. But when your Christian field of experience becomes a personal experience you come face to face with the question: "Lord, what do You want of me?" If God has a specific task for you, He will guide you on His way and accompany you. As you become aware of His guidance, you will become enthusiastic about the work that He has entrusted to you.

This enthusiasm is important in your prayers; it will help you to discern the will of God. If you are sincere in your wish to know the will of God, plead with Him for your enthusiasm to grow. In this way you will be inspired by new, creative ideas and methods for effective service that will unexpectedly fill your thoughts. If you are not sure that the path which you have chosen is indeed God's chosen path for you, ask Him to diminish your enthusiasm. Keep your thoughts open and your spirit receptive to the work of God's Holy Spirit. Allow Him to increase or diminish your enthusiasm so that you can determine your path through life.

Trying to find the will of God through prayer has the additional benefit of a more intimate relationship with the Lord. It means that you will keep your spiritual ear tuned to the voice of God. Even if it takes time, it keeps you from allowing your enthusiasm to dominate and confuse God's guidance in your life.

When I am desperate, Lord, I may simply come to You. You give me wise guidance through Your Word to show me what is best for me. Amen.

Hebrews 13:20-25

WHEN DARK CLOUDS GATHER

"Surely God is my salvation; I will trust and not be afraid. The LORD, the LORD, is my strength and my song; he has become my salvation."

~ ISAIAH 12:2 ~

It would be extremely naive to think that ominous clouds will not gather, darkening our lives during the course of the new year. It would be even more futile to try and ignore them in the foolish belief that, by denying their existence, they would eventually just disappear. Unfortunately, the storm usually erupts, whether you want it to or not. It is far better to trustingly prepare for it by standing firm in a living faith in the almighty God who also controls the storms and hurricanes.

Never allow your Heavenly Father to be ousted from the centre of your life. Then His place will be taken by fear. However threatening the circumstances may be, it is imperative that you will not allow anything or anyone to usurp God's pivotal role in your life. With Him as the centre you will be able to maintain your balance at all times.

When your entire being is consumed by reverence and love for God, you will make the wonderful discovery that fear no longer rules your mind. Uncertainty is replaced by trust. You then develop a faith in God that enables you to meet the future with joyful self-assurance. The ominous clouds might still be present, but you will always see the silver lining, and you will have the steadfast knowledge that, behind every cloud, there is a loving Father who sees to it that everything culminates in your salvation. God might not disperse the clouds, but He enables you to see that even when thunderstorms threaten, He is still carving the holy design of your life because He loves you with a Divine love.

Even when everything around me is shrouded in darkness, You will shield me. Thank You for supporting and shielding me through Your love – even though I do not deserve it. Amen.

Isaiah 12:1-6

SALVATION: FACT, NOT FICTION

... "Everyone who calls on the name of the Lord will be saved."

~ ROMANS 10:13 ~

Since its early foundation, the Church has been subject to fierce criticism by sceptics and cynical, false teachers. There are those who adamantly believe in fate, and those who deny its existence; those who practise religion, and those who maintain that it is the height of folly. There are those who believe in the profound mystery of the Holy Trinity, and others who are doubtful. Nevertheless, the church of Jesus Christ has withstood the onslaughts for ages, it has even defied vicious persecution and torture. The Word of God still has pride of place as the most widely read book of all times.

No other book enjoys, or will ever enjoy, the universal respect that the Bible enjoys. The faith emanating from the Word can never be surpassed by anything the world could offer. Regardless of who you are: saint or hardened sinner; regardless of what you may do: good or evil; the living Christ offers you salvation and eternal life in God's eternal kingdom. All that is required of you is to turn to God in repentance, confess your sins and embrace Him as your Savior and Redeemer.

For many, these demands appear to be too simplistic to be true. Therefore, they turn to intellectual methods to achieve understanding. They allow their suspicions to rob them of the greatest Source of Peace at man's disposal. Look around you to see how Christ has changed people's lives: they did not buy or work for their salvation, nor did they steal or borrow it. They received it freely through repentance and confession: *Salvation is found in no one else, for there is no other name under heaven given to men by which we must be saved* (Acts 4:12).

> Lord, You became man in order to come and find that which was lost, to save and to serve. Open my eyes so that I may see Your hand all around me. Amen.

Romans 10:5-15

EVERLASTING ARMS UNDERNEATH YOU

"The eternal God is your refuge, and underneath are the everlasting arms."

~ DEUTERONOMY 33:27 ~

B ecause of the uncertainty of life, in the year that lies ahead you will often experience adversity, making you feel as if your world has disintegrated. This is usually the case when you are visited by major financial setbacks, serious illness, the death of a loved one, or by a radical change in lifestyle. Think of the many elderly people who experience a feeling of measureless despair because they have reached a stage in their lives when they inevitably have to move to a home for the aged.

Whatever the negative circumstances may be, and no matter how difficult the situation may seem, never lose sight of the fact that God keeps a loving vigil and that He will take you in His care. He will always provide a sanctuary for your ragged soul, where you will experience peace of mind amidst the ups and downs of life. See Him in your mind's eye where He awaits you with outstretched arms, forever ready to embrace you with His eternal love and endless grace. Make the consolation of our text for today the maxim to guide you into a courageous new year, and experience the healing balm of His peace that transcends all understanding.

In every crisis and every moment of despair you must trust in the Lord. Give yourself to Him without reservation and find serenity in His faithful care. Let your daily prayer of thanksgiving be: *You hem me in – behind and before; you have laid your hand upon me* (Ps. 139:5). Praise the Lord in the blessed assurance that He will take you in His care – today and forever.

I dwell in You and Your arms keep me safe. I want to live and act through You, because You are my Savior and my King. Amen.

Deuteronomy 33:24-29

REACH FOR SPIRITUAL MATURITY

When I was a child, I talked like a child, I thought like a child, I reasoned like a child. When I became a man, I put childish ways behind me.

~ 1 CORINTHIANS 13:11 ~

Little children are wonderful creatures and they afford us much joy and pleasure. However, it is tragic when little children remain little children. Many people have a spiritual rocking-horse existence: there is a lot of movement, but little progress. We must guard with all our might against the law of atrophy: that which is not utilised, wastes away and dies. There are many people who never achieve mental or spiritual maturity. The grudges of yesterday are transferred to today, poisoning their attitude and confusing their thoughts – every new day granted to them by God.

We must forget the insults and grudges that we have nurtured over the years. To state that a grudge is so real that it can't be forgotten, is to aggravate and perpetuate the poisoning. It could cause untold harm to your spirit and your spiritual development. It is merely another way of saying that you will never forgive and forget. The most damage is done to the life that harbors the grudge.

The quality of your Christlikeness should enable you to overcome insults, grudges and vexations that hamper your spiritual growth. Today you have an opportunity to grow by God's grace, to put the negative behind you and to reach for a future of exuberant spiritual growth. God presented us with the gift of the Holy Spirit to be our Mentor and Guide and to lead us to spiritual maturity. If you open your spirit to the influence of the Holy Spirit and allow Him to find expression in you, a new lifestyle will open to you. One aspect of this growth in your spiritual life is that it enables you to forgive and forget. Then you can concentrate on those things that contribute to your spiritual maturity.

Lord, I cannot do anything without You. Fill me with Your Spirit so that my life may grow and I may experience fulfilment in You. Amen.

1 Corinthians 13:1-13

ℛEACH FOR THE SKY!

I want to know Christ and the power of His resurrection and the fellowship and sharing in His sufferings, become like Him in His death, and so, somehow, to attain to the resurrection from the dead.

~ PHILIPPIANS 3:10-11 ~

Ambition is a commendable characteristic, provided it does not become an obsession with you as its slave. You must not endeavor to fulfil your ambitions at the expense of other people and objects. The damage to yourself and other people is incalculable. Remember the words of Jesus: "*What good will it be for a man if he gains the whole world, yet forfeits his soul? Or what can a man give in exchange for his soul?*" (Mt. 16:26).

There is one ideal in life that must overshadow all others: to live in the image of Christ. This must be the greatest ambition of every follower of Jesus. It is, after all, the pinnacle of our expectations in our Christian pilgrimage. It is therefore also an ambition that demands complete surrender and commitment.

The pure joy of a life in Jesus Christ cannot be measured. Such life is priceless and precious. It cannot be expressed in words, because there are simply not enough sounds to describe the ecstasy and plenitude of the life that Jesus offers His followers. It must, however, be remembered that the price of discipleship is sacrifice: sacrificing yourself, your thoughts, as well as your volition and all your ambitions and dreams. These must be laid on the altar of the living Christ so that His life can be reflected in you.

Initially, it might be regarded too high a price to pay, but as the triumphant resurrection followed the crucifixion of Jesus, so will the abundance of a life in Him, and through Him, be compensation for your complete surrender to your Savior and Redeemer.

Lord, I want to devote my entire life to Your service and follow You wherever You may lead. Grant me the strength to do just that. Amen.

Philippians 3:7-16

ꜱRUE LOVE IS AN ASSURANCE OF FREEDOM

RUE LOVE IS AN ASSURANCE OF FREEDOM

He came to that which was his own, but his own did not receive him.

~ John 1:11 ~

ꜱhere are few experiences that hurt more than being rejected by someone whom you love dearly. To give love and then be rejected, is painful and difficult to handle. However, we must make sure that rejection is not the breaking of bonds that have bound someone to us so tightly that they did not have sufficient freedom and that their unique personality was smothered and stunted in its development by our love. Then, the only way to freedom is by rejecting your love. If you truly love someone, you will allow him the freedom that the spirit needs. It is only by setting someone free that the bonds of mutual love may be strengthened. It is love with a tender touch.

The principle of generous love forms the basis of the Christian gospel. God allows you the freedom of choice to either believe in Him or reject Him. Christ does not want to compel you to love Him. He invites you from His grace to accept Him and to associate with Him through a new relationship of love.

If you accept His love and make His new way of life your own, you will discover with delight that your imperfect love reacts to his Divine love. Your relationship with Him strengthens and deepens steadily. Such a love brings about freedom, joy and peace in your life. If you reject His love and turn your back on the gratifying life that He offers you, you not only accept a lower standard of living, but you also turn your back on God's love. He will continue to love you, even though you have rejected His love. In this way you sacrifice your precious freedom. Can you still afford to do so this year?

Take away my weariness, Lord, and allow Your strength to flow through me. Amen.

John 1:1-18

DO YOU TRULY BELIEVE?

"I do believe; help me overcome my unbelief!"

~ MARK 9:24 ~

It is extremely risky to face a new year lacking true and sincere faith. How great is your faith really? Have you diminished it to issues of attending church, singing songs of praise, listening to nice sermons and endeavouring to live a respectable life? Or do you believe that the dynamic and transforming omnipotence of a living God exists in the center of Christianity?

Your faith becomes reality when the external ceremonies of Christianity become a pulsating and powerful experience of the soul. Many people would justifiably say that faith becomes dynamic when Jesus Christ enters your life. In reality, however, it only becomes effective the moment when your attitude towards yourself changes. When, through the power of Christ residing in you, you no longer see yourself as someone defeated by some secret pet vice with which you are continually concluding an unholy compromise. It starts the moment when you feel yourself to be triumphant and completely in control of your own life, through God's Holy Spirit which resides in you and enables you to triumph over all sin.

It is true that salvation is God's liberating deed of grace towards mankind. However, it does not release you from the responsibility to accept Him with both your spirit and your intellect. You must develop the discipline to experience Christ's presence in your everyday life. Prayer, Bible study and fellowship in faith with other believers are the essential contributing factors in the development of a spiritual awareness and the attainment of a positive, living and dynamic faith.

Lord, You are my only shelter. When I feel powerless and afraid, You will lead me through the darkness and give me renewed courage. Amen.

Mark 9:14-29

WITHOUT GOD YOU HAVE NOTHING

"What good will it be for a man if he gains the whole world, yet forfeits his soul? Or what can a man give in exchange for his soul?"

~ MATTHEW 16:26 ~

Each one who values life, wishes to derive something special from it. From our teenage years onwards we dream about what we want to become one day and what we want to do, and those dreams dictate the quality of our lives. You can continue dreaming and, in doing so, allow the years to pass by unutilized and without achieving anything worthwhile. On the other hand, your dreams could inspire you to take action so that your character may be moulded by the creative matter of your dreams. You can place a sword in the hands of your dreams and conquer the world by realizing them; or you can remain an idle dreamer for the rest of your life.

It is important that the dream or ideal that inspires you is big enough to pose a challenge. If your dreams limit you to collecting earthly treasures, to living a meaningless social life, you are doing yourself a great injustice. Then you have forgotten that you were created in the image of God and you have probably not realized that God destined you for greater things. You are so busy collecting, inspired by what you see, that you lose all spiritual sensitivity and perception.

The ideal would be to nurture a growing realization of God's living presence in your everyday life. It is possible that your fascination with the things that you can see, touch and collect holds a greater attraction for you than the power and beauty of the living God. In the world which you inhabit, objects then become of primary importance to you, and that which is important to God, is set aside. It is only by a deliberate return to God, and by living according to His requirements and standards, that you can determine the true value of life. Remember: Without God you have nothing!

Thank You, Father, that I may inherit Your kingdom. Thank You for blessing me in ways that leave me speechless. Amen.

Matthew 16:24-28

ℱAITH IS A PROCESS OF GROWTH

But grow in the grace and knowledge of our Lord and Savior Jesus
Christ.

~ 2 PETER 3:18 ~

Christian life is all but static. While the revelation of God in Jesus
Christ was a unique and one-time miracle, man's reaction to this
manifestation of God's love is not something which just happens in a
person's life only to be forgotten in the long run. It is the dismal truth
that many Christians make little or no progress in their spiritual
pilgrimage after getting to know Christ as their Savior. They claim to be
Christians, but they have either forsaken their first love, or their faith
has fallen into a painful rut.

It is relatively easy to determine whether or not you are growing
spiritually: has Christ become a growing reality since coming into your
life? Is prayer an essential and dynamic force in your decision-making?
Do you regard the Scriptures as the revelation of God's will in your
life? Are you in any way nearer to Christ than what you were at the
time when you were born again?

It requires courage and total honesty to answer these questions. If
the Holy Spirit is invoked, your spiritual dereliction of duty will be
exposed in all its ghastliness. It can be an unsettling experience if it is
not a sincere prelude to a renewed momentum of your faith in Christ.
Regardless of the failures of the past, the whisperings of the Holy Spirit
will inspire you to develop an awareness of Christ's indwelling presence.
There is no end to this kind of growth and development, because the
more you become aware of Christ's presence, the greater your love for
Him becomes. This growth is the life-giving energy of your Christlikeness, enabling you to reach fruit-bearing maturity in His kingdom.

You are the true Vine, Lord. Keep me from evil and help me to be
truly fruitful in You. Amen.

2 Peter 3:12-18

Therefore we are always confident and know that as long as we are at home in the body we are away from the Lord. We live by faith, not by sight.

~ 2 CORINTHIANS 5:6-7 ~

Anybody suffering from visual disability will confirm the problem that they experience. The inability to read a newspaper or letter; uncertainty when walking; not being able to see the sun shining. These are only a few traumatic examples of this kind of disability. Maybe the worst experience of all is to be in a foreign environment, without being able to find your way or lacking the necessary self-confidence to move around.

It is possible to draw a parallel between this kind of situation and life itself. How often have you not experienced doubt, loneliness and anxiety? When an important decision had to be taken, it was impossible for you to do so with any measure of confidence, because you found it impossible to see ahead in order to weigh the possible consequences against each other.

If this has been your experience, and you want to be honest with yourself, you will be forced to admit that you are trying to rely on your own limited insight. Rather surrender your problem or future completely to God and leave it in His hands. Therefore, regardless of the circum-stances, put your plans, your doubt, your fears and your problems before the Lord's throne of grace and request Jesus to be your Guide. Be sensitive to the whisperings and stirrings of the Holy Spirit in your life, and face the future with faith and trust. You can rest assured that the living Christ will be by your side to lead and guide you.

Lord, let Your kindly light guide me. Help me to understand that I should take life one day at a time and seek Your guidance in everything I do. Amen.

2 Corinthians 5:1-10

ＨOW GREAT IS YOUR GOD?

How great is God – beyond our understanding! The number of his
years is past finding out.

~ JOB 36:26 ~

One of the biggest stumbling blocks in our spiritual development is
a limited perception of God. It could be that you believe that God
loves you and cares for you every day. You readily accept that He is
omnipotent and omnipresent. It is also possible that the very moment
when adversity strikes or when you are confronted with a seemingly
insurmountable problem, God is relegated to an insignificant position
in your life. You do not call upon His wisdom, serenity, omnipotence
and power, even though He has placed these qualities at your disposal.

Unless you remind yourself constantly of the unlimited resources
that God has placed at your disposal, and unless you make regular use
of them in times of need and distress, you will discover that your trials
and tribulations are always greater than your God. Therefore, it is of
utmost importance to broaden your vision of God when life is smooth
and prosperous. This could happen by immersing yourself in quiet time
with God and in broadening your interest in the world around you. Be
determined to grow in your perception of the greatness of God, as well
as of all the means of grace that He has placed at your disposal through
which you can get to know Him more intimately. Then, when the storms
of life erupt, which will happen without a doubt, you will have a spiritual
reserve, enabling you to keep your footing – regardless of how difficult
the moment may be.

When you have been united with the Great God, you will find that
in times of temptation He will give you strength; that your faith is not
merely a question of emotion, but seeing the Unseen. He assures you
of His presence, even in your times of indifference. Know that God is
great, and you will have great faith.

Lord, I am speechless when I behold the wonders of Your creation.
You are miraculous in Your greatness and I want to sing Your praises
all my life. Amen.

 Job 36:22-33

Pray continually ...

~ 1 THESSALONIANS 5:17 ~

℧he generally accepted thought regarding a disciplined prayer life, is that certain times of day should be put aside to be alone with God: early in the morning before the activity of the day, or at night before we go to bed. Over the years it has been proven beyond doubt that such practice yields many blessings for man. For countless people the suspension of this commendable practice will result in a loss and leave a void that nothing else in their lives can replace or fill.

It is difficult enough to create a pattern of prayer in your life. It is somewhat more difficult to cultivate a sustained prayer life. Every right-minded disciple of Jesus Christ, who has endeavoured to pray "continually", knows something about the feelings of guilt and the frustrations resulting from the knowledge that hours have passed without us sparing a thought for the Lord. The demands of a busy life and the fact that the human brain can only handle one thought at a time, prevent us from applying the practice of sustained prayer every waking moment.

Continual prayer does not mean a constant repetition of the same requests, because that would be a manifestation of unbelief. To keep your prayers constantly in your thoughts could also mean that you are so obsessed with your problems that you do not really want to let go so that God can take over. The motive behind sustained prayer is to listen to God and to be sensitive to His guidance through the Holy Spirit. In the quiet of your deepest being you will feel His presence and experience His omnipotence. Regardless of where you may find yourself, or what you may busy yourself with, you can lift your heart to God, even for a single moment and in a fleeting thought, and in doing so, experience the reality of His presence.

> Thank You, Lord, for hearing my prayers of supplication and thanksgiving, and that You bless those who wait on You in prayer. Help me to maintain a childlike trust in You – now and forever. Amen.

 1 Thessalonians 5:12-28

ℱIND YOUR STRENGTH IN GOD

... Be strong in the Lord and in His mighty power.

~ EPHESIANS 6:10 ~

ℰ vents in the world around us could have an unsettling influence on our personal lives. In times of war people become fear-stricken; recessions and economic crises result in concern and stress, and sometimes even suicide; the failure of a business venture or a set-back to your health could result in major anxiety and fear. When your lifestyle has to change as a result of changing circumstances, you are filled with premonitions and uncertainty. Most of us will concede that, at one time or another in our lives, we have experienced such circumstances.

If you desire not to be completely overwhelmed by anxiety and fear, or not to be unnerved by feelings of uncertainty and inadequacy, it is essential that you cling in faith to the living Christ and derive your strength from Him. Nobody other than the God of love knows you and your problems so intimately and completely, and nobody so loves you that He will keep a vigil of all-embracing love over you.

Armed with the assurance that you are supported and protected by the power and omnipotence, the love and mercy of God, you should be equipped to deal with any event which life might deal you. You have the steadfast realization in your heart that you need not handle situations on your own: the living and Omnipotent Savior is always with you. Therefore, always seek your strength in the Lord and His great power, and you will conquer fear, anxiety and adversity, and live a life of faith and trust. Then you can say amen to the words of the writer of Hebrews: "*The Lord is my helper; I will not be afraid. What can man do to me?*" (Heb. 13:6).

Thank You for providing me with armor, shielding me against the shrewdness of Satan. You are my power and my strength. In You I trust. Amen.

Ephesians 6:10-20

Say "Yes!" to Life

" ... I have come that they may have life, and have it to the full."

~ John 10:10 ~

The year ahead is the culmination of the years that were, but it is also a time of boundless opportunity to do good and to grow spiritually and intellectually. For you, the past may have been a tale of frustration and increasing bitterness, and you may feel that, at the moment, your life is void of inspiration and creativity, so that you cannot start anything that is constructive or worthwhile. When looking back at the past, you may find little reason for faith in either the present or the future.

But remember: the future belongs to you and you can do with it whatever you want to. God has given you freedom of choice. You can either live constructively or destructively; you can meet the future by being either positive or negative. The choice is yours. However, do not forget that God, in His grace, gave you life – with a sublime purpose. Every day is a gift from the loving hand of God, and you can only live life to the full when you subject yourself to God's purpose for your life. Attaining your purpose in life will eventually depend on your relationship with Him.

Naturally there are those who would want to deny this truth, but if life has a spiritual foundation, it must also have a spiritual objective. It is by acknowledging this truth and by its embodiment in your own life, that you are guaranteed complete deliverance, joy and fulfilment. And only then can you utilize God's precious gift of *life* to the full.

The abundant life belongs to God and, even though He is generous with this gift, He can only give it to those who are willing to receive and use it. Therefore, to say "Yes!" to life is your privilege, as well as your responsibility.

Thank You that I may have everlasting life through Christ's crucifixion. Not even death can make me tremble. Amen.

John 10:1-11

"Though the mountains be shaken and the hills be removed, yet my unfailing love for you will not be shaken nor my covenant of peace be removed" ...

~ ISAIAH 54:10 ~

$\mathcal{M}$ ost of us have first-hand knowledge of the radically changing circumstances of life that often have a dramatic influence on us, as well as on those whom we love. One moment we experience joy and ecstasy, and then we are suddenly swept into the depths of despair. How often has your world been disrupted by serious illness or death; by failure or financial disaster. A philosopher once said: "Nothing in life is unchangeable, except change itself." Most people will, from experience and with good reason, agree with this while endeavouring to maintain their balance against the instability of life.

Nevertheless, you have the assurance of God's love for you, regardless of unexpected events in your life. However despondent you may be about those events and circumstances, which are a cause of great concern for you and which shake the foundations of your existence, you must never lose sight of the fact the Jesus loves you with an unfailing, eternal and perfect love. He will deliver you from your burden and your weariness if you go to Him in prayer and faith. He will allay your fears and concerns and will present you with His Holy Spirit to give you comfort and lead you on a just path.

Regardless of the circumstances, or how dark the future may seem, if you take God at His Word and listen to His promises while turning to Him in times of affliction, you may rest assured that you will enjoy the blessings of the Lord, as well as His peace that drives out all fear (cf. 1 Jn. 4:18).

Lord, I feel safe in the shadow of Your hand. Thank You for sheltering me when the storms of life are raging about me. Amen.

Isaiah 54:1-15

Then he touched their eyes and said, "According to your faith will it be done to you" ...

~ Matthew 9:29 ~

$\mathcal{T}$here are people who regard faith as a mere commodity, something which you may have a lot of or very little, depending on the circumstances. In moments of strain and stress they wish that they had more faith, but they are not entirely sure where to find this essential commodity.

The fact remains that you have faith and that you do not need more faith, but rather a change in the quality of the faith that you already have. Maybe, for too long, you have put your faith in the wrong things, such as banks, trains, aeroplanes, television and newspapers. Maybe it is the tragic truth that you have greater faith in failure than in success. You hope for inner victory, but you believe that you are due for defeat. Your basic faith is not really a religious issue, but that which you, out of habit, expect life to hand you. This daily expectation, which once again is a different revelation of faith, is precisely that which is eventually produced in your life.

You should have an understanding of the importance and necessity of maintaining a disposition of expectation towards life. You expect only the most noble, as well as the best, with the certain knowledge that what you expect will, without doubt, eventually happen.

However, how is it possible to expect the best when standards are continually lowered and when the view of the future is dark? Only those who have an unfailing faith and trust in the Eternal God, who believe in His eventual redemption of the human race, can face the future with courage and serenity. This great truth, and the acceptance of it in your life, creates a stabilizing influence in your life and enables you to face the future with confidence.

Help me Lord, to be steadfast in my faith and to be forever devoted to Your work. Bless me in abundance and help me to use it to Your greater glory. Amen.

Matthew 9:27-31

⊙AKE A STAND

May our Lord Jesus Christ himself and God our Father, who loved us and by his grace gave us eternal encouragement and good hope, encourage your hearts and strengthen you in every good deed and word.

~ 2 THESSALONIANS 2:16-17 ~

Ⓟ aul calls on the Christians in Thessalonica to be steadfast in their faith. It is not always easy to live your Christian faith to the full every day, especially in modern times. Dubious and double standards, moral decay and the questioning of established truths, are the order of the day and accepted by many as the norm. Should a person then wish to take a stand in this environment, it becomes increasingly difficult, and you are regarded as the exception to the rule. As a result of this, and in order to avoid ridicule and rejection, many people find it far easier to go with the flow rather than displaying the courage of their conviction and taking a firm stand. It is imperative, in these ominous times, to take a stand for Christ and not to be ashamed of identifying with Him.

In every facet of life, the Holy Spirit is ready and willing to support and encourage the testimony of Christ. He enables you to overcome your feelings of incompetency and inadequacy, of fear and embarrassment, when you find yourself in the position where you have to reveal your loyalty to Christ in a positive fashion. When words fail you, He will enable you to speak out against that which you believe to be in conflict with His holy will. He will also guide you in distinguishing good from evil.

Therefore, maintain close contact with the living Christ and open you heart and life to the influence of the Holy Spirit. When the time comes to be counted, you will not be found wanting.

Lord, I so much want to live a pure and holy life. Strengthen me and allow Your will to guide me so that I may resist sin and evil. Amen.

2 Thessalonians: 2:13 – 3:15

May the grace of the Lord Jesus Christ, and the love of God, and the fellowship of the Holy Spirit be with you all.

~ 2 Cᴏʀɪɴᴛʜɪᴀɴs 13:14 ~

In these days of materialism and self-interest, it is a real problem for many people to appreciate a precious gift of untold value – which cannot be valued in monetary terms – let alone to accept it free of charge. Generally speaking, everything carries a price tag: be it cash, service or a favor.

Nevertheless, while you reflect on the sacrifice which God made at Golgotha, through Jesus Christ, for our redemption and salvation; the undying hope that He gave us through His triumphant resurrection from the dead; proffering us His power through the Holy Spirit who descended on Whit Sunday: surely that is a source of excitement and wonder and a call for joy and praise? That our merciful Lord, Master and Friend so loved us, that He freely gave these gifts to undeserving people like you and me?

There is no way in which we, as earthly creatures, could justly pay the Lord for His unfathomable love. However, we could, and should, open our lives to Him so that we could be instrumental in passing on His love to others. Indeed, it is Christ's command that we should love one another as we love ourselves, and as He loves us.

Because of our human weakness and insignificance, we could never do it from our own strength. Through the love of God and the grace of Jesus Christ, the Holy Spirit enables us to do His work and to spread His love amongst all that we come into touch with (cf. Acts 1:8).

> Lord, I always want to glorify You as my Father. Guide me through Your Holy Spirit so that I may be obedient to You in everything I do. Amen.

 2 Corinthians: 13:1-13

February

... For I have the desire to do what is good, but I cannot carry it out. For what I do is not the good I want to do; no, the evil I do not want to do – this I keep on doing.

~ Romans 7:18-19 ~

Prayer

Merciful God and loving Father through Jesus our Savior,

You are the Source of every precious moment of life bestowed upon us.

Merely one month of a new year has passed; it has flown by like a mere memory and I have to confess with shame that I stand guilty before You regarding the prospects and opportunities You have presented me with.

So much that I wanted to do, so many honorable intentions that failed miserably because I wasted my precious time: Prayer time in conversation with You; Bible study to discover Your will for my life; pondering Your greatness revealed in the wonders of Your creation; fellowship in faith with other children of Yours; meaningful church attendance to enrich my spiritual life; willingness to give freely of my love to others.

Thank you that You are a patient and merciful Gardener; that, time and again, You forgive and give me strength to live on a foundation of victory.

Lend me a helping hand to utilize this month – and the rest of my life – to the optimum in glorification and celebration of You, so that I may love You more; follow You more conscientiously, and serve You with greater loyalty.

Make me new, Lord Jesus and, through the Holy Spirit, lead me along Your perfect path.

Amen

GOD'S WAY IS THE PATH TO SUCCESS

Teach me your way, O LORD, and I will walk in your truth; give me an undivided heart, that I may fear your name.

~ PSALM 86:11 ~

To ask what success is, is a universal question. If we say that God's way leads to success, the cynic will give a condescending smile and declare that the Christian message is too idealistic to be of any productive value in our striving for success. Christ showed the way of love and, through His death, He not only emphasized the great demands of such a path, but He proved that, even in death, love could triumph and achieve success.

Although many people reject the way of Christian love, they have nothing of equal value to put in its place. They propose political and social systems as solutions for the world's problems, but success is not achieved through that. Every system that was proposed to solve the world's problems got stranded on the rocks of greed, the thirst for power and aggression. These are all contradictions on the path of love.

God's path to success is the road of common sense. If man could learn to love, the world's failures would disappear one by one or, at least, become manageable. God did not call man to an unattainable ideal or an impossible lifestyle in order to achieve success. It is only because he does not want to accept God's methods for achieving success that he remains blind to the truth and regularly fails in his foolishness. God did not put dreams and ideals in our hearts that are unattainable. However, God's way requires sacrifice, and those who risk putting it into practice will discover that it is the only path to true success.

Lord, I want to follow You because You are my King. Lead me along the right path so that I may see Your dwelling. Amen.

Psalm 86:1-13

DEPENDENCY ON GOD LEADS TO SUCCESS!

But I cry to you for help, O LORD; in the morning my prayer comes before you.

~ PSALM 88:13 ~

In these days of sophisticated advertising, the virtues of a variety of products are proclaimed. The listening, watching and reading public is invited to "start the day in the right way" with some kind of cereal or fruit juice. Various vitamin tablets and health salts are offered as the right way to prepare yourself in order to be able to cope with the day ahead. Every remedy on offer claims to be more successful than the next.

Each one of us needs help to successfully meet the demands of each day, especially in these competitive times in which we live. Modern life emphasizes super-speed, super-excellence and super-performance, which makes life more stressful and more tense. Nervous tension increases by the day. Consequently, there is an increasing number of people who experience a decline in their health and lifestyle, with the accompanying problems and failures.

There is only one sure way to meet every day with its tough demands successfully, and that is to face each day with peace of mind. In order to achieve this, it is essential to start every day in the quiet presence of God and with the living Christ. Reveal to Him your fear and anxiety and place those things that cause you most concern before Him. Somebody said that we should start each day in prayer, so that it would not fray at the edges. Seek Jesus Christ's help for whatever the day might bring, by asking Him to help carry your burden. Hand over the new day, your concerns, the day itself, and yourself to Him. Then face the day, shielded by His hand, with peace in your heart. Dependency on God leads to true success!

You make everything bright. Even the darkness becomes light. You are the Morning Star to which I lift my eyes. Amen.

 Psalm 88:1-14

WHAT IS THE SOURCE OF YOUR SUCCESS?

"But if it were I, I would appeal to God; I would lay my cause before him."

~ JOB 5:8 ~

Even carefully planned and thoroughly executed tasks can sometimes go horribly wrong and then the people involved might not understand what has happened. The matter might have been well researched in advance; every possibility was taken into account, and all obstacles and dangers carefully considered. With the groundwork and planning completed, the plan was implemented. Inspite of all the precautions, everything can turn into miserable failure.

When this happens and all those concerned become disappointed, disillusioned and frustrated, there is always the resounding question: *Why?* After all the effort that went into it, where did things go wrong and where did we err? Regardless of the nature of your undertaking; be it business or personal affairs; material or spiritual; whether it affects only you or others as well, never set about a task at hand on your own, because you will be doomed to failure. Jesus Christ offered you His helping hand to carry your burden (cf. Mt. 11:28-30). In this way, He wants to become your Partner in every undertaking that you launch. He wants to support you in every undertaking that is within God's will for you. Only then do you taste true success in life.

Take every plan and every undertaking in your life to God in prayer first, and ask Him to indicate in His unique way whether that plan carries His approval. When you have prayed and laid your plans before Him, open your mind so that you will be sensitive to the whisperings of the Holy Spirit, and then obey God's will. Plan your life in this way and you will not be disappointed, because the omnipotent God will be with you in all circumstances.

Lord, I put my trust in You, because Your promises are firm and true. Disaster will no longer trouble me. Amen.

Job 5:8-19

ASSESS YOURSELF

Do not think of yourself more highly than you ought ...

~ ROMANS 12:3 ~

*M*any people have a poor opinion of themselves and their abilities. When asked to perform a modest task, they summarily refuse because they cannot be convinced that they are indeed able to manage it. They refuse invitations because they have no self-confidence. Such people lead an unhappy and frustrated life, because that which you believe of yourself, is inevitably reflected in your way of life.

As a Christian disciple, you must, sooner or later, assess yourself in the light of God's Holy Spirit. It could be a disillusioning experience, but at the same time it could be a revelation. You will then see yourself as you really are: with pettiness, superficial self-pity and self-delusion. It could be an uncomfortable and humbling moment in your life. If you accept God's forgiveness for that which you had been in your own eyes, you will begin to see who you could become through His strength, wisdom and inspiration. The point of departure for success is: know yourself.

Stop disparaging yourself and convincing yourself that you will never achieve anything worthwhile. This leads to inner conflict, frustration and unhappiness. The fundamental truth is that you were created in the image of God and in His eyes you are invaluable. If you embrace this truth, the honest assessment of your life is about to begin. Instead of always expecting failure, start to live successfully, especially in your spiritual life. Despair is then replaced by hope. Your goal in life is then equal to God's assessment of your life. If you seek success, start here.

Jesus Christ, I am endlessly grateful to have been redeemed by Your blood. Through You I can inherit eternal life. Amen.

Romans 12:1-8

ACHIEVE YOUR GOALS THROUGH JESUS

"... observe what the LORD your God requires: Walk in his ways, and keep his decrees and commands, his laws and requirements, as written in the Law of Moses ... "

~ 1 KINGS 2:3 ~

The successful achievement of our ideals and ambitions in life is, by our nature, the highest goal for each of us. There are few, if any, who can honestly admit that success is of little or no concern to them, who can say that they would be content, regardless of what life has to offer. In fact, life would be empty and without purpose for the person who does not set goals for himself and who alleges that he has no ambition.

On the other hand, it could be a painful experience for those who are striving for success. It could cause an irreparable blow to their self-confidence should their ambitions fail. Many people have surrendered their future to despair and failure because they experienced a setback in the planning of their career.

On your pilgrimage through life, it is essential to acknowledge and accept that you cannot achieve success in your own strength. You need the support and guidance of Jesus to ensure that you make the right choice and take the right decision, so that you may follow the right path. If you embrace Christ as your Partner in every undertaking; if you always seek His will in careful obedience; if you live within His will for you; you can rest assured in the knowledge that you will experience fulfilment in life in everything that you do and everywhere that you go.

I want to sing Your praises through words and feelings, because You have absolved my sins. You give me strength and keep vigil over me so that I may glorify You. Amen.

1 Kings 3:1-12

He who was seated on the throne said, "I am making everything new!"
~ Revelation 21:5 ~

There are many mysteries surrounding the birth and resurrection of Jesus Christ that the ordinary believer finds hard to understand. The eternal love of God that gave rise to it cannot be fathomed. But the heart of the matter is that God entered human history in a physical form in the Person of the living Christ. He identified with humanity. It is a breathtaking truth and a mystery that has us kneeling before the omnipotent God in worship and wonder.

The fact that Christ can identify with you and me, and you with Him, opens new horizons of greatness that you have never seen before. God Himself came in Jesus Christ to take you from failure and despair into an environment where your spirit could reach maturity. When this happens, people's circumstances change radically and irreversibly. They are in a familiar environment, but with a new approach to their problems. Whether you change to new spheres of service or continue as you are, there is one irrefutable fact: you get a new concept of God; you have a new attitude towards your problems, circumstances and conditions.

Through the coming of Jesus Christ to our sin-drenched world, God came to explain the mystery of an Omnipotent Divine Being, so that even the most simple-hearted can understand it. This means that your life will never be the same again. If you embrace Jesus as your Savior and Redeemer, His coming will make "everything" in your life "new".

Lord, You are faithful and through Christ I am reborn. I want to praise and glorify You because You have forgiven all my sins. Amen.

Revelation 21:1-8

LIFE IN ALL ITS FULLNESS

... That you may be filled to the measure of all the fullness of God.

~ EPHESIANS 3:19 ~

We sometimes come across people who allege that life is empty and futile and that it is not worthwhile to carry on living. There are people who, because of circumstances or negative dispositions, as well as through their own doing, have descended into a mire of despair. They have lost interest in life and in the fullness that life has to offer.

While it is a known fact that, in life, we experience setbacks, which at times literally rock the foundations of our very existence, we must never lose sight of the Jesus factor. He came so that we may have abundant "life" (cf. Jn. 10:10). He assures us that, in every situation, He will be with us (cf. Mt. 28:20), He promised that He would carry our burden with us (cf. Mt. 11:28-30). The only requirement is that we must turn to Him in faith.

If you are depressed or pessimistic, it is necessary that you enter into an intimate relationship with the living Christ by means of prayer and meditation. Like a needy child, tell Him about all your problems and concerns. Share with Him your doubts and your fears. It has indeed been written, *Cast all your anxiety on Him because He cares for you* (1 Pet. 5:7). Do that and you will experience profound joy and peace. Through God's immense grace you will find meaning and direction for your life, and your life will be crowned with the success of God, ... *Be faithful, even to the point of death, and I will give you the crown of life* (Rev. 2:10).

> Lord, You sprinkle Your blessings over me like soft rain. You gladden my heart. Grant me the fullness of Your Spirit. Amen.

Ephesians 3:14-21

YOUR THOUGHTS ARE CRUCIAL

"The good man brings good things out of the good stored up in his heart, and the evil man brings evil things out of the evil stored up in his heart. For out of the overflow of his heart his mouth speaks."

~ LUKE 6:45 ~

Be grateful that God gave you a brain. Your brain may be bright, it may be slow or mediocre, but if you are a healthy person, you have the ability to think. This gives you the power and responsibility to decide what you are going to allow into your thoughts.

Many people do not take the trouble to make decisions and they just drift through life, driven by the feelings that rule their lives and not their minds. In any community such dependent people are usually loyal to the leader who can shout the loudest and who never demands them to think for themselves.

As a disciple of the living Christ, you are controlled by your love for Him and therefore your thoughts should be controlled by Him. This implies a follower of whom high standards of devotion are required. It requires the cultivation of spiritual life that grows continually; to learn to linger in the presence of the Master – not out of duty but because it is considered a joy and a privilege – so that your life may be gradually filled with His Holy Spirit.

Such a high standard of spiritual life is overwhelming and the prospective disciple may well ask with Paul: ... *Who is equal to such a task?* (2 Cor. 2:16). To follow Christ's doctrines and live in awareness of His holy Presence, cannot be achieved from our own strength. However, He has promised us His Holy Spirit. If you are united in faith with Christ, you will find that He controls your thoughts and you will start thinking creatively and successfully.

Holy Jesus, hear my prayer and strengthen my heart, my soul, my mind. Mould me to Your image so that my thoughts, words and deeds will be to Your greater glory. Amen.

Luke 6:43-45

Utilize What You Have to the Optimum

... For I have learned to be content whatever the circumstances.

~ Philippians 4:11 ~

Unfortunately, there are many people who never reach their full potential. They drag through life feeling discontent, because they know that there is more to life than what they have achieved. In most cases the reasons for their discontent are clear: they wanted to follow a specific career, but circumstances made it impossible; a responsibility which they could not dodge resulted in their having to sacrifice dreams and ambitions; other circumstances possibly contributed to cause a prolonged disappointment about what could have been. Many gifted and competent people feel frustrated because their dreams and expectations were never realized.

People, who suffer this frustration, often allow disappointments to determine their quality of life. It overshadows everything they think and do. They continually dwell upon what could have been and this prevents them from enjoying life or making a meaningful contribution.

The answer to this unhappy state is to take time to be quiet and to redefine what you already have. Count your blessings and be determined not to allow your past to determine your present and your future. Whatever disappointments may overshadow your past, the future is calling you and it is rich in promises. Do not allow memories from the past or failures that you had to bear to cloud your vision of the future.

One of the wonders of the doctrines of Jesus Christ is that they omit thoughts about the past and only deal with the present and the future. Jesus gives salvation *now* and this is a great truth. He is the Lord of the present moment. He will guide you, shelter you and inspire you in ways that you regard as almost impossible. The past is history; the future is bright with promise with Jesus as your Savior and Redeemer. He enables you to make optimal use of that which you do have.

I pray to You for peace in this world so that all who breathe will acknowledge and glorify You as the Lord. Amen.

 Philippians 4:10-19

$\mathcal{I}$T IS YOUR RESPONSIBILITY

May the Lord direct your hearts into God's love and Christ's perseverance.

~ 2 THESSALONIANS 3:5 ~

$\mathcal{W}$e cherish in our hearts the eternal truth that God's love is free and undeserved. Nothing that you have done or intend to do can earn you that. God loves you because God is love, and this is a great truth for which we are eternally grateful and for which we should glorify and thank Him. Because God loves with such a lasting love, we must guard against the Divine love becoming tawdry to us or mistaking it for a kind of sympathy that allows you to sin without being punished. The moment you realize that you are the object of God's love, you have responsibilities to fulfil if you wish to be worthy of that love.

Because it was God Himself who lit the flame of love for Him in your heart, you must do all you can to ensure that nothing will extinguish this inner flame in you. The only way in which you can achieve that, is to allow your life to be controlled by your love for Jesus Christ. For this your thoughts must be held captive by the Holy Spirit, our Teacher. Your daily inspiration must spring from your time spent quietly in His presence. Then your life will be an expression and revelation of your love for Him and you will become a channel for His love to your fellow man. Everything that you do will be done to the glory of the God of love.

God loves you with an everlasting love – just as He loves every other human being. As a disciple of Jesus Christ, it is your responsibility to reveal God's love as a practical reality in the world in which you live and work. If you fail in this, you cannot hope for spiritual success.

Verily, You are love! Your Son became man to demonstrate true love. Help me to radiate love in return. Amen.

2 Thessalonians 3:1-15

THEOLOGICAL BELIEF AND SPIRITUAL EXPERIENCE

Since we live by the Spirit, let us keep in step with the Spirit.

~ GALATIANS 5:25 ~

In these days of conflicting ideologies, when even theologians differ in opinion, it is often difficult for ordinary people to know exactly what to believe. In the midst of this confusion, cults proliferate by drawing dissatisfied members out of mainstream churches.

Although there are divergent interpretations of the teachings of Christ, there is only *one* Christ and all things that are preached in His name must conform to Him. The Living Christ can only be known through a personal relationship with Him, and by sharing in His love and power. This is achieved only through an intimate and personal relationship with Christ.

In the spiritual life, your primary loyalty must be to the Living Savior. How would He respond in situations in which you find yourself? What would He think of the underhanded business deal that you have just clinched? How does He view relationships that are broken because of your unforgiving spirit? The value of your faith and the depth of your spiritual experience can only be measured by their practical application in your daily life. You can spend hours at mass crusades; have the ability to pray in public; quote endlessly from the Word, but if you have not had a personal encounter with the Living Christ your spiritual posturing counts for nothing.

Loving Master, my love for You rises above my intellectual and theological knowledge, because it is founded on Your love and power. Amen.

Galatians 5:13-26

ALLOW FAITH TO DISPEL FEAR

He said to his disciples, "Why are you so afraid? Do you still have no faith?"

~ MARK 4:40 ~

There are few people who do not harbor fear in one form or another. It might be concealed in the complexity of their personality and they cannot explain it all that well. However, it reveals itself in a discomfort which they cannot control and which robs their lives of peace and stability. It is a strange fact that many people cannot explain the inexplicable fear that haunts them. The unknown future, an incurable disease, losing your job, the death of a loved one can cause comprehensible fear, but outside these things there often lurks a fear that is inexplicable. It affects the deepest stirrings of a man's spirit, refuses to be analysed, but is nevertheless a burning presence.

There is but one sure cure for a life that is dominated by fear, and that is a living faith in Jesus Christ. Fear and faith cannot co-exist in the same life. Should people try to accommodate both, conflict is created which undermines their peace of mind and eventually destroys them.

Faith nurtures faith and fear nurtures fear. Place your trust in God. At first, in the little things in your life His love and wisdom will be revealed and confirmed and, in time, the bigger things in your life will be under His control. Put God to the test, even if it is only in the little things, and you will soon find that He is actively working on the big issues in your life. When this happens, fear will subside until your whole life is free of destructive fear. You will increasingly be controlled by a positive faith and will taste success above fear.

As Your child, I know where to find veritable peace. Dispel fear and selfishness from my heart, so that I may serve You faithfully. Amen.

Mark 4:35-41

CONFRONT YOUR WEAKNESSES

But David found strength in the LORD his God.

~ I SAMUEL 30:6 ~

$\mathcal{M}$ ost people become aware of their imperfection at one time or another. The managing director of a company, in some cases, will be out of his depth in front of the stove or the kitchen sink, while a champion wrestler may not be able to win the 100 meters. Incompetence can manifest itself in any aspect of life and could be true of any type of person. There are few people who can honestly state that they are equipped to meet and handle any situation with ease and self-confidence.

The moment that you accept that there are areas in your life that you handle with difficulty, the next step is to take the action you need to handle the shortcomings that you experience in a positive manner. You must find a method to increase and restore your self-confidence. It will enable you to apply positive self-restraint while you honestly take issue with your problem.

Regardless of what problems you face or how imperfect or inadequate you might feel in any given situation – be it in the business world, on the home front, on the sportsfield, or even on a social level – you must surrender yourself in prayer to God. Ask Him to give you strength, through the living Christ, to handle the situation. If you accept this fact and believe that He can and will do it, you can move forward with confidence in the knowledge that God's grace is sufficient to enable you to overcome your weaknesses.

> Lord, even when I am filled with doubt, You are by my side. You give me strength to wrestle with daily temptation, so that one day I may behold Your splendor. Amen.

1 Samuel 30:1-10

⊘HE SOUND OF SILENCE

... And after the fire came a gentle whisper.

~ 1 KINGS 19:12 ~

We live in a time of deafening din and noise. Radios, cassette players and CD players make a tremendous onslaught on our hearing wherever we go. Some music is pleasing and soothing, but much of the noise that passes as "music" today is stressful on the ears and nerves of sensitive people. Because we have become used to the noise, we no longer know how to deal with silence. When confronted by a period of silence, we become restless and soon start whiling the time away with insignificant matters.

To enjoy and appreciate silence is one of the small successes in life. It is then that your spirit becomes receptive to the presence of God. If you share the fellowship of God in silence, you will be able to face life with self-confidence and dignity. A philosopher said: "Every evil under the sun has overtaken us because we do not sit quietly in a room sometimes."

You cannot enter silence with blank thoughts. To attempt that will lead to confusion and wandering thoughts. Enter the silence with a prayer that the Holy Spirit will fill your thoughts with a Christian quality. This can span the Master's omnipotence, majesty, or the omnipotence of His creation. It can be any aspect of His holy Being that specifically appeals to you at that moment.

When you are alone with God in silence and you become aware of His living presence, your time of quiet reflection becomes a time of spiritual empowerment and inspiration. There you may gather strength for daily life with its demands and responsibilities.

Lord, I will wait upon You in quiet trust. I know that You will disperse my doubts and strengthen my faith anew. You guarantee that through the blood of Christ. Amen.

1 Kings 19:1-12

QUEST FOR TRUTH

All a man's ways seem innocent to him, but motives are weighed by the LORD.

~ PROVERBS 16:2 ~

or many people, to win an argument is a matter of honor and self-assertiveness. In order to win, they ignore important facts, twist the truth and place the emphasis on the wrong issue all together. For many people a reputation for cleverness and prestige is of much greater importance than the truth. They have a twisted idea of success. All seekers for the truth must have a humble disposition towards the questions and problems of life. They must always be prepared to make new discoveries, and be willing to accept a deeper insight than the superficial and obvious.

No student has ever reached the terminus of truth, because truth has its fountain-head and fullness in God. Although the truth has many facets, they all originate from the holy omniscient Creator God. To deny this is to cut yourself off from the Source of Truth. All truth – if one can comprehend it – will lead you to a clearer understanding of the eternal God.

Even though no person can possess every truth, it is still possible for us to know the God of truth. Jesus Christ said, ... "*If you hold to my teaching, you are really my disciples. Then you will know the truth, and the truth will set you free*" (Jn. 8:31-32). Through obedience and devotion to the Lord, it is possible to be free from destructive forces; forces that tie you to ignorance and blind you to the concept of truth. To love and to serve the living Christ is the point of departure on the path leading to truth. Are you willing to follow this path for the sake of spiritual success?

Father, allow Your love to rule my heart. Let Your Spirit dwell within me forever and teach me the truth. I want to serve You with all my heart. Amen.

Proverbs 16:1-9

CONFIDENCE

Though an army besiege me, my heart will not fear; though war break out against me, even then will I be confident.

~ PSALM 27:3 ~

Confidence is, of course, not an art that many people try to cultivate. One can seriously consider what you are going to say to your superior when requesting a raise, or when you propose a scheme that will promote business, but when the time comes to speak up, you cannot find the words and then your entire disposition changes. You are not, by any means, comfortable and apart from the frustration that overcomes you, you regard yourself as a failure.

To allow yourself to become so unsettled and upset that you lack confidence and get confused, is totally unnecessary. It prevents you from developing your potential to the full. It is unnecessary to be influenced in such a negative fashion, because you hold the solution in your hands. Develop a higher regard for yourself and develop greater faith in your ability to achieve success.

There could be many and diverse reasons for lacking self-confidence: fear, uncertainty, inferiority, fear of rejection and other concealed symptoms; these could all contribute to your tense disposition towards life. The only way to control these destructive influences is to take refuge in a greater influence that can destroy all these things and win your whole-hearted confidence. You meet this "greater influence" when you discover Jesus Christ as the Lord of your life and when you start living in order to love and serve Him. When He becomes the centre of your existence, you will overcome your inferiority and lack of confidence. Your confidence will grow by the day and you will start to lead a well-adjusted life of self-confidence.

Confidence is all I have. Just confidence in You, and the knowledge that You will bring me salvation. You are my rock and You never falter. Amen.

Psalm 27:1-14

A FAITH THAT COUNTS

... The only thing that counts is faith expressing itself through love.

~ GALATIANS 5:6 ~

Different people have divergent points of view about what is most important in our spiritual lives. There are people who stick meticulously to a set of rules; they define everything in the finest detail and then desperately cling to it. Furthermore, their love is limited to those people who agree with them.

Your faith will prove itself to be insufficient and ineffective if it does not lead you to a more profound knowledge and awareness of God. To have an intimate relationship with Jesus Christ and love Him with such sincerity that His presence becomes a living reality for you. Those precious moments that you set aside to be alone with Him will convey inspiration to even the most orthodox of Christians. A positive faith in the resurrected and exalted Savior forms the basis of all Christian doctrines and religions.

Faith becomes alive and meaningful when it is expressed through love. Without love, faith becomes constrained and bigoted and then the height, depth and the eternal nature of God's love cannot be fathomed or experienced. This love is always associated with our heavenly Father. If our love then has to be acceptable to God in some measure, as well as fulfil its true function, it has to be inspired and confirmed by the perfect love of God.

When you possess a living faith that manifests itself in love, you have the basic qualities of a practical, inspired and effective religion that is acceptable to God. At the same time it is a source of blessing, not only for you, but also for your fellow man.

Lord, Your Word teaches me to love You with my whole heart, soul and mind, and to love my neighbor as myself. Grant me the strength to abide by these commandments. Amen.

Galatians 5:1-12

ABSOLUTE COMMITMENT

But whatever was to my profit I now consider loss for the sake of Christ.

~ PHILIPPIANS 3:7 ~

Your act of commitment to the Master, Jesus Christ, should never be taken lightly. If often happens that people set out on their walk with Christ with great commitment and enthusiasm. After some spiritual experience, they are on an emotional high and virtually ecstatic. It is, however, a dismal truth that, in many instances, this mountain-top experience is of relatively short duration. As soon as the initial enthusiasm, driving force and resoluteness start to wane, many people return to their old life, habits, friends and ways.

You must never forget that Christ, for the sake of your salvation, gave up everything – even His life! Nothing was more important to Him than His mission to save souls for God. He wanted to lead people from the darkness of sin and misery into the miraculous light of God. In order to achieve this, He put all personal desires and ideals aside, forsook all convenience and security and, for your and my sake, made the perfect sacrifice of His life!

As a Christian, it should be of immediate and obvious importance to you to live your life according to the will of the One who sacrificed His life for you. Commitment and dedication involve searching for God's will and remaining true to it throughout your life. It requires disregarding all you own preferences and desires and opening up your whole being to the influence of the Holy Spirit.

It might seem to be a demanding and unattainable prospect, but in the light of Christ's sacrifice for you, it is a small price to pay for the life that He sacrificed for you.

Lord, fill me with the warmth of Your love, come and dwell in my heart. I want to dedicate my life to You. Amen.

Philippians 3:1-11

OUR CALLING TO CHEERFULNESS

Rejoice in the Lord always. I will say it again: Rejoice!

~ PHILIPPIANS 4:4 ~

A good friend of mine always concludes his correspondence with "Philippians 4:4!" It is not merely a pious appendage, but an honest testimony of a characteristic that he possesses. Cheerfulness is a Christian obligation and, if we measure up to it, it brings us rich dividends in our spiritual life. It also announces to the world that we possess an indestructible Christian joy that carries us through life. It seems as though the majority of people are controlled by their emotions. When they are depressed, they spread dark unhappiness amongst everyone they come into contact with.

As a child of God, you can experience the joy and inspiration of the living Christ in your life, enabling you to overcome all moodiness when others harass you, and to rejoice in the spiritual experience that transforms depression into true cheerfulness.

When you are spiritually tuned, you really have no reason for despondency. Your daily walk with Jesus Christ, the glorious promises contained in His Word, the experience of God's profound mercy that transcends understanding; these will fill your life with joy, purpose and direction. If you live within the will of God, you *can* overcome frustration and truly appreciate all the blessings that God showers you with. You are a redeemed child of God. Jesus redeemed you from sin with His blood. The Holy Spirit dwells in you! You are on your way "home". Just thinking of that sounds the death-knell for all despondency.

Your cheerfulness is not a facade that you put up for certain occasions in order to impress people, but is the result of a heart and mind that are in harmony with God through Jesus Christ. The Christian must have a positive approach to life and the foundation for his joy is always his salvation through Jesus Christ.

Lord, You fill my days with joy. Your peace flows through me like a quiet stream. Even when I suffer, I know that You will deliver me. Amen.

Philippians 4:2-6

REALIZE YOUR DREAMS

... "Everything is possible for him who believes."

~ Mark 9:23 ~

People nowadays are inclined to ridicule and belittle the dreamer. They feel that such a person is unrealistic and removed from reality. The pragmatic person is glorified and we forget that in life one person is dependent upon the other. Before the pragmatist can live his life fully, somewhere in the background there must be a visionary and a dreamer.

The problem with many people is that they are content to remain dreamers. They build castles in the air but do nothing to turn them into reality. Visions and dreams *could* become reality if the hope that lives in our hearts becomes practical through living faith; when we stop our wishful thinking and actively start doing something about our dreams. We can do this through the inspiration that God wants to make ours. God not only grants us the ability to dream, He provides us with the energy, inspiration and driving force to realize our dreams.

If you have been an idle dreamer and have given yourself over to wishful thinking for so long that you believe nothing and nobody can help your dreams come true anymore, attempt, from this moment onwards, to do something constructive. This can be the first step to turn your dreams into reality. Your sincere dreams have been granted to you to be fulfilled and realized. Therefore, place a sword in the hands of your dreams, go out and turn your dreams into glorious reality.

Father, strengthen me and give me courage so that I may remain devoted to Your work. Make me instrumental in Your plan of redemption and let my conduct glorify Your name. Amen.

Mark 9:14-29

WHEN THINGS GO WRONG

... "Do not be afraid or discouraged because of this vast army. For the battle is not yours, but God's."

~ 2 CHRONICLES 20:15 ~

In every person's life there comes a time that can be frightening, because of personal isolation and loneliness. For reasons that are not easy to fathom, you suddenly feel that you are alone in everything that you do. Life then becomes a lonely battle and you think – because it would seem as though everything is against you – that there is no reason for you to continue the battle. It is then that people strongly consider admitting defeat and giving up the battle.

When these feelings get the better of you, you have most probably ignored God. Overwhelmed by the forces posted against you, you allowed the influence of evil to affect you negatively, even before the battle started. By displaying such an attitude, you subconsciously acknowledged that these destructive forces have greater control over your life than the omnipotence of your heavenly Father.

Hold on to the timeless truth, to your loyalty to God and to the things that He represents. Then you have joined forces with the dynamic power of justice and no negative or destructive force can stand against you. You cannot risk fighting the battle in your own inadequate strength. Find your strength in Jesus Christ and the sources of strength that your Father in heaven offers you and, through His mercy, puts at your disposal. Then you will always live successfully and victoriously and with profound awareness of His presence. Furthermore, do not underestimate the necessity of serious prayer in these circumstances.

Help me Lord to count my blessings during crises. You will never forsake me and never leave me alone. Even in difficult times I may count on Your blessings. Amen.

2 Chronicles 20:13-21

YOU ARE NEVER TOO OLD

Teach us to number our days aright, that we may gain a heart of wisdom.
~ PSALM 90:12 ~

As the milestones flash past on the road of life, many people feel that time is running out and that they are too old for new thoughts and new experiences. Many people are old before they have even earned the title of "the aged". Others seem to retain the secret of everlasting youth and discover, as they grow older, new worlds of thought and new undertakings. It is the quality of life that matters, not the number of years that you have lived.

Do you feel too old to enjoy new experiences? One of the secrets of life is to live every day productively and to the full. If you want to go somewhere, then go! If you want to do something, do it now! Are you too old to adapt because you have to change your lifestyle? Fear of the unknown, of a new environment filled with strange people, the grief of having to part with personal belongings because your place in the sun is shrinking to accommodate a new routine: these are all realities that you will have to learn to face with courage and faith.

If you have to move to a retirement home, the unfamiliar will soon be replaced by new friendships and fellowship with people of your own peer group. You will enjoy the knowledge that there are people caring for you and that your children do not have to worry about you. And wherever you may find yourself, God is there.

Are you too old to enjoy the beauty and wonders of nature? Have you cocooned yourself with the cotton wool of self-pity and labelled your life devoid of color? Life is a wonderful experience, especially if it is lived in the fellowship of God. Regardless of physical weakness or deterioration, you are still alive, by His grace. As the years speed by, think of eternity with God. As He has accompanied you every step of the way, He is with you now and He will be with you unto eternity.

> You are the rock of my foundation. Only You know the truth and only You can reveal the truth to me. Even in old age I will trust in You. Amen.

Psalm 90:1-17

WHAT IS THE FOCUS OF YOUR PRAYERS?

"Since you have asked for this and not for long life or wealth for yourself, nor have asked for the death of your enemies but for discernment in administering justice, I will do what you have asked. I will give you a wise and discerning heart, so that there will never have been anyone like you, nor will there ever be. Moreover, I will give you what you have not asked for – both riches and honor ... "

~ I KINGS: 3:11-13 ~

In the prayer life of the Christian there is a strong temptation to focus on the "self". Many people have the tendency to go before God with lists of requests. The serious danger of this approach is that your prayers soon become self-centred and that the praise and gratitude to God, as well as the interests of others, take a back seat in your prayers. The consequences of this will be disillusionment, while the strength of your prayer life will have to make way for requests for material objects. If your prayers then go unheard, it could easily cause alienation between God and yourself.

Every prayer that you send up to God must repeat the immortal words of the living Christ: " ... *Yet not as I will, but as you will*" (Mt. 26:39). This is the highest practice in faith: complete surrender of your prayers to the Lord, while you subject yourself to His will and devote yourself to Him. In this way you acknowledge His sovereignty over your life and all your circumstances – as well as over the lives of those on whose behalf you intervene.

When you succeed in committing your prayers completely to God, while trusting Him absolutely with your welfare and future, an untold feeling of peace will descend on your life. You will come to the realization that Christ has laid His hands on you and that the Holy Spirit has guided you onto the perfect path.

Lord, You guide me when words fail me in prayer. Your mercy intervenes and gives me peace. Guide my prayers now and always. Amen.

1 Kings 3:2-15

NEVER PUT THE BLAME ON GOD

A man's own folly ruins his life, yet his heart rages against the LORD.
~ PROVERBS 19:3 ~

God is often accused of things for which He is not responsible. It is His desire that everybody should live in harmony and have a peaceful and productive life, especially that our will should be in harmony with His will. Regardless of this truth, however, there are many maladjusted people and outcasts in society who blame God for their wretched state. This would probably not have happened if these unfortunate people had lived in closer contact with the Master, sought His will for their lives, and showed obedience.

The irrefutable truth is that every person is responsible for his own actions. This should have an enormous influence on each of us. It is a constant law of nature, and of spiritual life, that man reaps exactly what he sows. The fact that this law is often forgotten or ignored does not change the situation in the least.

If you are unhappy in an uncomfortable situation and display an aggressive disposition towards God and life, be sensible, come to peace with your disappointment, frustration and bitterness, and ask yourself where you have gone wrong. Co-operate with life instead of rebelling and kicking against it. Acknowledge the sovereignty of Christ over your life by co-operating with Him and allowing yourself to be guided by Him. Those who share in His life have been invited by Him to enter into a new dimension of life. They will approach their problems from a new perspective, the true values of life will find their rightful place and life will become meaningful because you will view it from Christ's perspective.

Lord, your kindness is everlasting! Even when afflicted by sin, You will not forsake me. I want to sing Your praises and I beseech You to lead me in Your truth. Amen.

Proverbs 19:1-8

GOD WANTS TO BE YOUR PARTNER

Devise your strategy, but it will be thwarted; propose your plan, but it will not stand, for God is with us.

~ ISAIAH 8:10 ~

In many of our lives, circumstances are something viewed with trepidation and even fear. It seems impossible that we could have landed ourselves in such a situation. We might be facing the threat of war against a mighty opponent, we might feel manipulated in the business world, or inevitable and dramatic changes might be on the way as a result of negative forces. Our personal lives may be threatened by circumstances completely beyond our control. In such, and other confusing situations, we might feel that we are under serious threat and so lose hope and admit defeat. The consequences are often disastrous.

The only safe way to venture upon life with any certainty is to do so in partnership with God. He created the world and everything in it – you as well. And He will not allow His creation to be overpowered. His love for you is so profound that He died for you in Jesus Christ. Hence, it is logical that He will deliver you from all evil.

In order to conquer your fears and anxieties amidst threats and in adversity, it is essential for you to have an intimate relationship with the living Christ. You must be one in spirit with Him so that, through the Holy Spirit, He could work in and through you. Then you will be able to face every challenge and danger in His ever-victorious Name.

Thank You, Lord, that You clothe me in armor so that I may remain standing in this world. You deliver me from evil and lead me to victory. Amen.

Isaiah 8:5-16

But now be strong ... declares the LORD ... and work. For I am with you, declares the LORD Almighty.

~ HAGGAI 2:4 ~

$\mathcal{I}$ n the initial exciting phase of one's new life, after you have made a complete surrender to Christ and started to live life as a Christian, the Lord's work is done with zeal and enthusiasm. We are filled with the joy of a new life in the living Christ and we wish to share our feelings and ecstasy with others. We so much want to be part of Christ's triumphal procession through the ages.

However, the problem that arises, is that few people are inclined to share in our enthusiasm. Some people are simply not willing to abandon their old and familiar ways for a new life in Christ Jesus. Others again, might already have been involved with the Lord's work for many years and they do not appreciate spiritually immature people encroaching upon their territory. Then there are those whose antagonism is reflected in their efforts to undermine and discourage by way of ridicule and scorn.

Whatever transpires, never succumb to the temptation to give up your work for Christ. Seek guidance from the Master at all times. When things go wrong and you feel discouraged, lay your problems in prayer before God and beseech Him to show you, through the Holy Spirit, where your conduct is wrong. Never be too afraid or too proud to seek and accept advice from mature Christians whose life and viewpoints you regard with respect. Seek advice, help and guidance at all times, but never allow discouragement to paralyze you in your honest pursuit to serve the Lord. Take courage and be steadfast in faith: through the mercy of Jesus Christ you will achieve success.

Your creation, Lord, will never perish; it is everlasting. Grant me strength and make me Your servant so that I may share in the fulfilment of Your will. Amen.

Haggai 2:1-9

... Where the Spirit of the Lord is, there is freedom.

~ 2 CORINTHIANS 3:17 ~

There are many people who feel disillusioned or disappointed by life. They complain about monotony, they show no interest in their work, even their leisure time drags by tediously. There is no inspiration and no meaning in their spiritual life. They become disillusioned and desolate while their lives have lost all dynamism.

Should you find yourself in this unfortunate situation, you must not attempt to find a worldly solution. It is true that there are many things that you can do to achieve temporary relief, but it is essential that you should look for the cause of your problems. Once you have established that, you will have no problem in finding the solution.

In all probability you will find that you have allowed your spiritual life to decline into a lifeless routine and that your faith has lost its splendor. It is essential that you open your life to the regenerating influence of Jesus the living Christ by practising regular and intimate fellowship with Him. Thus you enable Him to be your Partner in everything that you attempt and do. Once you are filled with His Holy Spirit, there will be new inspiration in your life, which means that it will also have new purpose and meaning. This is no temporary measure, because Jesus has promised to be with you always (cf. Mt. 28:20). Just make sure that you are always with Him.

Transform me, Lord, and allow Your Spirit to imbue me. Guide me in worship through Your power. Amen.

2 Corinthians 3:11-17

Is any one of you in trouble? He should pray. Is anyone happy? Let him sing songs of praise.

~ JAMES 5:13 ~

When one needs advice or help, you turn to somebody for help or assistance. You may seek the help of a well-qualified professional person, or you may turn to a trusty and wise friend for support. Regardless of who it may be, you go to the person with the belief in your heart that they will be able to help. Regardless of the course of events, you are habitually grateful for the assistance rendered to you and naturally you express your gratitude towards them.

When you confront a problem in life, you must never forget, amidst your anxiety and confusion, to go with your distress to the One who mercifully offered to be your Father. He invited all that are weary and burdened to come to Him, because He is willing to help (cf. Mt. 11:28-30). Find consolation and strength in Jesus Christ because He cares for you and He fully understands your distress and anxiety. Go to the Throne of Mercy and lay your problems before Him. Give yourself fully to Him in serious prayer and supplication. Then experience the serenity and peace of mind that only He can give you.

However, don't let the matter rest. While you experience the realization that Jesus is now in control of your life, thank God sincerely for the assurance that He loves you and cares for you, that you are special to Him and that He has laid His hands on you and guided you safely through the labyrinth of life; from your dark confusion to the wondrous light of Jesus' love. Praise the LORD, O my soul! His love is everlasting.

You are the only true Comforter. Thank You for inspiring me and strengthening me time after time. You are my refuge and my shelter. Amen.

James 5:12-20

ℒIFE BEGINS AND ENDS WITH GOD!

"I am the Alpha and the Omega, the First and the Last, the Beginning and the End."

~ REVELATION 22:13 ~

Ⓑe it a normal year or a leap year, life begins and ends with God. Regardless of what happens in your life, the most important and lasting impressions are made at the beginning and the end. Often the events that took place in between grow dim in memory, but you always remember what happened at the beginning and the end. When reading a book, watching a film, listening to a speech or a piece of music, the opening lines or notes have the greatest impact on your memory. The parts in between make little impression. If the beginning captures you and the end inspires you, any weaknesses that may come in between will disappear.

God reminds you of this when He tells you through His Word that He is the Beginning and the End. Your life is in His hands and He decrees your birth, just as He calls you "home" when your life is over. When you were a helpless baby, the love of Christ shielded you so that you were able to find a starting-place in life. Likewise, He was with you in the innocence and inability of your early youth. As you grew older and middle-aged, you were able to think for yourself and you lived your own life. We often tend to forget about this time with all its stresses and strains. It could well be that we forgot about God as well. If this is the case, remember that it is never too late. Turn to Christ today, either for the first time or in revival, and accept His love and forgiveness. In this way you prepare yourself for the encounter with the Omega in the eternal celestial kingdom of God.

You are the Alpha and the Omega, the First and the Last. I eagerly await the day of Your coming when the creation in its entirety will kneel before You. Praise the Lord! Amen.

Revelation 22:12-20

 March

He was despised and rejected by men, a man of sorrows, and familiar with suffering ...

~ Isaiah 53:3 ~

Prayer

Holy God, Your unfathomable love knows no bounds! You love us so, that You sent Your Son to walk the bitter Way of the Cross; even for me. Your love knows no bounds! Lord Jesus, Man of Sorrows, for my transgressions You were pierced; for my iniquities You were crushed; the punishment that brought me peace was upon You; and by Your wounds I was healed. How great are You! Your love knows no bounds. We follow you with holy admiration from the crib to the cross:

You were despised and rejected by men.

You were a man of sorrows, and familiar with suffering.

You walked the Via Dolorosa for me.

For me! The mind reels just to think about it.

It could only be love. Your love knows no bounds!

Lord Jesus, we follow You from Bethlehem to the cross:

from Gabbatha through Gethsemane to Golgotha;

we follow you to the grave and the resurrection.

We glorify Your holy Name. It was also for me.

Your love, Lord Jesus, knows no bounds.

Lead me in this month to new devotion and surrender to Your love, so that You and I may know: Your suffering was not in vain in my life. Man of Sorrows, Your love knows no bounds! We glorify and praise Your holy Name.

Amen

THE MAN OF SORROWS

He was despised and rejected by men, a man of sorrows, and familiar with suffering ...

~ ISAIAH 53:3 ~

Christ's suffering was unique and stands out in world history. It emerges from the plains of time as a monument of remembrance to the Man of Sorrows' suffering – for you and me. It reminds us that God's grace does not come cheap: the price was suffering, sorrow and blood, the blood of His only Son who became human for our sake.

The uniqueness of Christ's suffering did not lie so much in His physical suffering. We dare say that there were many of His followers who suffered physically as much as, if not more than He did. You only need to think of the martyrs who died at the stake; who were savaged by wild animals; who had molten lead poured down their throats; and suffered other unspeakable acts of violence. Christ endured indescribable suffering and was finally crucified. It is well known that crucifixion was the most barbaric and merciless of deaths in those days.

C.K. Schilder wrote a trilogy on the suffering of Christ that we can recommend as enriching reading material during the Passiontide: *Christ In His Suffering, Christ On Trial,* and *Christ Crucified.* In his writings, the author maintains: "The suffering of His soul was the soul of His suffering." He, the One without sin, in obedience to the Father, became "sin" for our sakes. The unbearable burden of the sins of all people through the ages was placed on His shoulders and He vicariously carried it to Golgotha.

Let us narrow down the suffering of Christ until it has me standing singularly, in the first person, helpless and in anguish before God.

Lord Jesus, it was for me that You had to endure scorn and suffering, for me that You had to be crucified. Thank You, Jesus, that You died for me so that I may inherit everlasting life. Amen.

Isaiah 53:1-12

ℐs Christ's suffering nothing to you?

Is it nothing to you, all you who pass by? Look around and see. Is any suffering like my suffering that was inflicted on me, that the LORD brought on me in the day of his fierce anger?

~ LAMENTATIONS 1:12 ~

ℐt is an innate characteristic of the human heart to feel compassion. If you see someone crying, hunched up in sorrow – even if it is a total stranger – your step is slowed down somewhat and you reach out in compassion to the person who grieves. It is only a callous person who passes "on the other side", like the priest and the Levite. Common humanity forces us to stop and empathize with the wretched.

I do not know how many Passion Weeks you have lived through. What has each meant to you? Christ did not always find the compassion of the Good Samaritan from all people, not even from all His followers on the Via Dolorosa. The words of our text for the day can rightfully be asked: "Is it nothing to you?" This reproach may never be true of you and me as His reborn children.

The latter part of Christ's life here on earth was an accumulation of bitter sorrows. What Jesus suffered, both in soul and body, cannot be compared to any other sorrow. He could rightfully say: *"Look around and see. Is any suffering like my suffering that was inflicted on me?"* In Gethsemane He wrestled with the cup of bitterness, and His sweat fell like drops of blood to the ground. With a diabolical kiss, one of His disciples betrayed Him, while another denied Him. He was shackled and led away like a criminal; He was derided, scorned, spat on, tortured and flogged. The Eternal Truth was denounced as a liar. He was sentenced to death although innocent. He was crucified between two criminals. For a while He was even forsaken by God.

And you who pass by on the Way of the Cross – is it nothing to you?

Lord Jesus, thank You for bearing the penance of sin on my behalf so that I may share in the joy of everlasting life. Remind me of the price You paid to redeem me from sin. Amen.

 Lamentations 1:1-13

The cause of Christ's suffering

But he was pierced for our transgressions, he was crushed for our iniquities; the punishment that brought us peace was upon him, and by his wounds we are healed.

~ Isaiah 53:5 ~

What, essentially, was the cause of Christ's suffering? Naturally, He could not have been punished for His own sins. He was holy, innocent, blameless and free of every sin. God declared from heaven: "*This is my Son, whom I love; with him I am well pleased*" (Mt. 3:17). What then is this Passion gospel that is preached?

It is that Jesus Christ took the sins of the world upon Himself and bore them vicariously and in atonement for us. God took our unrighteousness upon Him; our punishment was upon Him; by His wounds we were healed. God's wrath flared up because of our sins. Jesus suffered for the full extent of His life, from the crib to the cross, ... *Look around and see. Is any suffering like my suffering that was inflicted on me ...?* (Lam. 1:12).

What actually is God's wrath? It is the all-consuming blaze of His holiness that works to destroy sin. Some people do not want to hear anything about God's wrath. God is love, they say. We agree with this fully. But God is also holy and we dare not consider His holiness as less important than His love. Wrath is at its most severe when it is justly conveyed by love. God is just in His love. Therefore, He could not let sin go unpunished.

And that is why I implore you, look at Christ in His incomparable sorrow, brought upon Him by a just God in His wrath. It is terrible to fall into the hands of the living God, because the wrath of God is an all-consuming fire. Our God, who is endlessly just, is also endlessly great in love and grace. That is our hope and our salvation.

Lamb of God, the curse of sin nailed You to the cross, and yet, You were still patient and filled with love, because You knew that so many would be redeemed by this. Thank You that You intervened on my behalf as well as at Golgotha. Amen.

Isaiah 53:1-13

⊘HE LAW OF THE GRAIN OF WHEAT

I tell you the truth, unless a grain of wheat falls to the ground and dies,
it remains only a single seed. But if it dies, it produces many seeds.

~ JOHN 12:24 ~

What does Jesus teach us in the Passiontide with these words?
In the first place, He says: *Only through death may life be attained.* The grain of wheat must perish in the bowels of the earth; only then can it germinate to form new life. The Church of Christ was built on the blood of martyrs. When people are willing to die for something, great things always result. First, I must die to my sins, pride, self-justification. I must become less in order for Christ's life to be increasingly revealed in me.

In the second place, Jesus says: *Only when I give my life away, will I keep it.* Christ warned repeatedly that he who wants to save his life, would lose it. Evangelist Evans from Scotland always said, "It is better to burn while serving Christ than to get rusty while serving the world." If we desperately cling to life, we might "exist" longer, but we will not truly "live". Indeed, the Passiontide reminds us of a Man who lived for a mere 33 years, but through His death, history was irrevocably changed.

In the third place, Jesus says to us*: Only through service can true greatness be attained.* Those who serve will be lovingly remembered by the world. It is not what I "get out" of life that counts, but what I "put into" life by serving. That is what Jesus did when He died for us. Throughout His life He served and washed feet. What we need is the bearing of Jesus, the living Christ, in the body of a servant. Then the Passion of Christ would not have been in vain.

I praise You for the life that I have been given through the crucifixion,
Lord. You are my Savior and my God. Amen.

John 12:20-26

ⒷLOOD IS LIFE!

But if we walk in the light, as he is in the light, we have fellowship with one another, and the blood of Jesus, his Son, purifies us from all sin.

~ 1 JOHN 1:7 ~

Ⓦhen Napoleon was in exile on Saint Helena, he occasionally stood in front of a map of the world on which England was marked in red. He would point his finger resentfully to the red spot and say, "If it were not for that red blotch, I would have conquered the world." Likewise, Satan probably points to Golgotha and the blood that flowed there, and peevishly says, "If it were not for Golgotha and the blood of the Lamb, I would have conquered the world."

Time and again, Passiontide confronts us with Golgotha and the meaning of the blood that flowed there. We extol the virtues of the Cross and we pray on His blood. How is it possible that the blood of a man can purify? Because, from the start, no purification was possible without bloodshed. Blood is life. The blood from the Cross is the surety that Christ has paid the price for our sins in full. The Lamb was slaughtered and the angel of death passes by.

No one else could have done this for us. He had to die as the true God and as a real, just person, free of sin. Only Jesus could have done it. Therefore, the cry from my heart is, "Just give me Jesus, crucified for me." His blood "purifies". The sins of many people are concealed, covered up, and remain hidden. The blood of Jesus purifies ... all sins. No sin is too big or too small.

May you once again share in that purification during the Passiontide. Pray fervently with David, *Create in me a pure heart, O God ...* (Ps. 51:10).

Lord Jesus, drive every idol, every fear from my heart. Deliver me from sin, Lord, so that I may stand untainted before You. Amen.

1 John 1:1-10

⟁HE ABUNDANCE OF LOVE

While ... reclining at the table ... a woman came with an alabaster jar of very expensive perfume, made of pure nard. She broke the jar and poured the perfume on his head.

~ Mᴀʀᴋ 14:3 ~

⟁ his woman performed a service of love that was balm to Jesus' troubled heart on His painful road to the cross. *Her perfume, made of nard, was very precious.* It was made from a rare plant that was obtained with great difficulty from the faraway land of India. Its value was equal to a man's wages for a whole year. She does not only give a few drops as was the custom, but she gives in abundance *everything* that she has. She breaks the jar to ensure that she does not retain anything. She performs a deed of sacrifice. She does not only talk and promise, but she *does* something.

She made a sincere, unadulterated sacrifice. In those days there was no lack of diluted goods. It was therefore extraordinary to find someone who made a sincere, unadulterated and precious sacrifice. This sacrifice was the outward revelation of the true love in her heart.

Therefore her sacrifice emitted a lovely fragrance. Her deed could not remain concealed. Therefore her actions still speak to us and inspire us to similar sincere sacrifices. Her sacrifice was solely to the honor of the suffering Christ. On the one hand, she was sharply criticized for a deed that some regarded as a waste, but on the other hand, she set an example through the ages of sincere sacrifice.

Her perfume could only flow from a broken vessel. Likewise, we must be broken in ourselves as Christ was broken on the cross for us. She realized that the opportunity for sacrifice would be lost beyond recall. One of life's tragedies is that we suppress the impulse to do good, or we postpone it. True love does not postpone, but gives all, as the Man of Sorrows gave *everything* for us.

I lay myself before You, Lord. Use me to glorify Your Name. Amen.

Mark 14:3-9

When they had sung a hymn, they went out to the Mount of Olives.

~ Mark 14:26 ~

Is it not a crying contradiction in terms? Who approaches the cross with a song of praise on the lips? Jesus our Savior did so on the Thursday evening preceding that black Friday, which we commemorate as Good Friday, when He was crucified for us.

How could Jesus sing? Because His heart was in harmony with the will of God. He knew that God only wished the best for Him, as well as for all mankind. He could sing because He had a clear conscience. Many lose their song because sin silences their voices. Jesus could sing because He believed with conviction in His final victory. Just before He was taken captive, Jesus sang a song of praise, not a song of sorrow or suffering. He could sing under the bleakest circumstances because His hand was steadfastly in the hand of His Father.

What is Jesus' song testimony of? His unimpeachable obedience to the will of God. For Him it was a pleasure and not a burden. Jesus did not lament His fate. His song told of His complete surrender to His Father's wishes. It is a striking testimony to His voluntary sacrifice on behalf of us sinners.

What does one learn from Jesus' song of praise? That we should sing while performing our duties, regardless of how difficult they might prove to be. He teaches us that, even in the darkest of days, we should not lose our song, to sing even in the face of death. He is aware of the cross, but He is also aware of the glory to follow. God is faithful! In similar vein, the early Christians sang as martyrs on the stake and in the arenas; likewise, Paul and Silas sang songs of praise to the Lord, with scourged backs, at midnight, and in captivity. And so God's faithful and obedient children will sing through the ages, because the Master has showed us the way.

Father, remind me constantly that Your children are merely lodgers, strangers, on this earth. Let me celebrate in suffering, because I know that I am en route to a life of joy beyond words. Amen.

 Mark 14:26-31

SWORD OR CUP?

Jesus commanded Peter, "Put your sword away! Shall I not drink the cup the Father has given me?"

~ JOHN 18:11 ~

From the start, Jesus Christ was fully aware of what was awaiting Him on the Cross. He did not act in a moment of rash emotion. He lived with the unflinching knowledge of the crucifixion. In contrast, Peter and the other disciples were still hoping that He would be the anticipated earthly Messiah. In the moment of crisis, they were afraid and faint-hearted. The presumptuous Peter pulled out his sword to protect Jesus, but the Master taught him, and us, some Biblical principles.

- *He disapproves of the sword.* Christians do not answer violence with violence. He who lives by the sword will die by the sword. Survival of the fittest is the law in our world. But Jesus teaches us a better way: the law of love which is above the law of retribution. Our duty is to love God above all else and our neighbor as ourselves. Christ not only preached this, He demonstrated it.
- *He comes to terms with the cup.* He had another choice. He could have become an earthly king. However, there was far more at stake for Him than temporary popularity. Peter's deed could have resulted in swift death for the disciples, and Christ knew that after His death there was still a major task awaiting the disciples. A church had to be founded; a kingdom had to be built; the gospel had to be preached. He knew that a misguided deed in Gethsemane would result in lost sinners.

If we obey God's will conscientiously, everything will turn out well. The Cross gives meaning and purpose to our suffering and sorrow: the sword makes it futile and meaningless.

Greatest God, thank You for not giving me what I deserve: punishment for the sins that I commit. Thank You for delivering me from evil. Amen.

John 18:1-11

THE CROSS-CARRYING DISCIPLE

As they were going out, they met a man from Cyrene, named Simon, and they forced him to carry the cross.

~ MATTHEW 27:32 ~

It is remarkable how many people's lives were shaped because their paths crossed that of Jesus. Simon was one of them. We know very little about Simon from Cyrene. He had two sons, Alexander and Rufus, who were involved in the early church. He suffered a major disgrace: he came to celebrate Passover, and ended up carrying a cross. But Simon's shame became an enviable honor and he was rewarded with immortality.

Thousands of ordinary people, like Simon, bear the cross of Christ daily. He did not carry the cross because he was a disciple, but he became a disciple because he had carried the cross. Jesus Himself said: ... "*If anyone would come after me, he must deny himself and take up his cross and follow me*" (Mk. 8:34).

Our cross purifies us for heaven and brings out the best in us. John sees the cross-carrying disciples of Christ in heaven as people whose reward is great. To the Philippians, Paul says: *For it has been granted to you on behalf of Christ not only to believe in Him, but also to suffer for Him ...* (Phil. 1:29).

Therefore, we are also heirs to the suffering of Christ, and we should regard it as an honor and a privilege. Blessed are those who bear the cross of Christ, because they carry the instrument of their salvation. However, we must always ensure that it is the cross of Christ that we bear, and that we are not weighed down by crosses that we have taken upon ourselves. To carry a cross means inconvenience, sacrifice, disgrace, suffering and self-denial for the sake of Christ.

Let us then courageously pick up the cross and carry it cheerfully and without grumbling while we follow the Great Cross-carrier.

Lord Jesus, You know that I wish to follow You to the House of the Father. Strengthen me in my weakness and help me to fulfil my task here on earth. Amen.

Matthew 27:32-44

MISPLACED TEARS

... "Daughters of Jerusalem, do not weep for me; weep for yourselves and for your children."

~ LUKE 23:28 ~

$\mathcal{T}$he Man of Sorrows is on His way to Golgotha, part of a mournful procession. Jesus, with a scourged back, a crown of thorns on His holy head, the crude, wooden cross on His shoulders; arrogant and callous Roman soldiers; heartless high priests; an incited crowd, shouting themselves hoarse with cries of: "Crucify Him! Crucify Him!" But in the midst of this merciless crowd, a small group of women suddenly appears, mourning in great sorrow. And then we find Jesus' surprizing words to these weeping women. Why should they not have wept for Jesus, but rather for themselves and their children?

- His path, regardless of how painful it was, was the road of salvation for mankind. His suffering would yield glorious fruit in the lives of millions. After all, one does not grieve over the birth pangs of a mother, as they herald new life. Likewise, Jesus' sorrow brought new life to countless people. They should not have grieved for Him, because He was walking the road of obedience to God. If a heart lives in harmony with God, we do not have to weep for that soul.

- At the end of Jesus' Via Dolorosa, a glorious reward was awaiting Him. It is the end result of our suffering that is important, not the present sorrows. They should not have wept for Him, because His road of sorrow was also the road of His glorification (cf. Phil. 2:9-11). It was an ominous road with lurking dangers, but it led to unmeasured glory for Him and millions of others.

- Jesus was definitely not the most miserable person in that procession. He was on His way to Golgotha, He was carrying the cross, but He was definitely not pitiable. Everyone else was far worse off than Him and therefore they should not have wept for Him.

My Savior and Lord, You, King of the universe, were treated with hatred and derision so that I, and all the faithful, may have everlasting life. I thank You and glorify You for that. Amen.

Luke 23:26-32

"Daughters of Jerusalem, do not weep for me; weep for yourselves and for your children."

~ LUKE 23:28 ~

Why should the daughters of Jerusalem have wept for themselves and for their children?

- They formed part of the group on whom the curse of Gabbatha had fallen. Before Pilate, they brought the blood of Christ upon themselves and upon their children. Such a person could be mourned with bitter tears. They also had to weep because they were daughters of Jerusalem. But was Jerusalem not the city of grace then? For ten centuries the blood of atonement flowed in the temple court. It was there that the priests sent up sacrificial smoke while mumbling prayers. And now this city of grace was going to become a city of blood, because they had rejected the grace of God.

- They had to weep because they had rejected Christ. Like drowning persons they had cast the only life-jacket aside. For the likes of them salvation is no longer possible. This is to weep over, not so! They sinned against the highest love. The judgement passed on Jerusalem was frightening. In 70 AD Titus completely destroyed Jerusalem. The destruction of Jerusalem reverberated like a mournful cry around the world. Things could not be worse, it was said. Therefore, women who never experienced motherhood were regarded as fortunate.

- Tears of emotional pathos are not enough. Our tears must not be for the suffering of Christ, but for our part and involvement in it. When it is no more to us than tawdry tears of compassion, then Jesus, too, turns to us and says, "Do not weep for me; weep for yourself." Therefore, seek shelter with the Lamb, while it is still a time of mercy. Weep at His feet with tears of sincere remorse over the grief you also brought Him over your sins! Blessed are those who grieve like this, because they will be comforted.

Heavenly Lord, I can do nothing to be delivered from sin. Only You can save me. Amen.

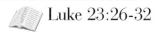 Luke 23:26-32

Gabbatha and the silence of Christ

But Jesus made no reply, not even to a single charge – to the great amazement of the governor.

~ Matthew 27:14 ~

You will remember that the officials who took Jesus captive testified: *"No one ever spoke the way this man does"* ... (Jn. 7:46). He who is not moved by the words of Jesus is definitely no longer open to any words of blessing. However, Jesus is not only powerful in His speech, but also in His silence. Isaiah prophesied: *He was oppressed and afflicted, yet he did not open his mouth* ... (Is. 53:7). Silence often speaks louder than words. Silence can be immensely positive. It can be a deed, a testimony, a warning or a cry. Often one can achieve far more with silence than with the most heated or bitter words.

It is important to know when Jesus is silent. He keeps silent when we lose sight of the truth. He does not defend Himself against the indictments of the Pharisees. He does not plead for justice, because they are not concerned about justice; nor about truth, because they have lost sight of the truth. They do not seek a solution, they seek His life. There are people who come to Jesus with all sorts of ingenious questions and then complain because they are not answered. Even if they did receive an answer, they would not react to it. They pray and ask and search, but they decide beforehand what the answer should be. They do not seek a solution, but an argument. Such questioners, without faith and love, face a silent Christ.

Jesus can also remain silent because He does not have anything more to say. Think here of Herod. When Jesus was brought to him, he was glad to see Jesus. He wanted Jesus to practise a little bit of magic like a magician. Jesus had nothing to say to that. There comes a time when Jesus does not have anything more to say. He finished what He had to say, and there was no reaction. I often fear that Jesus will remain silent in the lives of some people.

Almighty God, make my heart receptive to Your word and Your will and Your Spirit. Amen.

 Matthew 27:11-14

But Jesus made no reply, not even to a single charge – to the great amazement of the governor.

~ Matthew 27:14 ~

Jesus also keeps His silence when we live in sin willingly and without repentance. Think of David, the man after God's own heart. In Psalm 32 he tells us about the terrible silence of God. He committed adultery with Batsheba and had Uriah killed in the hope that he could silence the voice of God. The Holy Spirit revealed his sin and urged him to confess. However, David remained silent, and because he was silent, God kept His silence as well. God's silence drove David to distraction. The only thing that would help was confession before God. This he does in Psalm 32:5, *Then I acknowledged my sin to you and did not cover up my iniquity. I said, "I will confess my transgressions to the Lord" – and you forgave the guilt of my sin.*

Do not carry the burden of sin any longer without confessing to God. Then you will once again find a talking God, whispering to you: *"The blood of my Son, Jesus Christ, cleanses you of all sin."*

Jesus also keeps silence because He wants a miracle to take place in our lives and He is preparing us for it. Think here of Martha and Mary. They call on Jesus to come and see their brother, Lazarus, who is ill. They know that if Jesus merely utters one word, Lazarus will be healed. However, Jesus does not come immediately and, when He arrives four days later, Lazarus is already dead and buried. Although He loved Lazarus, He was preparing them for a major miracle. He breaks His silence with those powerful words of life, "Lazarus, come out!"

Often we do not understand Jesus' silence, but in His own time Jesus speaks and a miracle happens. Then we stand in silence and awe before a love so great, such omnipotence, such majesty. May the Holy Spirit guide you to understand the silence of Christ in your life.

Heavenly Father, You gave Your only begotten Son to die for our sins, so that not one shall be lost. Everyone may now know: God bestows peace. Amen.

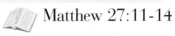 Matthew 27:11-14

GABBATHA: WHAT IS TRUTH?

"What is truth?" Pilate asked ...

~ JOHN 18:38 ~

or Pilate, this was not an honest quest for truth, because it was said with mocking sarcasm. It was not because Pilate could not find an answer to this universal and timeless question in all the philosophies of his time. He now had the opportunity to learn everything about truth from the only man in history who could state: *"I am the Truth!"* Pilate was never really interested in the truth. His guilty conscience caused him to yield to mass hysteria. He was a coward and could not bear to listen to the truth, because he feared that he would have to react to the demands thereof.

In the Passiontide, there are a few fundamental truths that we, as His disciples, can convey to a world in search of truth:

• All people are guilty before God. That is the truth. It is extremely difficult for man to say: I am a guilty sinner! People try to conceal their sins, to deny them or to shift the blame. However, according to the Word of God, the wages of sin is death. And that is the truth.

• Jesus Christ came to this world to deliver us from sin (cf. Jn. 3:16). This is a truth that carries a terrible price. This price was paid on the cross. It could have meant salvation for Pilate as well, if only he was sincere in his quest for truth.

• Every person must discover this glorious truth personally and then appropriate it. This calls for sincere repentance of our sins and turning to God through the Holy Spirit working in our hearts. The Passiontide reminds us anew of this truth: there is still time to discover the truth and respond to it.

The Lord is compassionate and gracious, slow to anger, abounding in love.

Jesus, You alone can truly set me free. Through Your Spirit, lead me into Your truth. Amen.

John 18:28-40

"What shall I do, then, with Jesus who is called Christ?" ...

~ MATTHEW 27:22 ~

One is required to make choices throughout life. As a learner, you must decide on subjects and a career. As an adult, you have to make decisions regarding your business, health, marriage and numerous other things. Furthermore, there are choices for eternity of which the most important is: What must I do with Jesus? My answer to this question will determine where I will spend eternity.

In reply to this question, I could *oppose* Him. I can call out with the crowds: "Crucify Him! Crucify Him!" Every day we hear such futile talk from people. They loudly deny the existence of God; they speak derisively about the Man of Sorrows. They put God's plan of salvation on the same level as the fairy tales of Hans Anderson. They kneel at the altars of opulence, authority, status and materialism. They are foolish enough to believe that they can live without God. He who opposes God, faces a powerful Opponent.

In reply to this question, I can also *ignore* Him. Like Pilate, I can take a basin of water and wash my hands, implying in a dramatic fashion that I do not want to be part of the matter. Religion is beneath people who ignore Jesus, and they will disregard Jesus. They lack a personal conviction of faith. They merely tolerate Christianity as they would a winter cold. They are neither warm nor cold; neither for Him nor against Him. However, you cannot wash your hands of Jesus and His suffering. By refusing to choose, you have already chosen against Him. The result of this choice will be catastrophic.

In reply to this question, I can *embrace* Him irrevocably as my Savior and Redeemer: ... *To all who received him, to those who believed in his name, he gave the right to become children of God* (Jn. 1:12). They accept His love, His peace, His salvation. If you embrace Him, you will be able to rejoice during this Passiontide.

My Savior and Shepherd, how my heart is filled with joy because I was cleansed from sin by Your blood! Amen.

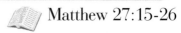 Matthew 27:15-26

GABBATHA: JESUS OR BARABBAS?

... "Which one do you want me to release to you: Barabbas, or Jesus
who is called Christ?"

~ MATTHEW 27:17 ~

At Gabbatha an election is being held: The choice is between the
innocent Man of Sorrows and Barabbas, the agitator, bandit and
murderer. The contrast is overwhelming: Jesus, the Prince of Peace, or
Barabbas, the agitator. The Light of the World or the child of darkness.
Christ's hands drip with blessings; Barabbas's hands drip with blood.
The King of Light or a murderer.

Barabbas was a sinner, but are you or I better than him? Have we not
sinned against God's commandments, rebelled against His supremacy?
As Barabbas stood before Pilate, we stand before God. Barabbas has
already received the death penalty. We deserve the same. Barabbas
had only one hope to be saved: Jesus Christ. Jesus is also the only hope
for us. Barabbas could only be saved by Christ's death; Christ had to
take his sentence, his cross, his death upon Himself. It is the same
with all of us: only the blood of Jesus Christ, cleanses us from all sins
before God.

Barabbas was acquitted without any merit. Similarly, every sinner
without any merit is acquitted. Barabbas was set free because of Jesus,
and nobody could touch him any longer. The sinner who embraces
Christ is completely liberated because Jesus takes his place. He picks
up our cross; He suffers our beating; He wears our crown of thorns; His
body is broken and His blood flows to liberate me.

The choice we face is: Jesus or Satan; life or death; salvation or
damnation. Each of us has to choose and our choices are for eternity:
eternal death or eternal life. Make your choice: "Only give me Jesus,
crucified for me!"

Lord Jesus, thank You for delivering me from sin. Help me to remember
that I must live Your salvation to the full by choosing life anew everyday.
Amen.

Matthew 27:15-26

GETHSEMANE – OLIVE PRESS!

Then Jesus went with his disciples to a place called Gethsemane ...
~ MATTHEW 26:36 ~

The word "Gethsemane" is filled with a holy awareness. Even in the vocabulary of the faithless world, it is used to describe utmost anguish. When we enter this garden, we find ourselves on holy ground. We cross the bridge over the brook of Kidron and walk into the shadows cast by the olive trees. Let us take off our shoes and bend our heads in deep adoration: Jesus, the Man of Sorrows was here.

Jesus came here to find strength and comfort in prayer. He has just prayed His High Priestly prayer for others. Now He prays for Himself to be prepared for His sacrifice; to make the impossible possible; to bear the unbearable. Although Golgotha was the crucible of His physical suffering, Gethsemane was the crucible of His anguish. The message of Gethsemane is one of steadfast obedience to the will of God.

It is a message for our times; a time in which licentiousness is called "freedom"; in which the word "obedience" has become a mockery of everything that is holy. Gethsemane speaks of absolute obedience to drain the cup of bitterness. When Jesus taught His disciples how to pray, He taught them to say, "Your will be done!" In Gethsemane He demonstrates this to His disciples and to all people through the ages.

Christ embraced sinful and sorrowful humanity to save us from eternal death. However, He knows that this embrace must culminate in His being forsaken by God. His sinless soul shrunk in this knowledge. We so easily sing, "Do only Your will, Lord, Your will with me." This is easy when we walk in sunshine, but when the dark shadows of Gethsemane close around us, and we are pressed by life, what then?

Shepherd of my life, You suffered in Gethsemane so that I will never have to endure the same suffering. Thank You for that, Lord. Amen.

Matthew 26:36-46

GETHSEMANE: NOT MY WILL

... "My Father, if it is possible, may this cup be taken from me. Yet not as I will, but as you will."

~ MATTHEW 26:39 ~

The poet, S.J. Pretorius, depicts the mystery of human suffering excellently in his poem entitled "Mechanic":

Life follows its whirligig on the black banks of eternity;
God carefully presses the heart against it
And hones it with the small sharp lunar caustic of sorrow.

When you enter your Gethsemane, remember that Jesus has been there before you and that He taught you the lesson of total obedience to and acceptance of the will of God. Gethsemane is the testimony of Christ's submission to death. Gethsemane proclaims that we are tried in God's crucible, but never destroyed.

Gethsemane brings us a message of distressing solitude: betrayal and renouncement by His disciples; rejection by His people. When David wept on the Mount of Olives, all his followers wept with him (cf. 2 Sam. 15:30). When Jesus was alone in Gethsemane, His disciples slept. He bears the world's sorrows and is forsaken by God. His sinless soul is crushed. He meets the Avenger of sins, He experiences the solitude of death, and yet prays, "As You will".

We utter these words like the fatalist, in spineless submission. With a shrug of the shoulders we claim to be in the hands of blind fate. "Que Sera Sera – Whatever will be, will be." That is the death-knell of all hope. That is passive resistance to God.

But like Jesus, we can also say, "As You will!" in a tone of pious acceptance. He knows that He is subjecting Himself to a love that will never forsake Him. Then we even accept that which we do not understand, because we are assured of the eternal love of God.

To You Lord, I sing a new song filled with praise and glory, because You redeemed us through the blood of Your own Son. Amen.

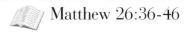 Matthew 26:36-46

GOLGOTHA: THE CROSS IN THE MIDDLE

When they came to the place called the Skull, there they crucified him, along with the criminals – one on his right, the other on his left.

~ LUKE 23:33 ~

Jerusalem is surrounded by mountains: Scopus in the south; Zion in the north; the Mount of Olives in the east; centrally there is Moriah. And then Golgotha, the smallest hill in Jerusalem, and therefore not readily mentioned amongst the mountains that surround the city of David. However, for us Golgotha is the "biggest", most precious, most meaningful of all the high and proud mountains on the entire face of the earth. On Golgotha there are three crosses: the cross in the middle is flanked by those of criminals. In the middle there is the cross of the Man of Sorrows.

Outwardly, the crosses look alike, but in essence they differ from each other as the dark night from the bright, sun-drenched day. The cross in the middle is actually meant for Barabbas, the biggest criminal of them all. The cross in the middle becomes the focal point of the universe, the center of our longing because of the Man hanging there: the Man of Sorrows. In Him, the guilt of all people is nailed to the cross.

Nevertheless, He is untainted and pure: Pilate testifies that He finds no guilt in Him; Pilate's wife says He is a righteous man; Judas declares that he has shed guiltless blood; His fellow-crucified declares that He had done nothing wrong; a Roman officer at the foot of the cross says: *"Surely this was a righteous man"* (Lk. 23:47). In fact, it is *our* cross that He hangs from. He bears *our* guilt, sin and penance. That is the cross of redemption. Barabbas, here Jesus dies on your cross and you are exonerated. Here, all our guilt was redeemed – forever and ever. At the cross in the middle salvation, forgiveness and redemption by God were brought to pass. Let us kneel at the cross in the middle as if it were the gate of our city of refuge: Eternal life!

> Jesus, You have brought me peace with the knowledge that You have already appeared before the Father and born His penance for sin. I praise and glorify You, Lord. Amen.

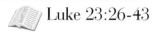 Luke 23:26-43

GOLGOTHA: CRUCIFIED WITH JESUS

... (There) they crucified him, along with the criminals – one on his right, the other on his left.

~ LUKE 23:33 ~

To the left of Jesus is the cross of one of the criminals. This cross is a cross of rebellion and revolt. This is a serious warning to everyone who has followed the Way of the Cross all the way to Golgotha. Here hangs a man who is rebelling against God right up to the moment of death. He is a robber, a rebel and a murderer. He deserves to die over and over again. However, this is not the worst that one can say about this man. Next to him hangs the Savior of sinners. If only he would admit and confess his guilt. But the appalling thing about this man is that he does not experience any guilt, nor does he admit to any injustice. He mocks in unison with the crowds. He has been hardened by sin and therefore he goes unsaved, not because his sin was so great, but because he had an impervious heart. He hangs next to the almighty Savior, and yet he remains unsaved.

Do you hear this terrible thing: one can live close to the Savior and still go unsaved. The river of grace can flow right past you and you can die of thirst when you refuse to drink the water of life.

To the right of Jesus, there is a cross of comfort, of confession, of guilt and of repentance. On this cross there also hangs a villain, no better than the other one. His wasted life will soon come to an end as well, but he gains eternal life. This criminal cast himself upon the grace and love of Jesus. He acknowledges the omnipotence of Jesus and admits his guilt. For him the night of sin is transfigured into a glorious daybreak of salvation. Jesus awaits him at the gates of eternity and guides him, as the very first fruit borne of the cross, into heaven. The angels rejoice in this one sinner who has been redeemed. The cross of Christ therefore becomes a sign of separation, a plus sign for those who want to embrace everlasting life, and a minus sign for the unrepenting.

Thank You Jesus, that I was redeemed through Your blood. Amen.

Luke 23:26-43

GOLGOTHA: WHY?

... "My God, my God, why have you forsaken me?"

~ MATTHEW 27:46 ~

There are countless "whys" in life. Why do bad things happen to good people, and good things to bad people? Why do babies die? Why war, terrorism, murder and hatred? Does God know about it – and if He knows, does He care? Yes, a thousand times yes! He knows and He cares. That is why there was a cross on Golgotha where His own Son had to sob: *"My God, my God, why have you forsaken me?"*

Why the cross, the most cruel and inhumane form of torture and death? Why did Jesus have to die on a cursed tree?

- Because the wrath of God demanded it. Man, created in the image of God, was reduced to sin and the penalty for his trespass was his life: the wages of sin is death. Here God's holiness and righteousness are seen. God is an all-consuming fire and He cannot be untrue to Himself. The ghastliness of man's sins ignited God's wrath.
- Because the love of God required it. Man's sins had to be paid for. This demand of a righteous God could not be evaded. The love of God required a sacrifice of His Son: To take our sins upon Himself and to pay for them with His body, the Man of Sorrows had to suffer hammer-strokes and nail holes.
- Because Christ willed for it to be so. Christ's obedience to the Father caused Him to leave heaven; He became a man like us, except without sin; He suffered sorrow and grief and He eventually died on the cross at Golgotha.

What is your answer to the "Why?" of Golgotha? He did it to redeem us. Golgotha draws our attention to the ghastliness of sin so that we can flee from it forever. Golgotha teaches us that God's love is unfathomable so that we can seek shelter with Him and, in doing so, gain eternal life. Have you done so yet?

> Heavenly Lord, a love as great as Yours deserves my all, my body, my soul and my spirit. Amen.

 Matthew 27:45-56

WORDS FROM THE CROSS

Jesus said ...

~ LUKE 23:34 ~

The seven sayings spoken on the Cross are like seven windows through which we get a glimpse of the soul of the dying Savior. In essence, they are a reflection of God's plan of redemption. Seven times Christ spoke on the cross. Seven was the perfect number for the Jews. It is the number for rest following tiresome labor. God labored for six days and rested on the seventh day. Through the seven sayings spoken on the Cross, the Man of Sorrows eventually finds rest in God. He rests from His wearisome suffering and preaching. On the crude cross, that becomes His deathbed, Jesus teaches us to die with dignity. A person dies as he has lived. To die was not Jesus' fate, but His privilege.

The seven words spoken on the Cross by the Master, can be clearly divided into three parts:

1. Three were spoken before darkness fell.
   - *"Father, forgive them, for they do not know what they are doing"* (Lk. 23:34).
   - *"I tell you the truth, today you will be with me in paradise"* (Lk. 23:43).
   - *" ... Here is your son ... Here is your mother"* (Jn. 19:26-27).
2. One was spoken when darkness descended on the earth.
   - *"My God, my God, why have you forsaken me?"* (Mt. 27:46).
3. Three were spoken after the darkness had lifted.
   - *"I am thirsty"* (Jn. 19:28).
   - *"It is finished"* (Jn. 19:30).
   - *"Father, into your hands I commit my spirit"* (Lk. 23:46).

Therefore, let us listen to that which the Master wanted to teach us from the cross.

Through Your death, heavenly Savior, I was given life. I thank You for that. Amen.

Luke 23:26-35

CROSS: PRAYER FOR FORGIVENESS

... "Father, forgive them, for they do not know what they are doing."
~ LUKE 23:34 ~

𝓘n the first three sayings spoken on the Cross, Christ manifests the depth of His eternal love, first towards His enemies, then towards one of His fellow-crucified; and thirdly towards His mother. In His moment of deep sorrow, He utters a prayer; not a prayer for revenge, but one of sympathy and redemption.

It is a prayer to His Father. His was the greatest sorrow of all times, but in the midst of His suffering He knew that He had a loving Father. That is His anchor of rest and peace. And He is our Father as well. In our deepest sorrow we too can pray to Him. He will understand, because His Son's sorrow was also His sorrow. Therefore He is a safe haven for us in our suffering and grief. With the death of his son, a father once called out, "Where was God when my son died?" Softly the minister replied, "Exactly where He was when His own Son died."

It is also a prayer of sympathy and empathy. *"They do not know what they are doing."* Their understanding of values has been limited and clouded by sin. Jesus prays for others, not for Himself. He pardons, rather than condemning them. He does not want to destroy; He wants to redeem. During His ministry on earth, He preached love: now He demonstrates it. And He expects every disciple of His to do the same.

It was an intercessory prayer of redemption for others. He knows that the sinner's salvation lies in the forgiveness of God. Until the very end He loved and forgave. And He is still interceding for us. He does not desire our death, but to pardon our sins that we can live.

As His disciples, we need to forgive in all our human relationships. As we have been forgiven, so we must forgive.

Thank You Father, for forgiveness of sins; that You erase everything against my name. Amen.

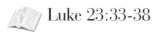 Luke 23:33-38

SECOND WORD SPOKEN ON

THE CROSS: THE FIRST FRUIT

... "I tell you the truth, today you will be with me in paradise."

~ LUKE 23:43 ~

nlike Matthew, Luke maintains (cf. Mt. 27:44) that it was not both criminals who scorned Jesus on the cross. The one on the right acts considerably differently. He acknowledges that they are both guilty, but that Jesus has done nothing wrong. He does not agree with the callous scorning of Jesus by the priests and the Roman soldiers. He acknowledges the Messiahship of Jesus, as well as His innocence. He therefore calls upon Jesus to think of him when He takes up His Messianic Kinghood.

This man truly believes that Jesus can save him, even in the last moments of his dismal life. He also confesses that he believes that Jesus' death does not mean that He is not the Christ. The crucifixion is precisely the evidence of it. This means that he knows that Jesus does not necessarily save Himself because He is the Christ. Through the work of the Holy Spirit, he has an awareness of who Jesus really is.

Jesus breaks His silence and replies to the repentant criminal with the promise, *"Today you will be with me in paradise"*. This glorious promise was not for the distant future, but for the immediate present. This means that, on that day, he would have been led into heaven by the hand of his Savior, as the first fruit of the crucifixion of the Man of Sorrows. There definitely would not have been a period of waiting.

Here is a man who literally embraced the grace of God with his last breath. Therefore he hears from the mouth of Jesus that his prayer has been answered. This is a wonderful example of God's eternal grace to everyone who wishes for it.

You called me to confess my sins, Lord, and therefore I pray once again that You will forgive my sins. Amen.

Luke 23:39-43

Third Word Spoken on

The Cross: Loyalty and Love

When Jesus saw his mother there, and the disciple whom he loved standing near by, he said to his mother, "Dear woman, here is your son," and to the disciple, "Here is your mother."

~ John 19:26-27 ~

The cross on Golgotha links the two most influential words on earth: Jesus and mother. We find two important elements: the loyalty of a mother and the love of a child.

The loyalty of a mother is demonstrated beyond compare by Mary. From before His birth, she kept everything that was said about Him in her heart. She was there for Him during valleys of His life. Painfully she witnessed how the people rejected their Savior; she saw Him carry His cross to Golgotha; she saw how they nailed Him to the rough cross. She witnessed His death. The sword that Simon prophesied pierced her heart. She was with Him as He died, even though her heart was broken. His disciples forsook Him, His friends denied and betrayed Him; His enemies sought His blood. But His mother stood at the foot of the cross. The crowds jeered, mocked, the soldiers were merciless and callous. But His mother remained at His side. That is the true, eternal loyalty of a mother.

The incomparable love of a child is also shown. Jesus knew what His mother had to suffer and that she would stand by Him till death. He did not think about Himself; His love saw only His mother faithful to the end. His last command on this earth concerned her. He forgot about Himself, His own sorrows and needs. Never was He more grateful, more tender and more sensitive towards His mother than here. John rightly said that He loved His own to the very end.

With this, Jesus shows us that our relationships carry responsibilities – even after death.

Through Your example I once again realize that love serves, Lord. Make me a servant to my neighbor. Amen.

John 19:23-27

ᴊOURTH WORD SPOKEN ON

THE CROSS: SORROW AND LOYALTY

"My God, my God, why have you forsaken me?"

~ MATTHEW 27:46 ~

At noon it turns dark on Golgotha and a superstitious silence hangs over the crowds. Only the sorrowful whimpers of the crucified are heard. The air is cleaved by a cry of terror, *"My God, my God, why have You forsaken me?"* In this way Jesus was, for a while, forsaken by God so that we will never be forsaken by God again.

"Forsaken." Is there a more dismal word in the English language? Forsaken by your friends; by your parents; by your family; by your people: Jesus knew it all. But the worst He experienced now: forsaken by God. To be forsaken by God is to be blighted. That is why Schilder says, "The soul of His suffering was the suffering of His soul".

Because He has experienced what it means to be forsaken by God, He can identify with us when our lives turn dark. In His fathomless sorrow, the morning star of Jesus' unyielding loyalty to His Father shines brightly. God's righteousness demanded that He turned His back on Jesus. Our sins demanded it, our salvation could not become reality without it.

Despite His fathomless sorrow, Jesus never falters in His loyalty to His Father. He is steadfast in His faith. It remains, "My God". It is easy to trust God when the sun is shining; to stand the test of darkness is more difficult. The true Christian lives and dies by his faith. Christ knew that the salvation of all people throughout the ages was at stake. Through His unyielding loyalty He sanctified the shame of the cross. By keeping quiet when God was looking for him, Adam caused the gates of paradise to close before man. By invoking God in His deepest despair, Christ once again opened the gates to paradise. Yes, He was forsaken by God so that we will never be forsaken by God again.

Jesus, I thank You that through Your crucifixion You have once again opened paradise to me. Amen.

 Matthew 27:45-53

$\mathcal{F}$IFTH WORD SPOKEN ON
THE CROSS: INTENSE THIRST

Later, knowing that all was now completed, and so that the Scripture would be fulfilled, Jesus said, "I am thirsty".

~ JOHN 19:28 ~

"$\mathcal{I}$ am thirsty!" These are words used by millions of people across the world every day. However, few people know what physical thirst, at its most extreme, really entails. Those who have suffered it tell blood-cudling tales of terrible suffering. Think of people with empty water bottles getting lost in the desert stumbling along in the searing sun with cracked lips and a swollen tongue, while the vultures start circling above them. It is an unspeakable suffering and a ghastly death to die of physical thirst. But then there is spiritual thirst – that "other thirst" – man's thirst after God, after salvation and after eternal life.

Jesus has already spoken three times. He cannot survive much longer. The feverishness of infected wounds on His holy body, where He hangs from the cross in the blazing Eastern sun, is accompanied by an all-consuming thirst. It is common knowledge that this was one of the most painful aspects of the crucifixion. Jesus has already been on the cross for more than three hours.

For whose sake does Jesus suffer this human thirst? For the sake of us sinners to protect us from eternal thirst and suffering in hell. Revelation 22:17 invites us, *The Spirit and the bride say, "Come!" And let him who hears say, "Come." Whoever is thirsty, let him come; and whoever wishes, let him take the free gift of the water of life.*

After what must we thirst? At God's fountain of living water the notice clearly states, " *... Whoever drinks the water I give him will never thirst ... "* (Jn. 4:14).

Father, I thirst after You. Please grant me Your abundant life. Amen.

John 19:28-37

Sixth Word Spoken on the

Cross: Mission Accomplished

When he had received the drink, Jesus said, "It is finished."

~ JOHN 19:30 ~

That which in English requires three words, is only one word in Greek: *Tetelestai*. It is the victorious cry of the victor. It comes forth from the mouth of Jesus the overcomer. It is directed at all people through the ages and at all evil spirits. What was finished and what gave rise to this victorious cry?

- The Old Testament prophecies are fulfilled. Jesus Christ was born in Bethlehem of a virgin from the lineage of David. He was counted amongst the poor and the criminals. He was pierced, His clothes divided and the die cast over them. He enabled the lame to walk, the blind to see, the deaf to hear and the dead to rise. As prophesied, all of this happened – and much more.

- The work of symbolic archetypes is complete: Joseph was betrayed and sold by his brothers; Joshua liberated his people. As High Priest He sacrificed Himself; as the Sacrificial Lamb He laid His life on the altar. As scapegoat He took the blame of humanity upon Himself. He was the perfect sacrifice.

- Victory over the enemy is finished: Darkness turns to shining light. Satan's power is broken and destroyed. Death is dead, because Christ is resurrection and life. He went to prepare a place for us and will once again return in glory to take us to be where He is.

- Man's salvation is complete. The demands of God's righteousness are met. He redeemed us with His blood. Our debt has been paid, the receipt nailed to the cross. Sin no longer rules us. Jesus Triumpher conquered Satan, sin, death and hell. It is finished!

How can we escape if we trample such great salvation under our feet?

On Golgotha, Lord, You triumphed over Hell and Death. Thank You that I may know that I no longer have to be afraid – through You I have everlasting life. Amen.

John 19:28-37

Seventh Word Spoken

ON THE CROSS: ACCEPTANCE

"Father, into your hands I commit my spirit."

~ Luke 23:46 ~

The last word spoken on the Cross speaks of surrender to the will of God. Through obedience the Man of Sorrows has triumphed. The darkness in His soul has vanished, the work of redemption is complete, death holds no fear for Him. God is still His Father. His faith in God remains steadfast.

At the deathbed of Jesus, which consisted of a rough wooden cross, He teaches His followers the way to die. In one of his essays, Bacon says, "Men fear death as children fear to walk in the dark". This is simply not true of the Christian disciple, because we have a Counselor and an Example who taught us to die fearlessly. The valley of the shadow of death no longer holds any terror for us, because He has already been there and He will accompany us to the other side.

Jesus bowed His head when He died. It was symbolic of His humble obedience to the will of God. Regardless of everything that He had to suffer, He quietly accepted the will of the Father. Everything that was heaped upon Him and done to Him, He accepted as the will of God and He committed His spirit to God. To die was not His inexplicable fate, but His privilege and joy because it was the will of His Father.

Those who do not know God as a loving Father, cringe with terror in their dying hour. Their spirit is rebellious and accusations are flung at God. They do not find acceptance in His perfect will. In contrast, God's faithful children, like their Master, simply accept and die, in peace. Everyone who offers assistance to the dying, has experience of both these groups.

How are you going to die? May it be in quiet acceptance like our Savior and Redeemer.

Thank You, heavenly Lord, that I may now call You my Father and that I may know that nobody can tear me from Your hand. Amen.

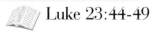 Luke 23:44-49

Ｓｅｃｒｅｔ Disciples

Now there was a man named Joseph ... He came from the Judean town of Arimathea ...

~ LUKE 23:50 ~

Now there was man ... named Nicodemus ... He came to Jesus at night ...

~ JOHN 3:1-2 ~

Ｊesus had died and what had to be done had to be done quickly. The Sabbath was drawing near and then no work was allowed. Jesus' friends were too poor to give Him a proper burial. Now two secret disciples came to the fore: Joseph of Arimathea, who provided the grave, and Nicodemus, who provided the fragrant oil and the death shroud. Sufficient fragrant oil to bury a king. In the conduct of these two people there was both tragedy and glory.

The tragedy lay in the fact that both were secret disciples of Jesus. What would it have meant to Jesus if these two members of the Sanhedrin gave testimony on His behalf when false accusations were flung at Him? But they were afraid. It is true that secret discipleship is impossible. Either your discipleship destroys the secret, or the secret destroys your discipleship. Loyalty and support while Jesus was alive would have meant infinitely more than a grave, a shroud and spices.

But there was also glory. The death of Jesus held more meaning for these two than His life did. Suddenly they had conquered their fear. Joseph of Arimathea personally approaches the Roman governor to claim the body of Jesus and Nicodemus brought his offerings without shame. All cowardice and fear were something of the past. The power of the cross had already started functioning. That is what Jesus personally promised. *"But I, when I am lifted up from the earth, will draw all men to myself"* (Jn. 12:32). The Cross turns cowards into heroes; sceptics into purposeful witnesses.

Lord, become King of my life and grant me Your peace that I so yearn for. Amen.

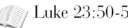 Luke 23:50-55 & John 3:1-13

At the place where Jesus was crucified, there was a garden, and in the garden a new tomb, in which no one had ever been laid ... they laid Jesus there.

~ JOHN 19:41-42 ~

ℸhere are four graves on Golgotha:
- The grave of Jesus was there. There we mourn His suffering, sorrow and God-forsaken state. We weep for the sins of mankind and our own. But it is also a grave where we rejoice. The grave is empty – He is not there. We do not worship a dead Lord, but a living Savior who ensured our salvation. The grave of Jesus proclaims that we are not destined for death, but for eternal life.
- My grave also lies on Golgotha. Paul says, *For Christ's love compels us, because we are convinced that one died for all, and therefore all died* (2 Cor. 5:14). In Christ, I die to my former self; to my pride, self-righteousness and lovelessness. All that He suffered, I should have suffered; all His sorrows should have been my sorrows. If the grain of wheat does not fall into the ground and die, it remains alone. Have you died with Christ on Golgotha?
- On Golgotha we find the grave of Satan. There the final battle was won. Christ suffered and conquered death. He crushed the head of the snake. We need not live as though we are still trapped by the power of Evil. Christ lives and Satan's grave is on Golgotha.
- On Golgotha we find the grave of death. Here, life bloomed as it does with the advent of Spring. Christ is by my side, even in the darkest depths of death. Christ went to prepare a place for us and will return to fetch us. Eternal Life! That is why Paul rejoices in 1 Cor. 15:54: ... *"Death has been swallowed up in victory."*

Over all the graves on Golgotha Jesus stands as the Victor. The living Savior who says, *"... I have come that they may have life, and have it to the full"* (Jn. 10:10).

> Thank You, Jesus, that I may proclaim that You live and therefore I do not fear death, because through You I inherit life. Amen.

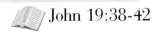 John 19:38-42

April

Prayer is the absolute requirement for everything that God wants to do in this world.

~ Dr Andrew Murray ~

Prayer

Holy God, and my heavenly Father in Jesus Christ: I belong to this world, but I especially belong to You. I yearn to communicate with You. Thank You for providing for that need through *prayer*. We form part of this world, but also of Your world, and I find traces of You everywhere in our beautiful world. It helps me to talk to You in prayer!

My life has its own quota of problems, Lord, and therefore I rejoice that I may bring them to You in prayer. I praise You that prayer keeps my relationship with You healthy and fertile. Lord Jesus, You were our Example in prayer. You taught us to say, "Abba! Father!" so that we can come as close to God as a little child comes to his father. Thank You that it is as easy for us to talk to You as a child to his father.

Help me to pray continually, as Paul commands, because we have the privilege to talk to You in any place at any time.

O, Holy Spirit, teach me the discipline of prayer, to find a time, place and objective in my prayer life to which I can faithfully commit myself.

Thank You for the glorious privilege that I may talk to You under any circumstances, knowing that You listen and hear. How wonderful is Your love, my Lord and Savior. I glorify and praise Your Name, because there is nothing that I cannot pray for, and You will provide all that I truly need. You know what is best for me and what is not. I rest myself in Your holy will.

It is such a wonderful thought that we never really become fully accomplished in prayer; that there are always new mysteries in prayer, waiting to be discovered. Therefore, I humbly plead with Your disciples of old: "Lord, teach us to pray!"

Amen

PRAYER IS SPIRITUAL DISCIPLINE

After he had dismissed them, he went up on a mountainside by himself to pray. When evening came, he was there alone ...

~ MATTHEW 14:23 ~

Everyone who yearns to develop a meaningful spiritual life must be willing to subject himself to discipline. Without that, faith is an emotional gimmick, filled with admirable emotion, but lacking the quality that lends it the constancy that is so essential for spiritual growth.

The most important component in the development of a stable and positive Christian faith is the nurturing of a living and strengthening prayer life. This means that your devotional appointments with your heavenly Father should be kept faithfully and conscientiously, even when there seems to be no reason for it. Lack of time, pressure of appointments, the unwillingness to pray, or simple laziness, are all destructive factors in the development of a positive and disciplined prayer life.

It is important to note that the Master, our Example in prayer, kept conscientious watch over His times of personal prayer. We read that He dismissed the people – His most intimate friends as well – and sought solace in the mountains to be alone with God.

If you are a serious student and practitioner of prayer, take care that this glorious privilege does not become servile duty, something that you believe you *have* to do, otherwise something very bad will happen to you. The wonder is that God is waiting for you at all times to meet you in private. He is Omnipresent and Omniscient – He is aware of your ever-changing circumstances. Therefore, pray – even if you do not feel like it. The effectiveness of your prayers does not depend on your feelings, but on the comforting realization that the Father is always available when you discipline yourself to meet Him.

I call out to You, Lord, and cast my sorrows, my doubts and my needs upon You, because I know that You will hear my prayer. Amen.

Matthew 14:22-32

PRAYER IS UNAVOIDABLE AND ESSENTIAL

Very early in the morning, while it was still dark, Jesus got up, left the house and went off to a solitary place, where he prayed.

~ MARK 1:35 ~

Some of the Master's children are hopelessly too busy. It may be that they are busy building the kingdom of God, and they are involved in meetings, commissions and seminars. As a result, they sometimes neglect their families and their prayer life, laboring under the delusion that they are serving the cause of the Lord.

Being so "terribly busy" is often merely a concealed attempt to fill a spiritual vacuum; an effort to show to God and your neighbor where your loyalty and dedication lie. Jesus Christ does not ask of you to get feverishly involved in His service, or that you should accept all the demands made on you in His Name. Through example and command, He emphasizes the utmost necessity of prayer. You cannot fulfil your spiritual duty without prayer. Aircraft often move at high speed under difficult circumstances, but this cannot happen safely and effectively without conscientious care and preparation by the ground staff. You may be extremely busy in the service of the Lord, but unless, while so hard at work, you are supported by the power of faithful prayer, you run the risk of a complete breakdown and burnout of your spiritual life. You are flying around without sufficient preparation. Eventually the stress becomes too much and a disastrous situation develops.

Prayer is the encouragement and inspiration for Christian service. It gives a seal of sincerity to everything that you embark upon in the Master's Name and gives you the deep satisfaction that you cannot get from any other source.

Father, through Your favor, may I experience more comfort in times of adversity, more sorrow over sin, more joy in my labors. May I be inspired by prayer and pursue Your example diligently. Amen.

Mark 1:32-39

ℙREPARE YOURSELF FOR LIFE THROUGH PRAYER

Pray continually ...

~ 1 THESSALONIANS 5:17 ~

𝒯he future is the great unknown and you do not know what it holds for you. However, there is nothing preventing you from preparing for it. The only effective way of doing this is by developing a healthy prayer life. This means a prayer life that enables you to maintain your balance when it seems as though the world around you has been turned on its head. It will provide you with strength in moments of weakness and comfort in times of sorrow. This is not achieved overnight, but is the precious fruit of ample time spent in the presence of the Lord.

As a wise sailor does not start repairing his sails when overcome by a storm, but already ensures in the calm of the harbor that they are in good condition, the pilgrim on the spiritual path will empower himself in the practice of prayer while he can devote his attention to it, without the pressure and influence of external problems.

Many people will tell you that praying is a natural instinct. This may be true, but an effective prayer life is the result of a disciplined and creative disposition before God. If you are sincere, you will not only pray when you feel like it, but you will rejoice in the privilege and share each fleeting emotion and feeling with your Master. Share your joy in prayer with God while the sun shines, and there will be no feeling of panic when the storm comes up. You will merely share in the quiet conviction that your God is in full control and that you have prepared adequately for every situation in life through prayer. God will do the rest!

> How wonderful, heavenly Father, to praise and to glorify You. I wish to sing the praises of Your great love and faithfulness for all nations to hear. Amen.

 1 Thessalonians 5:12-28

"And when you pray, do not keep on babbling like pagans, for they think they will be heard because of their many words."

~ MATTHEW 6:7 ~

$\mathcal{T}$here are many people who do not give serious thought to the prayers that they send up to God. They have a fixed pattern that was meaningful to them at one time or another in their lives, but through repeated use they have lost the former meaning. Still, they persevere in repeating over-familiar phrases while thinking about other things.

When you spend time in the presence of the living God, and you are sharing your fondest wishes with Him, you must be seriously mindful of the guidance of the Holy Spirit. Ask Him, while you pray, if there is anything that you can do to make your prayer life fertile. To send up high falutin phrases to Him without rhyme or reason and not be prepared to do your share to have those prayers answered, refutes the sincerity and reality of that which you are saying to God.

If you pray for prosperity but refuse to develop a generous spirit, your attitude will prevent you from becoming affluent. If you hanker after peace of mind and spirit but harbor unforgiving thoughts against anybody, you prevent God from bestowing the desired peace upon your life. If your only wish in life is to be happy, but you cause unhappiness for other people by a lack of consideration and greed, true happiness will always evade you.

Do not ask things of God that you can acquire through your effort. Believe in your prayer and, if you have done everything in your power and your prayer still remains unheard, leave everything in God's hand and see how He will be at work in your life.

Father, through Christ I wish to glorify You as my Father. Grant that I, through the guidance of Your Holy Spirit, will be obedient in my quiet time with You. Amen.

Matthew 6:5-15

RATHER SEEK GOD'S COUNTENANCE

"I revealed myself to those who did not ask for me; I was found by those who did not seek me. To a nation that did not call on my name, I said, 'Here am I, here am I.'"

~ ISAIAH 65:1 ~

W hen disaster suddenly strikes, the cry is often heard, "Why has God allowed it to happen?" Whether it is a personal tragedy or a national disaster, there are always those who are ready to blame our loving God and then even question His existence. They base their misleading argument on the false premise that, if there were indeed a God, He would not have allowed something like this to happen.

If we take a closer look at the tragedies and disasters that occur, we will find, time and again, that the human element is always present. Look carefully and honestly at every situation, and you will find ample evidence of indifference, greed, neglect, a search for status and influence, combined with all the other elements that collaborate to create the ingredients of disastrous situations that so often hit us.

Especially in these turbulent times, there is a desperate need to turn to God in prayer, to seek His will and guidance for ourselves, as well as for our country. It is necessary that we should listen to the voice of God as a matter of urgency, and obey that voice, so that, by staying within His will, we can live our lives in "the peace of God, which transcends all understanding". It is by seeking God in sincerity – not by blaming Him – and then obeying Him, that we will do our share to make this world a better place to live in.

Heavenly Father, hear my prayers, and assist me to abide by Your commandments and glorify Your name forever. Amen.

Isaiah 65:1-10

BREAK DOWN THE BARRIERS

I pray that you may be active in sharing your faith, so that you will have a full understanding of every good thing we have in Christ.

~ PHILEMON VERSE 6 ~

One of the most destructive forces that is undermining the church of Christ, is discord. Through the ages, differences of opinion on issues of interpretation and dogma often became so serious that they caused friction and bitterness between denominations. As a result, in many instances, those affected by it grew further and further apart, erecting barriers that resulted in antagonism and bitterness.

It is a sad and lamentable state of affairs, because those involved caused untold damage to the church of Christ. Today still, consciously or subconsciously, through their conduct and actions, they support Satan in his merciless attack on the church.

Regardless of your theological convictions, you must not lose sight of the fact that, as Christians, we worship *one* God who, through Jesus the living Christ, commanded us to love one another as He loves us.

God's holy love is all-inclusive, forgiving, understanding and tolerant. This should be the same quality of love that Christians foster and display towards each other if we want to thwart and conquer the onslaught of Satan.

Lord, Your Word asks of me to love You above all and my neighbor as myself. Grant that I will pursue these two commandments throughout my life. Amen.

Philemon 4-22

A Devotional exercise

Be joyful in hope, patient in affliction, faithful in prayer.

~ Romans 12:9-21 ~

Is your devotional time what it should be? Do you derive maximum spiritual satisfaction from it? These are pertinent questions and you are the only one who can answer. How you answer this question can make a world of difference between an ineffective prayer life, or one filled with an awareness of the presence of God.

While praying, you will undoubtedly think of your family and friends, and of those organizations in which you have a devotional interest. It may be part of your devotional pattern that has already become a habit. It could also be possible that you go further in your prayers than these established thoughts. Yet, the entire world is desperately crying out for prayer. Every newspaper is a prayer manual in itself. You can pray for the editors and for those who form public opinion, for those who are in distress, for those who are victims of violence and crime and, if you are magnanimous enough, even for criminals. If you look for it in the daily press, you will even find something to thank God for.

While moving around in your everyday life, the opportunities for prayer become incalculable. Send up brief prayers for those who seem to be tired or disillusioned, for the dissatisfied and for beggars. Pray thoughts of joy with those who are joyful and thank God for the joy that they radiate. You never need to be at a loss for things to pray for, provided you practise prayer in every situation in life. The big advantage of broadening your devotional base, is that your devotional time and quiet time with God become more profound. While practising praying for others, you are strengthening your ties with Jesus Christ.

Lord God, thank You that I may come to You in prayer for advice and guidance. Thank You for Your Spirit that teaches us to pray. Amen.

Romans 12:9-21

ᗷE PATIENT IN PRAYER

I will stand at my watch and station myself on the ramparts; I will look to see what he will say to me, and what answer I am to give to this complaint.

~ Habakkuk 2:1 ~

So often people complain that their prayers remain unheard. In many instances they start losing patience with God – to such an extent that their faith weakens and they run the risk of getting lost in the wilderness of spiritual stagnation. This is one of the tragic consequences of man's misconception regarding prayer.

It is an established and irrefutable fact that God hears *and* answers our prayers. However, we need to know His Word to understand that His answer comes in His perfect time and in His perfect way, according to His perfect will. This is also done according to our needs. Not your will and your wishes, unless they are in accordance with those of God.

Truly effective prayer often requires us to wait and watch. We must patiently wait for God to give us guidance, and we must wait willingly for a sign from Him that may manifest itself through circumstances, through another person, or even through the directions of your own heart or intuition as the Holy Spirit conveys it to you. If you allow Christ to enter and rule your life, you will develop the ability to remain patient and calm in all circumstances. God *will* reveal Himself to you and show you His way. Our strength lies in being quiet and having faith.

Father, grant that in times of doubt I will turn to You, that I will hold on to Your constancy and on to the assurance that I have in Jesus Christ. Amen.

Habakkuk 2:1-4

ARE YOUR PRAYERS BEING ANSWERED?

"And I will do whatever you ask in my name, so that the Son may bring glory to the Father. You may ask me for anything in my name, and I will do it."

~ JOHN 14:13-14 ~

Let us get back to those people who insist that God does not answer their prayers. They insist that they have taken their requests and prayers to Him, in accordance with His loving and merciful invitation. Yet, despite all the assurances in the Scriptures, their prayers remain unanswered and their wishes unfulfilled.

One all-important fact that is often overlooked, is that Jesus invites you to ask "in My name". This does not mean that all you need to do is to add the Name of Jesus to your devotional wish out of sheer habit. It has never been assumed that the Name of Jesus has magical powers and that it is a formula for the answer that you seek.

Prayer in the Name of the Living Christ implies that you will place your faith and trust implicitly in Him and surrender yourself entirely to Him so that He can provide in your needs as He sees them, and not as you wish.

You must practise patience. Prayer is not an alarm button that you push to call out an answering service. True prayer implies that you take your problems and needs to the throne of grace and wait for God to react to them at His perfect time and in His perfect way. He will do this in a way that is best for you because He loves you, cares about your welfare and only wants the best for you.

God, my Creator, I praise and thank You for Your eternal grace, for Your unfaltering love, and that You faithfully hear my prayers. Amen.

John 14:1-14

℘EACE IN PRAYER

Devote yourselves to prayer, being watchful and thankful.

~ COLOSSIANS 4:2 ~

 here are many people whose lives are ruled by anxiety, worry and fear. They may be concerned for themselves or for another. They may worry about their own future or that of their country or the world. In many cases, violence, crime, civil unrest, terrorism or political and economic instability are the cause of their fears and anxieties. How does one handle a situation like this?

It seems as if the apostle Paul provides the answer to these questions when he says: *Do not be anxious about anything, but in everything, by prayer and petition, with thanksgiving, present your requests to God. And the peace of God, which transcends all understanding, will guard your hearts and your minds in Christ Jesus* (Phil. 4:6-7).

Especially in circumstances of adversity, there is absolutely nothing that you can do from own strength to solve your problem. Jesus said that without Him we can do nothing, but He also said that in God, all things are possible.

Regardless of how difficult, or how bleak the future may seem, your peace of mind is assured if you seek Jesus in quiet prayer. Prayer and meditation, accompanied by praise and thanksgiving, is the only infallible method to ensure that you will be able to confront and handle life. Do not deny yourself the opportunity to find peace in prayer with Jesus, your Savior.

How wonderful, Lord, that I may come to You when I am filled with sorrow and when I repent of my sins; that I may come to You through songs of praise. Thank You for hearing my prayers with love. Amen.

Colossians 4:2-10

WISDOM COMES THROUGH PRAYER

If any of you lacks wisdom, he should ask God, who gives generously
to all without finding fault; and it will be given to him.

~ JAMES: 1:5 ~

M any people regard prayer as a spiritual exercise for those who
are inadequate in themselves and who lack the courage to face
the challenges of life. It is true that God grants confidence to those
who lack it, and helps those who are helpless, but true prayer is far
more than a spare wheel to be used under critical circumstances. It is
not a last resort under despairing conditions.

Prayer holds many advantages for those who make it part of their
daily routine. To wait patiently in the presence of God creates an
opportunity to experience the Holy Spirit. It can transform a time of
senseless words into a source of strength and wisdom that restores
balance in your life.

Seen though the eyes of a person with a stable prayer life, this life
takes on a complete new meaning. The hasty and foolish assessment
of a situation makes room for calm and balanced judgement. You start
to do things according to God's way. You see the patterns of your life
unfolding. It is breathtaking how God guides those who turn to Him in
prayer and listen in obedience to what He has to say.

God talks to you through prayer. Regardless of whether you are
plagued by doubt or confusion, or whether you find it difficult to make
a decision, the person who prays will be enlightened and guided. Prayer
confirms the existence of God in your heart and brings with it a new
experience of life and wisdom.

Jesus, Savior, Your burden is light and Your yoke is easy. Help me to
take up my cross and follow You. Amen.

James 1:1-8

ℐT IS YOUR RESPONSIBILITY TO PRAY

"... Then the Father will give you whatever you ask in my name."

~ JOHN 15:16 ~

When one scratches the surface a bit, you will discover that there is always a reason for people complaining that their prayers are not being heard. They take their needs, wishes and desires to God and they demand to be heard in the Name of Jesus Christ. Then they are deeply disappointed because their prayers are not being answered. They cannot understand why God's promises are not being fulfilled in their lives. According to them, they have conscientiously followed the guidelines set in the Bible.

It is completely true that the omnipotent God *can* and *will* hear prayers. Many grateful disciples can testify to glorious experiences of how, in their personal lives, God mercifully answered their prayers. The Lord's response to our petitions and intercession has already changed many a life radically and brought great joy and relief. Throughout the ages, Christians have been able to testify to this with hearts bursting with gratitude.

Remember when claiming Jesus' promises about prayer, that you are drawing near to God in the Name of Jesus Christ. In other words, before praying in the Name of the living and resurrected Savior, it is important for you to be completely convinced in your own mind that whatever you are asking of God is in accordance with that which Christ Jesus wants for you. This simply means that nothing unchristian may be included in your prayers or thoughts, which should always be ruled by love and a desire to stay within His will, as revealed to you by the Holy Spirit.

> Heavenly Father, thank You for Your gift of the Holy Spirit; that He acts as our Advocate with You and gives testimony on our behalf; that He leads us in prayer and strengthens us. Amen.

John 15:9-17

$\mathcal{P}$OSITIVE THINKING AND POSITIVE PRAYER

"For I know the plans I have for you," declares the LORD, "plans to prosper you and not to harm you, plans to give you hope and a future."

~ JEREMIAH 29:11 ~

$\mathcal{W}$ e live in times when grandiose psychological terms are often used, even by people who know little about the working of man's mind. It is often said that a shy person suffers from an "inferiority complex", and the necessity of "positive thinking" is emphasised in and out of season. Seemingly important phrases are used euphemistically to disguise sin. It is a defect, a weakness, but never is it referred to as sin.

While positive thinking has many advantages, and its benefits have been proven beyond doubt, it must not be confused with positive prayer. One can be an agnostic or even an atheist and still believe in positive thinking. Positive prayer is the sole possession of the believing child of God.

The inspiration of true Christlikeness is prayer; prayer that helps you to envisage the presence of the Master. Once the image of the living Christ has been implanted firmly in your mind, your prayer life will be protected against negative and meaningless phrases, and you will have the assurance that creates a positive disposition towards life.

Positive prayer is creative, but it should always focus your thoughts on God's will and not on what you want. This subjugation to God's will might sound restrictive, but it is not so at all if you keep reminding yourself that God's will for you is always best for you. To pray within God's will requires discipline, and this is never negative. It always results in a life of complete contentment if it is lived in the power and love of the living Christ.

Holy Lord, change my heart into a throne-room for You. Direct my life so that I may live as an example of a child of the God Most High. Amen.

 Jeremiah 29:10-19

..."Lord, teach us to pray ..."

~ Luke 11:1 ~

Most Christians are deeply aware of their own inability to pray according to the will of God. They realize that they should pray more regularly and ask the Master to grant them a more meaningful prayer life. However, they forget that having a vital and pulsating prayer life also depends upon themselves, and not only on the Master.

Christ sacrificed Himself unconditionally for all who embrace Him in faith and trust Him as their Savior and Redeemer. He gave Himself freely, but He will enrich your life only as far as you will allow Him to. The depth and quality of your devotion will be reflected in the power of your prayer life. A weak and superficial devotion can never yield a living and pulsating spiritual life. The whole truth is that if you desire complete dedication to your Master, the responsibility rests squarely on your shoulders.

If you seriously deepen your surrender to Christ, your awareness of His living presence will become an ever-increasing reality in your life. You will discover and open up channels of communication with Him that you can use anywhere at any time. If this happens, your prayers will surpass your former devotional time and will become the driving force of your everyday life. It does not mean a thing to ask God for a meaningful and positive prayer life unless you do your share to develop it.

Lord, teach me not to fret about what tomorrow may bring. Teach me to quietly trust in You, because You are good and all-wise. Amen.

Luke 11:1-13

℘RAY POSITIVELY

Surely the arm of the LORD is not too short to save, nor his ear too dull to hear.

~ ISAIAH 59:1 ~

We live in times of violence and crime and every right-minded person is shocked by the atrocities taking place all over the world. Murder and the slaughter of innocent people have become an everyday occurrence and people wonder where it will all end and if God is still in control, whether He really cares about what happens to us.

Under these circumstances, people are often inclined to pray for the restoration or healing of nations and for spiritual guidance for rulers and people in positions of authority. We commit our country to God's custody and pray for wisdom for our leaders. While all of this is necessary and praiseworthy, it is also tragically true that we do not pray that certain shortcomings will not manifest themselves in leaders, that they will not be corrupt and heartless. Power corrupts and absolute power corrupts absolutely, a wise man said. It is therefore necessary for us to pray with fire and conviction for those in positions of authority.

If you sincerely yearn for peace in our country and the world, it is of utmost importance to do an inventory of your own spiritual life. What does your relationship with others, regardless of race, color or creed, look like? You must be reconciled with your neighbor and show love and tolerance to all whom you come into contact with. It is necessary that you pray for the ability to respect the standpoint of others and to accept the fact that all people have been created in the image of God. Live your life as Jesus commands and you will experience the saving grace of God in your relationships with others, and share in His peace. For this you must pray persistently and positively.

Thank You, Father, that I may come to You when I do not know how to carry on. Thank You that I may rest assured in the knowledge that You will never forsake me. Amen.

Isaiah 59:1-8

And being in anguish, he prayed more earnestly, and his sweat was like drops of blood falling to the ground.

~ LUKE 22:44 ~

℘ rayer is not always an edifying experience. Obviously, there are those enriching moments when God becomes a glorious reality to you and you experience a feeling of oneness with Him. Then prayer creates an intimacy and joy that cannot be put into words. If, however, you have only experienced this aspect of prayer, you have not yet experienced all the qualities and depth of true prayer.

The large majority of the Master's disciples remain in the category of "give me" prayers. They tell God what they want and expect a quick answer. If a reply does not come quickly and in the way they want, they are disappointed but not very surprised, because they did not really expect an answer.

When you petition God to show you His way, to transform you into His image, to use you in His service, you experience the full impact of the challenges of prayer in all its depth. While such prayers are mainly between you and God, it will not be long before you realize that your prayers also involve other people. When you pray and experience God's presence, you will entrust those in distress to Him in prayer: maybe a straying child or young person, a hungry person who is alone and forsaken, the suffering, and all people of whom you become aware through the Holy Spirit.

As God entrusts people and circumstances to you, you start to realize the deep responsibility of true prayer. Sharing in this privilege enables you to identify with Christ's caring intercession for people. This takes you to the depths of prayer and only the Holy Spirit can lead you there. Between the opposite poles of height and depth, your prayer life will improve and mature.

Triune God, I wish to glorify You with my prayers, because I am reconciled with You through Jesus Christ. Amen.

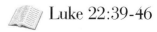 Luke 22:39-46

LET YOUR PRAYER LIFE FLOURISH

But grow in the grace and knowledge of our Lord and Savior Jesus Christ.

~ 2 PETER 3:18 ~

℘ rayer is easy! Prayer is difficult! If you have ever tried nurturing a meaningful prayer life, you will know that both these statements are equally true. With the best intentions you often put aside time to spend quietly in the presence of God, but as soon as you settle down, something suddenly destroys your precious privacy. It could be the telephone ringing, a knock at the door, a sudden thought about something you have forgotten to do. Satan will do his utmost to prevent you from praying.

It might help if you make these disturbing influences part of your prayers. In this way you will find that your prayer life expands. Take the obstacles that Satan places in your way and turn them into objects of prayer. In this way you will thwart Satan and his evil plans.

Prayer is not static, but a living, pulsating power that should be used constantly and continually in order to draw you closer to your heavenly Father. If your prayer life is weak and ineffective, or if you have stopped praying altogether, you are like a car battery that has not functioned for a long time. It cannot perform the task for which is was made. Regularly recharge your devotional batteries through uninterrupted prayer. And then joyfully experience your prayer life flourishing in all aspects to the benefit of your entire spiritual life.

Without You, Lord, I cannot do anything. Fill me with Your Spirit so that I may hold onto You. Amen.

2 Peter 3:8-18

... (Daniel) went home to his upstairs room where the windows opened towards Jerusalem. Three times a day he got down on his knees and prayed, giving thanks to his God, just as he had done before.

~ Daniel 6:10 ~

If your thoughts start to wander during your devotional time, you are merely one of the multitude of struggling disciples of Jesus Christ who wrestle with the same problem. There are few, if any, of Christ's followers who are not enticed by wandering thoughts during their quiet time. It seems as though the Evil One becomes increasingly active the moment someone strives for an intimate relationship with God.

Wandering thoughts during devotional time is not a state that you should accept as unavoidable. Self-imposed discipline, as with Daniel, can enable you to triumph. Do not be shy, afraid or hesitant to walk in the footsteps of the devotional giants from the past. You will be able to learn something different from each of them. In most cases they fought the same fight as you, and they fought until they gained victory.

There is no particular virtue attached to unprepared impromptu prayers. You may need a stimulus prayer to enable you to start praying. A prayer from the Bible or from an inspirational book will help to get you going so that you can talk from the heart in a meaningful way to God. Your imagination could be a wonderful facilitator in your prayer life. Fill your mind with images of Jesus your Lord. See Him as He walked amongst the crowds and imagine yourself as one of those present. You will find a modern translation of the New Testament to be a great help in this. If you make a habit of this, you will soon become aware of the Master's presence and your prayer life will be pulsating and dynamic, set free from negative and wandering thoughts.

Almighty God, make Your servants one when we gather to glorify You. Amen.

Daniel 6:1-13

$\mathcal{D}$O NOT FORGET TO SAY THANK YOU

One of them, when he saw he was healed, came back, praising God in a loud voice.

~ LUKE 17:15 ~

$\mathcal{I}$t is probably correct to say that a high percentage of people's prayer life consists of requests directed at God. In one way or another, we all ask things of God. We pray for healing, for guidance, for salvation, for peace, and that God will provide for our daily needs. Prayer involves the weather, family life, journeys and business undertakings. We seek God's help in matters of the church and state. Think about this while analyzing your own prayers, and you will find this to be true.

Obviously, this is not totally wrong, because Jesus himself invited us to come to Him with all our burdens and cares. What is our reaction when God does answer our prayers? How do we react when He does provide for our needs, heals us, takes away our cares? Or when, in His wisdom, He does not grant us exactly what we have asked for? Or if He gives us something else which we do not necessarily want at a particular moment, but which is clearly within His will for our well-being?

Paul encourages us to present all our requests to God by prayer and petition. And then, significantly, he adds *with thanksgiving* (cf. Phil. 4:6). Then, he continues, we will enjoy the peace of God, which transcends all understanding. Therefore, when you submit your prayer to God, let it be with thanksgiving, within His will. Be grateful that He hears, understands and, in His own perfect time and way, will answer your prayers in a way that is best for you. Accept everything that Jesus has in His heavenly storehouse for you and be at peace with God, your fellow man and yourself.

Lord, I wish to sing Your praises, I wish to glorify You and exalt all Your wondrous works. Amen.

Luke 17:11-19

But when you pray, go into your room, close the door and pray to your Father, who is unseen. Then your Father, who sees what is done in secret, will reward you.

~ MATTHEW 6:6 ~

W hen you isolate yourself to pray, you will often find that you are doing all the talking. Thoughts tumble over each other to be expressed. If you then return to the world with all its activities, you are not at all more refreshed or strengthened than you were at the beginning of your devotional time.

One reason for this is that it is an extremely difficult discipline to wait for God, especially for the disciple who has just been converted. It is far easier to talk to God than to listen to Him in silence. Wandering and annoying thoughts, bitterness in your heart, false pride that nurtures unforgiveness to somebody who has transgressed against you, and many other confusing and destructive thoughts hijack the precious time that you want to spend in God's presence.

Your thoughts do not exist in a vacuum. Therefore you have the responsibility to select your thoughts with care. In the time that you put aside to be alone with God, your thoughts should be completely focused on Him. It is therefore of crucial importance to exclude the world. That is why the Master, in our example of prayer, commands us to isolate ourselves behind closed doors in God's presence. In isolation you are then completely focused on the Father and a two-way conversation. It does not matter if it is physical doors or merely complete isolation. Then we talk to God in private and we listen to what He conveys to us through the Holy Spirit. Never underestimate the value of a closed devotional door in your spiritual life.

Eternal Rock, in You alone I trust, because You will help me. Your kindness and love are abundant. Amen.

Matthew 6:5-14

ⵕHE HOLY SPIRIT AND PRAYER

Live by the Spirit, and you will not gratify the desires of the sinful nature.

~ GALATIANS 5:16 ~

How often we feel disgruntled and frustrated with our prayer life! We long to conduct a meaningful conversation with God, set aside more time for Him, grow in our intimate relationship with Him, but time and again we fail in our good intentions. We sigh with Paul: ... *When I want to do good, evil is right there with me* (Rom. 7:21). This is especially true in the lives of those people who honestly desire a deeper devotional relationship with God and, in obedience to Christ's command, want to accept the challenge of prayer and do battle unto victory. Time and again, these good intentions are thwarted by Satan and we fall short of carrying out our intentions.

To triumph over Satan's temptations, interruptions and wandering thoughts in our prayer time is not all that easy. It requires a strong will and strict self-discipline. There are relatively few people who are able to exercise this self-discipline in their own strength. Consequently, it leads to an even bigger temptation, and that is to stop praying because we have failed, and then to slip back into prayer habits and practices that are not beneficial to our spiritual growth.

Jesus stated clearly and unequivocally that we would not achieve success without His help. However, with the help of God, we can do everything (cf. Phil. 4:13). He even went further and promised the help of the Holy Spirit to those who embrace Him as their Lord and Savior: *... The Spirit helps us in our weakness. We do not know what we ought to pray for, but the Spirit himself intercedes for us with groans that words cannot express* (Rom. 8:26).

Open yourself to the influence of the Holy Spirit, be obedient to His guidance, and you will find that your prayer life will change dramatically for the better.

Lord Jesus, let me always pray, give testimony and serve with love. Teach me to act according to the guidance of Your Spirit. Amen.

 Galatians 5:13-26

PRAYER DOES NOT MAKE YOU
A STRANGER TO THIS WORLD

With this in mind, we constantly pray for you, that our God may count you worthy of his calling ...

~ 2 THESSALONIANS 1:11 ~

P rivate prayer is a wonderful source of spiritual inspiration and strength. Without it, nothing worthwhile is ever achieved. In His example and command, Jesus emphasized the necessity of an intimately personal relationship with God. It is only when you have nurtured an awareness of His holy presence that you can value the power of prayer.

However, we must guard against prayer becoming so personal that it becomes an expression of selfishness, "Lord, please grant me!" "Lord, bless me and mine!" "Lord, if you do this for me, I will do that for you!" Such self-centered requests run the risk of making a mockery out of prayer.

To love, value and worship the eternal God in private prayer is an enriching experience. But while doing it, you become aware of the external world calling for a spirituality that can only be satisfied by the ministering of intercessory prayer or intercession. A person who prays does not only have a responsibility to God, but also to the world in which he lives. In true prayer, you experience something of the despair of the people around you, and you are under obligation to place that despair before your heavenly Father in prayer.

There is a time to be alone with God, but there is a time when you must bring others to Him, even if it requires taking out the roof tiles. This ministering of intercessory prayer is very close to the Master's heart, because He regularly practised it Himself.

Loving Father, teach me to love my neighbor as You meant me to; that I may lend assistance to those who need it, that I will comfort my neighbor in sorrow, and serve him with love. Amen.

2 Thessalonians 1:1-12

ℒord, hear my prayers

You will need to persevere so that when you have done the will of God, you will receive what he has promised.

~ Hebrews 10:36 ~

There are people who propound the "God is dead" theory and maintain that there is no God who hears prayers. Then there are those who believe that God has retired from this world, and no longer has any interest in it, and therefore does not answer prayers. They base their assumptions on the fact that those things they ask of God in prayer never materialize. Consequently, they are disillusioned to such an extent that the flame of their faith burns low and, in some cases, is even extinguished.

It is important to realize and accept that prayer is not a convenient answering service, where you merely push a button and God is at hand to do your will. Prayer should never be regarded as an instant solution to all your problems.

While it may be true that there are instances where God immediately answers prayers in a miraculous way, you must, at the same time, acknowledge that He knows what is in your best interests and that He only wishes you the best. If you accept this fact, it is important that you leave your devotional requests in His capable hands and surrender yourself in faith and trust to His loving care. He will, in His perfect time and way, provide for your needs.

God's timing is perfect. If you have placed your prayers before Him, be patient and wait for the Lord to answer you, through the Holy Spirit, in His infallible way. His answer will always be in your best interests.

You were crucified for *me*; for *me* You were forsaken by God so that evil and sin are triumphed over forever. Thank You for that, Lord Jesus. Amen.

Hebrews 10:22-39

So he left them and went away once more and prayed the third time, saying the same thing.

~ MATTHEW 26:44 ~

Ⓞn Gethsemane, the living Christ taught us an endless amount about prayer. There are many people, including devoted Christians, who experience problems with their prayer life in one form or another. They wonder why the discipline of persevering, fervent prayer is necessary, if God is all-seeing and omniscient. They feel guilty about the fact that they "trouble" God time and again with issues that He is already aware of.

Firstly, many things about various people are known to you as well, but you do not interfere until you are asked for help. However, when asked, you react. If you therefore feel that a particular matter deserves God's intervention, you must not hesitate to place it before Him. Keep Him in remembrance of His promises and request Him to take care of the situation.

Secondly, if you feel that something is worth praying for, it deserves more than just a passing reference before God. Your prayers should be placed before Him in all earnestness. Attempt to identify yourself as intimately as possible with the object of your prayers. True prayer implies honestly giving of yourself. Jesus gave Himself to such an extent that His sweat was drops of blood falling to the ground. Your time and emotions are given on behalf of someone or something. God will never tire of listening to you if you come to Him in the Name of Christ. The Holy Spirit teaches you fervor and perseverance, and therefore you should learn to be sensitive to God's voice through the Holy Spirit. It requires fervor and perseverance of a special quality.

In distress I call to You, oh Lord, because only You can grant me peace. Thank You for hearing my prayers and for always answering my cry for help. Thank You, almighty Father. Amen.

Matthew 26:36-46

ℐN THE HEAT OF DEBATE

I want men everywhere to lift up holy hands in prayer, without anger or disputing.

~ I TIMOTHY 2:8 ~

How do you react in the heat of debate? It is sad that, in some instances, a stranger would have no idea that he was at a Christian gathering, unless previously notified. Too often, high-level church meetings become explosive and people's emotions get the better of their reason. The more serious the debate becomes, the higher the emotions run. Irritation and short tempers are displayed when church leaders are criticized or questioned about their standpoints.

It is an atrocious disservice to the church of Christ when Christian disciples allow their emotions to get the better of them. What untold damage is frequently done to the work of Christ when love is replaced by anger, and harmony by petty differences?

If you get involved in a situation where it seems as though matters are getting out of hand, turn to God in prayer. If you are in discussion with others, suggest that you temporarily adjourn the meeting for a few moments of prayer. If your request is denied, send your own silent prayer to the Throne of Mercy for guidance, wisdom, tolerance and understanding. Do not succumb to the temptation to give expression to your anger. Ask the Holy Spirit for the strength to demonstrate the love of Jesus Christ in your words and deeds. There is simply no better way to heal wounds and restore peace.

> Almighty God, grant that my conduct glorify Your Name. Let Your Spirit guide me in every moment so that I may conduct myself like a child of God Most High. Amen.

1 Timothy 2:8-15

... But the Spirit himself intercedes for us with groans that words cannot express.

~ Romans 8:26 ~

⟨I⟩t is a laudable desire to be skilled in prayer, but, so often, starting to pray leads to frustration. Take heart, every unspoken wish could be a prayer.

God does not expect high falutin and learned words, fancy phrases or superficial eulogies. He asks a life that sincerely seeks Him and your yearning for Him is an indication that your thoughts are turned to God. It is of utmost importance that you should put time aside for prayer and meditation. If you suspend your own efforts and become quiet before God, you will become aware of His nearness and presence. We must never forget that meaningful prayer is a continual exercise that may be practised at any time, anywhere.

Prayer is a practical experience of your mind and spirit that can be practised at all times and under any circumstances. Your prayers should be simple and natural. It is not irreverent to talk to God as you would to a trusted friend. Such intimacy will, without a doubt, bring joy to His paternal heart. You are then not busy using artificial language, but you pour out your spirit and thoughts in a simple manner to Him. God is not so much interested in your "style" of worship, as in the sincerity of your heart.

If you truly want to pray effectively, allow your most honorable thoughts to be the foundation of your prayer life. Then you will develop a growing intimacy with your Father and the Spirit will pray in unison with your spirit.

> Father, the heart is so easily misled. Come and rule in my heart and life, Lord, to the greater glory of Your Name. Amen.

Romans 8:18-30

ℙRAYER IS A LIFE-ALTERING POWER

So Jacob was left alone, and a man wrestled with him till daybreak.

~ GENESIS 32:24 ~

... "Your name will no longer be Jacob, but Israel, because you have struggled with God and with men and have overcome."

~ GENESIS 32:28 ~

ℐn the final analysis, prayer is what *you* make of it. For thousands it is comfort in sorrow. Others again, experience immense power when they spend time with God. Nobody can question the effectiveness of true prayer.

Unfortunately, there are those for whom prayer is a routine without any power or meaning, despite what God has meant prayer to be. Some people pray because they are afraid that something terrible will happen to them if they should stop praying. Others again suspend their devotional time because they feel that they do not want to continue with a practice that, according to them, serves no useful purpose.

Effective prayer is much more than asking God for things that will enrich your life. Or to use flattering words to satisfy an erratic God, in order for Him to grant you that which you ask from Him. True prayer is a pursuit of a clearer, deeper and richer vision of God your Father. Your prayers may be weak and imperfect, but it is your spirit that reaches out to the eternal God. He accepts your motives before judging your prayer. The wishes of your heart are of greater importance to God than the way in which you express yourself in words.

Realize, that while your heart is yearning for God, He is waiting to meet with you and manifest His love for you. He does not only wish to comfort and console. He wishes to challenge you to faith and trust so that you will accept His will unconditionally. Then you are motivated in your devotional time by hallowed ideals that are confirmed by His Holy Spirit. Then you are a reborn creature in Jesus Christ.

> Lord Jesus, You triumphed over sin. I glorify and praise You that, through Your sacrifice, I may share in this. Amen.

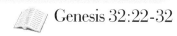 Genesis 32:22-32

Is any one of you sick? He should call the elders of the church to pray over him ... And the prayer offered in faith will make the sick person well; the Lord will raise him up...

~ JAMES 5:14-15 ~

$\mathcal{N}$ever underestimate the power of prayer in a case of illness. While in any way we do not detract from medical science, we must never lose sight of the fact that miracles have been performed in the past – and are still performed today – through God's healing power brought about through intercession.

Too often prayers for the sick are mechanical and superficial. Often no attempt is even made to determine the cause of illness. Nothing is asked about the sick person's identity. The seriousness of his condition is not determined, neither the circumstances in which he finds himself. If you study Jesus Christ's devotional procedure, you cannot but notice how intimately He identified with the sick person seeking healing. He even felt how strength flowed from His own body when the healing process started.

True prayer for healing is not an experiment in trial and error. It was never intended to be merely a matter of minor importance. It requires the highest form of trust in God on the part of the person who prays, sufficient to entrust the patient to God's caring mercy in order for Him to manifest His perfect will in the sick person. Complete involvement on the side of the intercessor, and total acceptance of God's will on the side of the patient, will lead to the greatest miracle of all healing: the peace of God, which transcends all understanding.

> Eternal Father, will You guide me to say prayers to Your greater glorification with faith that could move mountains. Amen.

James 5:13-20

ℬE POSITIVE IN PRAYER

"What do you want me to do for you?" ...

~ Mark 10:51 ~

𝒰 nfortunately, there are many people who are extremely sceptical about the value of prayer, and they deny themselves one of God's greatest gifts of mercy to mankind. They will point to everything that is going wrong in the world, to those who suffer failure upon failure, to the unfortunate victims of disease and illness, to those whose lives are in ruin. Inevitably, they will then question the value of prayer, as well as the love of a God who allows it all to happen.

When you come in prayer before God, it is essential to be explicit and crystal clear in your requests, and that you reveal faith and trust that will enable you to entrust your petitions, or the person for whom you are praying, to God's sublime will. When you have stated your requests, you must trust in God to take them up and answer them in His time and way. It will most certainly be in the best interests of all concerned.

Do not be vague, half-hearted or unsure when you pray. It is a sign of lack of faith if you pray negatively, because you are subconsciously, without realizing it, finding a loophole to hide behind if what you seek does not transpire. When you are in the presence of God, place all your fears and concerns before Him. Ask Him to guide you and allow the Holy Spirit to determine your thoughts. If you have been honest and sincere with God, then leave the matter in His loving hands. Be filled with expectation and await His answer. He will not disappoint you.

> Almighty Lord, cleanse me, make me holy and pure, so that I may draw near to Your throne. Amen.

Mark 10:46-52

... But God has revealed it to us by his Spirit. The spirit searches all things, even the deep things of God.

~ 1 Corinthians 2:10 ~

𝓜 any of the Lord's most devoted children have demonstrated the value of "darting prayers". These are short, but sincere prayers, sent up to God in moments of extreme distress. Experience has shown, time and again, that God honors such prayers with an answer. In the development of the discipline and art of prayer, we will become aware that these fleeting prayers are not sufficient for an effective prayer life. An instant prayer is evidence that you are reaching out to God, but it usually leaves insufficient time for God's presence to become a positive reality to you.

Prayer is like a two-lane highway. You reach out to God and God seeks access to your spirit and thoughts in order for you and Him to unite. Such intimate identification, even when accepted in simple faith, takes time to develop. It takes time to become aware of God's presence and to become sensitive to His guidance and will.

To identify with God in prayer, is much more than simply a religious theory or an emotional experience. In order for it to reach maximum potential, it must result in service. Prayer that does not manifest itself in your daily life, fails miserably in giving expression to God's will in human situations.

Through prayer, you can grow in the image of Jesus Christ. When you receive His Holy Spirit, through His grace and power, you are not only able to identify with Him, but also to convey His values in life to others.

God Most High, recreate me, transform my heart, so that in my words and conduct I may increasingly conform to Your image. Amen.

1 Corinthians 2:6-16

May

So we rebuilt the wall till all of it reached half its height, for the people worked with all their heart.

~ Nehemiah 4:6 ~

Prayer

I thank You, loving God and heavenly Father, that I have a task to perform.

Grant me the grace to put my heart in it and to do it as though I was doing it for You. Thank You Master, for finding joy and pride in my labors to Your greater glory. Lord Jesus, You spent the first years of Your life in a carpenter's shop, performing Your holy labor. Therefore we know that You will understand.

Preserve me from a mindless day-to-day routine. Grant me inspiration, enthusiasm and creativity for my task.

Prevent me from getting into a dusty rut. Make every day and every task new and challenging for me. Elevate and enrich my relationships with my fellow-workers. Grant that they will see from my labor and my life that I am Your child.

Make me conscientious in every detail and dedicated to every assignment I receive; loyal to my employer, provided that my loyalty to You is not negatively influenced. Help me not to get involved in petty quarrels, unfair incitement and destructive conduct.

Thank You, Lord Jesus, that the people whom You called upon to be Your co-workers were ordinary people like me.

Open my heart and ears so that I may hear Your voice above the droning of machinery and technology.

I pray this in the Name of Jesus, my Lord,
My Example and Counselor in life.
Amen

WORK SATISFACTION

So I saw that there is nothing better for a man than to enjoy his work,
because that is his lot ...

~ ECCLESIASTES 3:22 ~

People often find their work monotonous because the initial fascination with their task has gone and only frustration and boredom
remain. This attitude has become an everyday occurrence, due to
electronic resources and technological equipment that work and think
for man.

You must utilize the special talents and aptitudes that God entrusted
you with in your chosen profession, so that you can do your share,
regardless of how elementary or routine it may be, in order to achieve
the eventual objective and to facilitate the completion of an important
project. All surgeons are dependent on the theatre staff, and they are
essential to the success of the operation, even those who have the
humble task of attending to the hygiene of the operating theatre. The
success of the world-famous pianist would be impossible without the
painfully conscientious attention of the piano tuner to his task.

Whatever task you are called upon to perform, do not neglect to
thank God that He has chosen you to do it. Dedicate everything you
do to Him and ask the Holy Spirit to guide and comfort you, so that
whatever you are called upon to do, you will find perfect joy in the
knowledge that you are doing it well because you are doing it to the
glorification of your Master.

Help us, Lord, to glorify Your Name forever in everything we do.
Help us always to recognize Your hand in our lives. Amen.

Ecclesiastes 3:18-22

Be kind and compassionate to one another, forgiving each other, just as in Christ God forgave you.

~ EPHESIANS 4:32 ~

ℐn our everyday labors we are often entangled in relationships with other people. These relationships contribute positively or negatively to the quality of our labor. There are certain things in life against which you have to protect yourself: complacency, selfishness, foolish pride, unhealthy thoughts, ridicule that hurts others and many more disparaging dispositions that inflict pain on other people.

It is general knowledge that hardening of the arteries obstructs the free flow of blood. However, by hardening your disposition against calls for help, forgiveness and allaying the distress of others, you could harden your spirit and prejudice your personality. There are many reasons why people harden their hearts towards people less fortunate than they are. One is simply meanness or small-mindedness; another is that they think that by offering understanding, love and possible financial aid, they would be exploited. Nobody enjoys being exploited. We don't want to be taken for granted.

The way to overcome a heartless and uninvolved disposition is to approach life with the attitude of Jesus Christ. It requires of you not to condemn; but to have sympathy for, and understanding of, the frustrations of those less fortunate, as well as the will to think and act constructively.

Displaying such a compassionate attitude helps to establish sympathy and meaningful and lasting relationships; it allows the Spirit of God to work through you and, once again, bring you to the realization that only through being a blessing to your fellow man can you receive the love and blessing of God.

Sometimes we are so uninvolved. Help us, Lord, to comfort those who are filled with sorrow. Help us to support them in neighborly love. Amen.

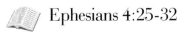 Ephesians 4:25-32

INSPIRATION FOR YOUR GOD-GIVEN TASK

"Listen to this, Job; stop and consider God's wonders."

~ JOB 37:14 ~

When you feel unworthy and incapable of the task set for you and to which God has called you, find courage in the fact that many of God's greatest servants felt unworthy of their calling. The Bible repeatedly tells of people who tried to avoid the calling that God had for them.

If you feel convinced that God has called you to a specific or special task and you still feel unsure of yourself, nevertheless do everything in your power to prepare yourself for that task. Clear your mind of all negative thoughts and emotions and spend intimate time with God. Be quiet in His presence so that you may become attuned to His holy presence. This spiritual exercise will make you aware of God's way of working. You will see God at work in changing circumstances and conditions and you will gain the confidence to wrestle with problems that could cross your path.

The inspiration and self-confidence that you receive from God are much more than a superficial form of emotion. If your spirit plummets the depths and your vision of what God wants you to do is vague, quietly wait on Him and then you will be assured that the task you have been set, can be accomplished, if you draw from the Source of wisdom and strength. Put all your thoughts before God and ask His blessing and clear guidance. Then a path will certainly open before you and you will receive everything required to perform the task to which God has called you.

Your omnipotence knows no bounds, Your creations are perfect. The universe in its grandeur belongs only to You. Amen.

Job 37:13-24

⊘HE FOLLY OF PRIDE

An unfriendly man pursues selfish ends; he defies all sound judgment.
~ PROVERBS 18:1 ~

Selfishness is the twin brother of pride. There are people who always want their own way and this is obvious in every facet of their lives; especially in conversation. They state their case dogmatically and do not tolerate any contradiction or argument. When they are questioned, they become aggressive and unpleasant.

Such people are often found in company and work situations. They normally volunteer to serve on committees. The opinions that they propound are normally concealed behind grand-sounding phrases and almost incomprehensible language. They are forever busy talking about principles of vital importance that are at stake. The truth is, however, that they are not in the least concerned about defending a principle, but merely their own haughtiness, pride and selfishness. They regard losing an argument as personal humiliation and are more concerned about winning an argument than reaching a peaceful settlement.

It is a wise man who does not allow selfish pride to become a stumbling block between him and his co-workers. His quest for the truth is more to him than scoring points in a debate, and he is big enough to admit defeat when it is in the interest of everybody.

Where the Spirit of Christ reigns in a person's life, constructive humility develops in place of a negative mind that forever creates problems of selfish pride between people. To be truly humble is to co-operate at all times for the sake of the general benefit of all. It is also a sure way to destroy foolish and selfish pride.

Sometimes we are so proud. Help us to stand before You small and humble and to glorify Your great name with sincerity. Amen.

Proverbs 18:1-9

DO NOT JUDGE

Do not take revenge, my friends, but leave room for God's wrath.

~ ROMANS 12:19 ~

Many people pass judgement because of their preconceived ideas. They accept a one-sided opinion that is both untrue and unwise. When dealing with complex situations, it is important for you not to be influenced by hearsay or wild speculations. There are always people who are more than willing to foist their unfounded opinions on you. If you listen to them, you will remain unsure and dissatisfied, until you have weighed your findings against your own opinions and experiences.

Avoid judging others, as you will never really understand their circumstances because you have not experienced identical circumstances yourself. Who gave you or me the right to judge? Judgement belongs to God; He said so himself. If you attempt to judge, you will merely create conflict in your innermost being, because you burden your mind with condemning thoughts. To walk in the shoes of the one who is being judged creates wise insight. Is your motive to judge born from love or from a desire to see another being humiliated? If you form your opinion with the attitude of Jesus Christ, your judgement will have healing qualities that are constructive and edifying.

Before passing judgement, consider your own shortcomings and weaknesses. Think of the love and wisdom of your Savior when He said that the one without blame should cast the first stone. If judgement, however, is required, it may only be passed with a Christian attitude of love and compassion.

Help us to glorify Your Name in everything we do. Please soften our hearts and help us to show compassion towards others. Amen.

Romans 12:9-21

ᗰON'T LOSE HOPE

... Never tire of doing what is right.

~ 2 THESSALONIANS 3:13 ~

ᕼ ow often have you met people who feel that there is little or no sense in trying to do "the right thing", or to live a life of caring about other people and their problems? These are people who might have reached out in friendliness to others, only to be rebuffed, or they might have offered their assistance to somebody and their friendliness was abused. They might have made sacrifices that went by totally unnoticed, or maybe they have supported somebody that left them in the lurch to their own detriment. Under these circumstances the benefactor is inclined to withdraw into himself, fearing that he might be hurt once again.

Regardless of how justified you might feel, you must realize that this attitude will inevitably lead to self-centeredness and a feeling of complacency. Moreover, if you want to be honest with yourself, you will have to admit that it clashes directly with the doctrines of Jesus Christ. In spite of the thankless disposition of people, He gave His all to mankind and never gave up on people.

In today's world, it is not easy to display the disposition of Jesus Christ. However, you must remember that what you do for other people, you also do for the Master. The gratitude or lack thereof, cannot nearly be compared to the satisfaction you experience as a devoted servant of Jesus Christ. Indeed, Jesus said, *"... In this world you will have trouble. But take heart! I have overcome the world"* (Jn. 16:33).

Lord, please strengthen us. Give us a steady hand, in order to never cease doing Your work. Amen.

2 Thessalonians 3:6-18

ALWAYS BE YOUR BEST

I urge you to live a life worthy of the calling you have received.

~ EPHESIANS 4:1 ~

People are inclined to display a personality in the workplace that is different to who they really are. They wear a mask. A Christian must be himself and strive to be the best he can be – to be that which God meant him to be!

Some people feel it serves no purpose to live as a Christian. For a long time you have endeavored to maintain the appearance of Christlikeness. You sinned, pleaded for forgiveness and sinned again, until it degenerated into such a routine that you made a mockery out of God's forgiveness. You know who you should be through the mercy and power of Christ, and you also know who you really are, because of disobedience, sin and self-centeredness. This knowledge is so discouraging that you feel inclined to put an end to all efforts to be the Christian that you should be.

There may be a number of reasons why you regard attempts to be a true Christian as a useless exercise. However, there are also many good reasons to persevere and to keep on trying. Jesus loves you and wants to be your Friend. The love He has for you is greater than the ebb and flow of your emotional experiences. His love is steadfast and constant. In contrast to your weakness, He puts His strength at your disposal and asks you to draw this strength into your life through prayer, meditation, Bible study and positive thinking (cf. 2 Cor. 12:9).

As the love of Christ becomes an increasing reality in your life, your faith will grow and become powerful and creative. Do not be discouraged: the Master believes in you. For His sake, be your best self. He will strengthen and comfort you at all times.

Please mold my heart, my strength and my reason every day. Let everything I do, say and think bear testimony to Your presence in my life. Amen.

Ephesians 4:1-8

GUARD AGAINST GREED

"Watch out! Be on your guard against all kinds of greed; a man's life does not consist in the abundance of his possessions."

~ LUKE 12:15 ~

Greed is seldom mentioned by name. It is regularly disguised in order to cover its awful face and to give it an acceptable appearance. Rich people are seldom content with their wealth, because they are constantly looking for ways to multiply that which they already possess. To gather riches for the sake of riches, or for the sake of the security it offers you, never yields the satisfaction expected.

Underprivileged people can also be guilty of greed. Hoarding more possessions than you need and refusing to share with others due to a fear of the future, is not in accordance with the will of God. To allow greed, regardless of its form, to rule your life, is to renounce your faith in the generosity of your heavenly Father. The abundance of God's generosity is breathtaking, but one of man's biggest sins is that he abuses God's gifts through his greed and thus creates an unhealthy economic state.

God did not limit Himself to the giving of gifts. He gave Himself. This quality of Divine generosity is far beyond our comprehension. But those who, in faith, embrace God's gift of Himself in Jesus Christ, are completely delivered from the kind of greed that imprisons one's spirit and affects one's personality for the worse.

Break the bonds of greed and start to give, not only of your material possessions, but also of yourself. Then you start living the life of benevolence that God meant for you, and then you allow God to smile on your life.

We know that You will always provide in abundance. Help us to do Your will at all times and to know that You will provide for our needs. Amen.

Luke 12:13-21

THE DYNAMICS OF THE SPOKEN WORD

A word aptly spoken is like apples of gold in settings of silver.

~ PROVERBS 25:11 ~

In the workplace, various ways are used to communicate with various people. Communication mostly takes place through conversations. A single word can make a major difference in a person's life. How these words are spoken is therefore of utmost importance. Some people have a special flair for words and, by choosing the right word at the right time, they can make an untold difference to another person's life. They can fill others with a glowing feeling of wellbeing. However, it is equally true that a wrong word and bad timing can have a devastating effect on someone's life.

There are times when people yearn for a word of encouragement or compassion, when an expression of love or interest can make a world of difference and brighten their day. A word of praise or well-meant advice is never wasted; even constructive criticism or a concerned reprimand is acceptable and beneficial to the receiver.

The most important thing for you as a Christian is that, through the power of the Holy Spirit, you should choose your words prudently and determine their timing with utmost responsibility and care. Be sensitive to the state of mind of the person you talk to. Avoid needless flattery and, equally important, heartlessness. Always be sincere in what you say and speak with the love of Jesus Christ in your heart. In this way you will enrich not only the life of the person you are talking to, but your own life too.

Your Name is so holy and great. Help me, Lord, to never say or do anything that will disgrace You. Amen.

Proverbs 25:1-12

STAND BY YOUR CONVICTIONS

Do not conform any longer to the pattern of the world, but be transformed by the renewing of your mind.

~ Romans 12:2 ~

There is a growing number of people in the labor market today who do not remain true to their highest ideals and principles. For many it is merely a form of weakness and laziness, because the standards set for them are too high. Such people have noble dreams that will never be realized.

There are many people who bow to societal pressure and so suppress their ideals. If the moral and spiritual standards of the community in which they live are low, they are embarrassed to take a stand that is in direct contrast with popular opinion. If love and truth form an integral part of your character, and you live in a society where neither is honored or respected, you will eventually find yourself in disharmony with your fellow man.

Such disharmony could be a time of testing. You could suppress your high ideals and meekly accept popular opinion. In this way you violate your God-created character. On the other hand, you could stand by your convictions. What you believe in is then of crucial importance and becomes the only way for you to achieve true freedom in life. If you are true to yourself, you may be scorned or rejected, but you will enjoy the satisfaction of knowing that you do not live a double life. It is only when you are at peace with yourself and when you strive to please God rather than your fellow man, that you will be able to live a life of quality and contentment.

Bless our labor in You, Lord. Help us to be steadfast and strong, and always filled with fervor towards You. Amen.

Romans 12:1-8

How do you deal with aggression?

A gentle answer turns away wrath, but a harsh word stirs up anger.

~ Proverbs 15:1 ~

Even the most placid person can, at times, be irritated by someone's aggression. A sense of humor and a positive disposition can handle minor annoyances, but if these are accompanied by repulsive aggression, they become more difficult to deal with. First, you become upset and soon you become aggressive. The problem with aggressiveness is that it wakens similar attitudes in the one at whom it is aimed. Harsh and unfriendly words are bandied about, later leading to bitter remorse.

No matter how aggressive another person may be, it is neither a reason nor an excuse for you to act in similar vein. Keep yourself under control and count to ten before responding. Most aggressive people attempt to conceal feelings of inferiority or a lack of self-confidence. Even though it may seem as though they are seeking confrontation, what they really need is understanding and sympathy, even though they may be unaware of this.

As a Christian, you have promised Christ your love and devotion. Therefore no matter how aggressive a person may be, your loyalty to Christ should allow you to rise above the reproaches heaped upon you, and enable you to act with understanding and compassion towards a confused personality. To live and act in the Spirit of Christ, is to possess an inner calm that always enables you to deal with the aggressive person in a constructive manner, and to defuse the situation with a friendly word.

Jesus, we complain so easily, but You endured the worst suffering without a murmur and without seeking revenge. Please help us to be as forgiving as You. Amen.

Proverbs 15:1-15

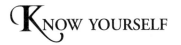
So if the Son sets you free, you will be free indeed.

~ JOHN 8:36 ~

It is surprising how many people are strangers to themselves. They act without being able to account for their behavior. They say things they do not really mean, and they often hate themselves for the attitude they show towards those who love them and care about them. It sometimes seems as though these people have been separated from themselves, wondering what has caused their behavior.

Unless you are completely honest, you cannot discover the truth about yourself. This honesty is not easy to attain, because man is a master of self-deception. By trying to justify these realities, they deceive themselves: Dishonesty and theft are labelled "borrowing", and sin is referred to as a "weakness". Beautiful names conceal ugly characteristics and situations.

Honesty towards yourself requires conviction and guidance by the Holy Spirit; not as you desire others to see you, but as you really are. Your weaknesses, flaws and sins are exposed and you must face them and deal with them. Some Christians abandon the challenge rather than accept the harsh reality about themselves.

As you become increasingly aware of the true "you", the picture need not only be dark and discouraging. The Holy Spirit grants you insight into what you can become through Christ's power and through the wisdom of God in your life. While you grow in the Holy Spirit in the knowledge of yourself, your weaknesses and shortcomings will fall away through His grace and you will be able to live with confidence, freed from all the bonds that restricted your personality. Free indeed, because Christ has set you free.

Your miraculous love redeems even the worst sinner. Thank You that we may live with You in truth as Your children. Amen.

John 8:31-43

TRUE WEALTH

" ... 'You fool! This very night your life will be demanded from you. Then who will get what you have prepared for yourself?' This is how it will be with anyone who stores up things for himself but is not rich towards God."

~ LUKE 12:20-21 ~

So much in life depends on your understanding and fundamental values. Many people make wealth and possessions the first priority in their lives. Money can buy things that can be seen and handled, and it can buy the services of people. Without a doubt it is also true that wealth lends people prestige in society.

Wealth in itself is no sin, just as poverty per se is no virtue. But the rich man must regard it as a transitory trust that cannot be used towards his own selfish ends. The issue is not "how much" you collect, but rather how you can use it to best serve your fellow man. What matters is not the money that you possess, but the disposition that motivates it and the way in which it is spent. Therefore, true wealth is not the collecting of bonds, houses, property or money, but your attitude towards these things. It also enriches those with whom you come into contact, because you are not only giving of your money, but especially of yourself as well.

To share in a disposition rich in the blessings that God conveys, means that you must also live in His fellowship to such an extent that His standards also become your standards. It is only when everything that you possess is dedicated to your Lord and Master, and when you use it to His honor and with the holy purpose in mind, that you possess wealth of a much higher quality than those who only count their wealth in material terms.

In Your care, Lord, we are not in want of anything. Help us to be there for one another, just as Jesus is with us in our sorrow. Amen.

Luke 12:13-21

GOD REMAINS IN CONTROL

He is before all things, and in him all things hold together.

~ COLOSSIANS 1:17 ~

In matters of state, of a business undertaking, in the workplace and in your private life, there comes a time when it would seem as though everything is going wrong. The future seems uncertain and the present is unstable and leaves much to be desired. Under such circumstances the temptation arises to look back at the past in nostalgia and to yearn for "the good old days".

Regardless of what problems might be upsetting your personal life or the world around you, look back over history. You will discover that nations and individuals have struggled through difficult times that can be compared with what we are experiencing in our times. Disasters, hardships and dangers existed in the past. People were confronted with sorrow and adversity, just as we are confronted today by situations in which we have to do battle. And yet the world has remained standing.

Before giving in to despondency, and before starting to sing in the grand choir of the despairing, first acknowledge the greatness, glory and constancy of God. He called the world into existence, He created man, He has kept vigil over His creation and cared for us through the ages and sheltered us in every disaster. He is the Creator God who shall never abandon His workmanship. In His unfathomable love, He gave His Son to this world, so that whoever believes in Him shall not perish but have everlasting life (cf. Jn. 3:16). Therefore, hold on to His promises; place your entire trust and faith in the living Christ. Through Him you will survive all dangers and adversity, to His greater glory.

You are eternal, Lord, and the workmanship of Your creation bears testimony to Your greater glory. The universe celebrates Your great Name. Amen.

Colossians 1:15-20

YOU ARE SPECIAL TO GOD

For God does not show favoritism.

~ ROMANS 2:11 ~

God has no "favorites". Whether you are an ordinary person or a celebrity, a leader in the business world or a laborer, whether you are honored by society or considered a non-entity, in God's eyes you are special because you are one of His creatures, His child, and He loves you. You are a unique creation of His hand and you have special value in His eyes.

There are so many people who torture themselves with the thought that they are completely unworthy, or that they have disappointed God, or that they have neglected their religion and that God is therefore angry with them. They feel unworthy in comparison to others who live a more devoted life. As a result, they regard themselves as unworthy and feel that they have drifted out of the sphere of God's love and trusty care.

Take a moment and look at life in the days when Jesus walked this earth, and you will soon realize that all people have received the same love, care, grace and compassion. The living Christ reached out to both the worthy and the unworthy. He loved His disciples, even though they disappointed Him in His time of despair. He forgave His enemies, even though they nailed Him to a cross. He chose Paul to be His powerful testimony, although he had persecuted Christians and killed them.

Do not give in to feelings of inferiority, feeling unworthy of God's love. He chose you because He loves you and because the Redeemer came for the salvation of "all" people, both the righteous and the sinners. You belong to God; you are His child whom He loves. Value being a child of God, and value your heritage.

> I know that You live and that You have forgiven my sins. Through Your precious blood I have inherited peace. Amen.

Romans 2:1-11

CONTROL YOUR ANGER

"In your anger do not sin": Do not let the sun go down while you are still angry ...

~ EPHESIANS 4:26 ~

There are moments in life when anger could rectify societal and social evils. Our society would have been that much the poorer were it not for people who were motivated into justified anger and dismay by the directives of their hearts. Such anger can be creative when the person displaying it keeps his initial purpose in mind.

One of the disasters of unbridled anger is that you lose control over it. Reason is displaced by panic, planning by confusion, and the vision of the greatness of life is attenuated to the nastiness and small-mindedness of the moment. The greatest tragedy of self-centered anger is that it isolates you from God. When you feel hurt or humiliated because other people enjoy privileges above you, you have allowed anger to incite your spirit and you will consequently feel that God is far away from you.

The solution to this unfortunate condition is to place God back where He belongs: in the center of your life! When He is there, it is breathtaking to see how anger subsides and balance returns to your life. When anger is then experienced, it will not be in response to a personal insult, but for the sake of God's glory or an injustice committed to your fellow man. Unbridled anger could destroy your entire life, but the potency of justified anger that is under control, could be a powerful weapon of justice when controlled by the Holy Spirit.

Help us, Lord, to control our emotions. Please grant us the armor of Your light to fight the good fight. Amen.

Ephesians 4:25-32

GOD IS ALWAYS WITH YOU

For men are not cast off by the Lord for ever. Though he brings grief, he will show compassion ...

~ LAMENTATIONS 3:31-32 ~

It is a sorrowful experience to meet people who maintain that they are totally "alone" in this world. They feel that they have no family or friends, and that there is no one to turn to for help and comfort in times of distress, sorrow and tension.

Although it is undeniably true that there are people who do not enjoy the warmth of a family life or the company of intimate friends and who, in human terms, have "no one" to share their deepest life experiences with, it does not mean, in any way, that they are "alone" in life. For many it might sound ridiculous, but it is an irrefutable fact that God is always with you. There are countless people who have personal experience of the fulfilment of Jesus' glorious promise when He said, *"... And surely I am with you always, to the very end of the age"* (Mt. 28:20).

If you feel lonely and alone, turn to Jesus this very moment and, upon entering the calmness of His presence, remember: *"Be strong and courageous. Do not be afraid or terrified because of them, for the LORD your God goes with you; he will never leave you nor forsake you"* (Deut. 31:6).

You are so patient, Lord. You will never forsake man in his feebleness, but You will always be by our side in compassion. Thank You for Your presence. Amen.

Lamentations 3:21-33

... But one thing I do: Forgetting what is behind and straining towards what is ahead ...

~ PHILIPPIANS 3:13 ~

ᴄᴵ If you are haunted by thoughts about "what could have been", you cannot experience the freedom of spirit that is your spiritual heritage. A foolish decision or misguided action probably robbed your life of peace and joy. The words, "confession" and "remorse", are completely out of step with modern thinking. Everything they mean and everything they represent are as relevant today as they were in the distant past. This means to "turn around", to be converted, to mend your old ways and to choose a new path and a new life. Conscious of what you were, you see a vision of what you could become through the merciful atonement of Christ. The past might cause you to feel burning shame, but the shining halo of the future supersedes the dismal gloom of the past. That which you once thought to be totally impossible, suddenly becomes gloriously possible.

When confronted by the challenge of the living Christ and, when you take the reality of your confession seriously, a new life opens before you. Revelation 21:5 states: ... *"I am making everything new!"* Former flaws and sins that have mortified you for so long no longer have any hold or control over your life. By embracing salvation through Jesus Christ, His Spirit fills your spirit with peace even with regard to the past.

When this transformation takes place in your life, you are looking ahead to a "vivacious", sparkling, twinkling future in the presence of God. This means that you start every day anew with God, undisturbed by negative thoughts about failures and flaws of the past, and visibly aware of the restored future awaiting you. Then you enter the future in the presence of God.

We cannot cease praising You for Your miraculous works of redemption. Through Your mercy even Your weakest child is redeemed. Amen.

Philippians 3:7-16

DEEDS SPEAK LOUDER THAN WORDS

"Not everyone who says to me, 'Lord, Lord,' will enter the kingdom of heaven, but only he who does the will of my Father who is in heaven."

~ MATTHEW 7:21 ~

The Name of Jesus Christ is glorified by countless people across the globe. The reverence in which they hold Him is displayed in beautiful buildings, in communities bearing His Name, and in a civilization that, although it falls far short of His standards, nevertheless has deference for His holy Name. Despite the reverence in which the Name of the living Christ is held, the practical implementation of His message of salvation has not nearly been accepted yet. Nations still do not trust one another, class and racial hatred are still rampant and many of His disciples have greater loyalty towards the world than that which they display towards their Lord and Master.

The sad truth is that not everyone who says, "Lord, Lord!" has made Him the Lord of their lives. In order for the Christian faith to impact modern society, it must first take root in the lives of people who call themselves Christians. It is folly to talk about putting Christian ethics into practice, before a personal experience with the living Christ has taken place in the lives of Christian people. It is impossible to have a true Christian society before you have people who know that the living Christ rules their lives.

In the midst of pressure for the preaching of a social and political gospel, personal faithfulness to the supremacy of Jesus Christ must always receive priority. This is done through divinely inspired deeds and not through idle words.

Help us, Lord, to always abide by Your commandments and to please You. Please help us always do Your will. Amen.

Matthew 7:15-23

DEALING WITH ADVERSITY

"And now, do not be distressed and do not be angry with yourselves for selling me here, because it was to save lives that God sent me ahead of you."

~ GENESIS 45:5 ~

There must have been many a time in his life when Joseph felt that God had forsaken him. There was the hatred of his brothers when they tried to destroy him and his dreams, he experienced bondage and banishment in a foreign land. All of that surely had him wondering how God, or his father, Jacob, could still be of any help to him. When, after many years, he became a prince in Egypt, he could state with conviction that God had been working positively in his life all the while.

Being a child of God does not safeguard you against adversity and misfortune in your daily life. You are subject to the same trials and tribulations as those who show absolutely no loyalty towards their heavenly Father. When you are gloriously aware of the fact that God is your Father, you will realize that He even uses problem situations to your advantage. This truth strengthens you with the spiritual ability to survive, which prevents your heart from hardening and you from becoming embittered.

As you grow in the knowledge of God, you will be able to see Him at work in the ordinary things in life. Instead of complaining when overtaken by problems, you will steadfastly hold onto the conviction that God demonstrates His omnipotence, even in the most trying circumstances in your life. In your adversity you then understand that you see only the unfinished pattern of your life, but that God sees it in its entirety. Therefore, display the patience to allow Him to carve out His holy purpose with your life and, despite all your disappointments and problems, He will achieve His perfect objective with your life.

You are my only shelter, Lord, and I am helpless before You. You deliver me from evil and guide me when I am surrounded by darkness and devoid of all hope. Amen.

Genesis 45:1-11

GOD PERFORMS HIS WONDERS THROUGH YOU

Cast all your anxiety on him because he cares for you.

~ 1 PETER 5:7 ~

Sometimes incessant worries beyond your control prey upon your mind. You may be concerned about your job or your co-workers, about an increase in taxes or rent, or about the conduct of a loved one. You only see gloom and premonitions attesting to an unsure future. When your life is ruled by paralyzing fear, you cannot experience the freedom and joy that fall to those who love God and trust in Him.

If you are anxious and worried about a personal matter, you must remember that your God is greater than all the circumstances and situations that could befall you. For a moment, you might have allowed clouds of anxiety, fear and uncertainty about the future to obscure your image of God. However, He is forever constant and He desires to share the deepest experiences of your life with you.

In a spirit of thanksgiving, take your anxieties, fears and worries and share them with your merciful God. Give these things over to Him unreservedly. You will experience an untold feeling of deliverance. This could be brought about by a single episode of prayer in your life. Accept the challenge to follow God's plan of action. God's omnipotence will sweep away all petty thoughts, and all uncertainty will disappear. The true greatness of God is not only revealed in His majestic universe, but also in His measureless love and concern for people like you and me.

Your works are perfect, Lord and, even when I drink from the cup of bitterness, You will never forsake me, but You will help me to understand eventually that with You, I will survive forever. Amen.

1 Peter 5:5-11

GOD'S METHODS ARE FAULTLESS

For the foolishness of God is wiser than man's wisdom, and the weakness of God is stronger than man's strength.

~ 1 CORINTHIANS 1:25 ~

There are people who scorn those who adhere to their Christian faith and values. It is regarded as out of step with modern life and the world of business. They are therefore inclined to regard those who steadfastly hold on to the standards of Jesus Christ with contempt or view them as amusing anomalies.

When you look at the lives of people who have left their imprint on life – be it in the economy, in the sporting arena, in a social sphere or in the field of politics – you will find that those who have made a lasting impression and boast major achievements, are those people whose lives are anchored to the Rock of Ages.

It is true that people whose lives are ruled by God, through steadfast and sound Christian principles, enjoy a stable self-assuredness and peace of mind that does not have its foundation in mankind, but is solely derived from their faith in Christ. Any act or achievement that is in conflict with the principles and standards of the living Christ, will eventually show signs of weakness and failure.

There is no short cut to spiritual victory in order to obtain joy and prosperity from life. It is essential to nurture a personal relationship with your Savior and to allow Him to guide you and influence you in everything that you do.

> You deliver us from the bondage of sin, Lord, so that we may rejoice in Your work and know that everything You do is perfect. Amen.

1 Corinthians 1:18-31

GROW IN WISDOM BY SERVING GOD

The fear of the LORD is the beginning of wisdom; all that follow his precepts have good understanding ...

~ PSALM 111:10 ~

To be educated is definitely an advantage in life. The greater your education, the broader your outlook on life. You possess a deeper understanding of life's mysteries. However, we must not forget that it is possible to be highly educated while suffering from spiritual want. For the Christian, sanctification must always receive priority over education. This is a comforting truth for the devoted child of God who, for whatever reason, has been denied a good education.

You may experience disappointment about not having been able to obtain a good education and feel inferior to others because you perceive them to be "cleverer" than you are. However, you must always remember that your inability to obtain a higher academic education should not clip your wings of spiritual growth and service to the Master. A person who is in the process of developing spiritually is closer to the heart of God and, therefore, he is more skilled in understanding God's ways than the person who is intellectually brilliant, but nevertheless denies the existence of God.

A spiritual person has discovered the true Source of wisdom in life. There is purpose in his service to God. He possesses peace and inner strength born from the fellowship of the Holy Spirit, and lives his life in such a way that he gains deep-rooted contentment and inspiration. Therefore, make time to get together with God, not only to put your requests before Him, but to allow the "atmosphere" of God's life to penetrate your life so that you may serve Him in truth, and so that His wisdom, peace and strength may flow through you.

I am nothing without You, Lord. Help me to spend every day in Your fellowship and to experience the fullness of life through You every day. Amen.

Psalm 111:1-10

Do not be anxious about anything, but in everything, by prayer and petition, with thanksgiving, present your requests to God.

~ Philippians 4:6 ~

Of all the Christian doctrines, prayer is probably most commonly practiced and, in all likelihood, the least understood. So many people regard prayer as a life-jacket to be used in desperate situations, when everything else has failed. Or as a method to tell God what they really wish for and to obtain His blessing for that which they have already decided upon. With this attitude, it is small wonder that so many people maintain that their prayers go unanswered.

At first, as with every other relationship, a relationship of prayer with God has to be established. Failing that, your prayer life will never develop in a meaningful way, nor become a significant experience. You have to develop an affinity for the living Christ by constantly acknowledging His presence in your daily life. Grow ever closer to Him while studying His Word, and meditate in the quiet presence of the peace of God.

Always remember to thank and praise God for the privilege of prayer, and then cast all your cares, fears, problems and requests upon Him and ask Him to grant you that which He deems necessary, as well as for the grace to be able to handle any situation that might arise. Then wait patiently on the Lord and be sensitive to the whisperings of the Holy Spirit that will lead you onto the path of peace. Then God's destiny will unfold itself and the way forward will become clear with God as your Governor and Guide.

> From Your hand You grant us more than we could ever ask for. We can always have the blessed assurance of Your love and know that Your promises hold good. Amen.

Philippians 4:2-9

ℬAD HABITS START ON A SMALL SCALE

Train a child in the way he should go, and when he is old he will not turn from it.

~ PROVERBS 22:6 ~

We are all creatures of habit, whether we are ordinary laborers, professional craftsman, ministers, doctors or professors. Some habits are good, some less so, and others again are extremely bad. Some are the product of our early education and many are the products of our own making. What we are at this moment, is the culmination of many years' practice in forming habits.

One of the most glorious facts of the Christian gospel is that it helps you to break bad habits. Christ breaks the power of repeated sins and sets the prisoner free. If you have a habit that is destroying your character and demolishing your personality, you can overcome it by acknowledging the sovereignty of the omnipotent Christ in your life. He can radically change the direction of your thoughts and deeds.

Christ is a Master in the art of changing lives. He provides the initiative to start a new life. He promises this to all who follow Him and dedicate their lives to Him. If you have done this personally and acknowledge the truth that the Holy Spirit dwells in you, new life will flow into your entire being and you will become aware of His power that makes it possible for you to overcome every bad habit in His name. Habits that are acceptable to God and that contribute to your spiritual and moral wellbeing, are encouraged by the Holy Spirit and you know the joy and vitality of your Lord Jesus the living Christ, who enables you to do anything.

We are so sinful, Lord, but Your Spirit always supports us so that we may live in Christ. We are so grateful that You lead us to a new life. Amen.

Proverbs 22:1-10

SEEK TO PLEASE GOD, NOT PEOPLE

For they love praise from men more than praise from God.

~ JOHN 12:43 ~

or a great many people their status in society, the business world or on the sports field means infinitely more than anything else. They are willing to go to great lengths to be acceptable in social circles, or to achieve success in business, or to stand out as a hero on the sports field. Often this hankering after success results in these people compromising their principles or forsaking former friends, whose life-styles are a stumbling block in the way of fulfilling their selfish ambitions – at any cost.

When people take such a direction, their relationship with God inevitably becomes increasingly ineffective. In many cases they turn away from Him and give up the principles ordained by Jesus Christ, because their efforts or the goals that they have set for themselves oppose these. It has been proven time and again that man is unreliable. Dispositions and loyalties may easily change. Promises are easily broken and relationships become stale and fragile. Somebody who one moment extols your virtues and flatters you, can just as easily reject you the next moment.

The only way to achieve the very best in life and to develop the feeling of self-confidence and fulfilment that is so essential to your peace of mind, is to stay true in all things to your high calling in Jesus Christ. He is constant – yesterday, today and for all eternity. He will never forsake you or fail you. Place your full trust in Him and not in fallible people. You will never be disappointed.

We do not always understand it Lord, but Your way is always best. You will never forsake us and we know that we are safe in You. Amen.

John 12:37-50

GOD HEARS YOUR CALL OF DISTRESS

I call on the LORD in my distress, and he answers me.

~ PSALM 120:1 ~

In the business world, in the workplace, on the sports field and in the family circle, problems and difficulties present themselves from time to time. At times like these it is a great comfort to know that there is somebody to turn to. To know that there is a friend or confidant who is willing to help, to give guidance and advice, gives you peace of mind in moments of despair and distress. Unfortunately there are people who have no friends to lean on and who seem to lead a lonely and troubled life.

It is essential for you to realize that you are never completely alone and that you are not without friends in this harsh world. Jesus, the living Christ, has undertaken never to leave nor forsake you (cf. Heb. 13:5). He offers you His friendship and all that He asks from you is obedience to His commandment of love. Secure in this knowledge, you have the assurance of His constant presence in your life. He has already heard your call of distress and answered your prayer (Ps. 120:1).

In order to enjoy the benefit of this relationship, you must maintain this contact through prayer and meditation. Live in His fellowship at all times. If you do this, you will in various ways become aware of the wonderful answer to your call of distress. Through the Holy Spirit, follow the light of His guidance and you will walk a safe and fulfilling path.

You know our deepest sorrow and hear our sighs. Help us, Lord, never to forget that You alone are our salvation and support. Amen.

Psalm 120:1-7

UNITY IS WITHIN REACH THROUGH CHRIST

Accept him whose faith is weak, without passing judgment on disputable matters.

~ ROMANS 14:1 ~

At home, work or in leisure time activities, we meet people from different denominations and different religious convictions. A personal, steadfast religion is then of vital importance. Without it you will drift from one theological school of thought to another without much spiritual progress. To know what you believe is of crucial importance. However, you must be careful that your doctrine does not become so dogmatic that it denies other Christians the right to believe what they perceive to be true.

There are many interpretations of the Christian gospel. Some of them have already caused serious rifts between sincere disciples of Jesus Christ. An undeniable sign of spiritual immaturity is when religion causes a rift between followers of Christ.

A steadfast faith in Jesus Christ is essential to your Christian life, but of even higher priority is practising Christ's message of love in a positive way. Your love for your resurrected Savior and the practising of that love, especially towards fellow believers, must receive priority over your theological views.

Religions can divide people, but Christ's love unifies. Therefore, the litmus test of any Christian faith is not tradition or historical importance, but the quality and quantity of love that it generates for God and fellow man. Such a love is not founded by human effort, but by the love of Christ, which is an important fruit of the Holy Spirit. If your life is filled with the love of Christ, you will feel one with all who embrace Christ as their Savior and Redeemer.

You are the faithful Shepherd who always guides us in love. Help us, Lord, never to stray. Amen.

Romans 14:1-12

BE GRATEFUL FOR WHAT YOU HAVE

When they received it (the money), they began to grumble against the landowner.

~ MATTHEW 20:11 ~

Why do so many people waste time and energy on insignificant and unimportant things? They persevere in this until it becomes part of their personality and their way of life. Strangely enough, they are usually attracted to people who are similar to them in this respect. When people are united by incessant complaining, they do themselves a major disservice and make no positive contribution to the community to which they belong.

You do not have to look very far to find something to complain about, if you are that way inclined. However, a wise person always tries to restore the balance by thinking about something for which he can be grateful. Remember, for everything that causes grievance, there is something for which you can be eternally grateful.

If you have developed a grateful heart, you have discovered one of the great secrets of co-operating with life. Then your personality starts developing for the better. Try to find something that you can be grateful for and praise God for it. Then incorporate the thought into your way of life, so that your disposition becomes one of grateful praise to God. Look for His co-operation in every sphere of your life. Once you have done that, you will experience an inner change. It will seem as if all the powers of goodwill are competing to be revealed through you, and you will experience an untold feeling of amazement and contentment with the ways of God.

I sometimes complain about such trivialities. Jesus, You endured Your suffering in silence so that I may be free. Please cleanse my heart and purify me through suffering. Amen.

Matthew 20:1-16

... Respect those who work hard among you, who are over you in the Lord and who admonish you.

~ 1 THESSALONIANS 5:12 ~

Through the ages of its existence, the church has suffered from internal strife, arguments and discord. In the Acts of the Apostles, mention is already made of how the apostles argued amongst themselves. In some cases the quarrels were about crucial dogmatic and theological differences, but in the vast majority of cases it was matters of a personal nature that originated from a clash of personalities, jealousy and other trivialities.

In order for a society to function in a proper and orderly fashion, good leadership is essential. This is even manifested in the animal world. Somebody must have the authority to take decisions in the best interest of others in order for the whole group to be able to make a well-organized living.

In this regard, Christians do not differ from other groups, except that the responsibility resting with church leaders and members of the church is very grave, because it primarily relates to the wellbeing of the kingdom of God. In order to ensure that a harmonious and effective testimony for Christ is given by your denomination, fellowship or congregation, leaders must be elected in accordance with the will of God, as has been revealed after serious prayer. If it is certain that this is the case, we must persevere in prayer for them, so that the heavy burden of responsibility could be lightened by Jesus Himself. However, the main point must always be the exaltation and glorification of the King of the church, Jesus Christ.

Even though we might feel threatened by danger every day, and even though our faith sometimes falters, we can live in the knowledge that You will never forsake us. Your support was allotted to us. Amen.

1 Thessalonians 5:12-28

REMEMBER GOD'S SHARE IN YOUR SUCCESS

But by the grace of God I am what I am, and his grace to me was not without effect ...

~ 1 CORINTHIANS 15:10 ~

There are many people who declare that they are "self-made people" and they are rather satisfied with the product. If they think about the success that they have achieved in their careers, they claim all credit for themselves and they are inclined to look back on their achievements with a high measure of complacency.

It is indeed a foolish person who convinces himself that the honor is his alone for that which he has achieved in life. Regardless of how successful your career may be, there were indeed times when you faced problems and stumbling blocks, and that the future looked gloomy and unsure to you. If God's hand of grace was not shielding you, if He did not grant you good health and a clear mind, you would never have triumphed over problems and adversities. You can therefore be sure that your success can mainly be attributed to the grace and guidance of God, whether you were always aware of it or not.

In order to lead a fulfilled life, blessed with peace of mind, it is necessary to acknowledge your complete dependency on the living Christ. Then you will start to realize that He also forms an integral part of your secular life, as He does of your spiritual life. By gratefully acknowledging God in your achievements and by thanking Him for His grace and goodness, an extra dimension, that you have not yet experienced, will be added to your life. It will fill your life with joy and happiness to know that the living God has a major share in your success.

You bless us so undeservedly Lord, and more so than we can ever expect. You are our salvation and courage for each day. Thank You for blessing us so abundantly. Amen.

1 Corinthians 15:1-11

June

"As long as the earth endures, seed time and harvest, cold and heat, summer and winter, day and night will never cease."

~ Genesis 8:22~

ᗅrayer

Winter has its own charm, but also its inherent anxieties.

Thank You for wind, rain and cold; for time to read and reflect.

Thank You for nature that is drowsily waiting on new life and growth.

Let me remember in winter to make time for You, to become quiet in Your holy presence.

Slow down my pace so that I may have time to think about those things that have eternal value and that really count.

Heavenly Father, winter also claims its dues relentlessly: the elderly and the poor who suffer hardship; the unemployed who suffer for want of bread; the hungry who walk past me with pleading eyes; the homeless who are forced to sleep in the bitter cold and have to endure the icy stares of their fellow men.

Help me, Master, to give love like You and to lend a helping hand. Cloak our snow-covered world with the spirit of Christmas in June!

We pray this in the Name of the One who is filled with Compassion, Jesus Christ, our Lord and Savior.

Amen

ʜE IS ALIVE! JESUS IS ALIVE TODAY!

"He is not here; he has risen, just as he said..."

~ MATTHEW 28:6 ~

Early on the Sunday morning following the crucifixion, the women arrived at the grave of Jesus, carrying spices. How great was their surprize and bewilderment when they arrived there! An earthquake, a messenger from heaven and a tombstone that had been rolled away. There was no sign of death, only of pulsating life. The messenger spoke to them, "Do not fear!" Glorious comfort from God to a sorrowful, anxious, tense and dumbfounded humanity. Luke then carried on, ... *"Why do you look for the living among the dead?"* (Lk. 24:5). Our religion is not a death cult. Our Lord lives.

It was a prodigious moment in the history of the world. We are elevated from mortality to true "life". He that died for *our* sins is not dead. He lives! We do not talk about Him in the past tense, but in the present tense. He *was* not, He *is*! He *did* not live, He *lives*! We know where He is: in the heaven of His glory where we will live with Him forever. Through His Spirit, He resides in the blessed Gospel that brings hope to our despondent hearts. He is here on earth, to strengthen us, to guide us, to govern us and to inspire us to new life. Through His Spirit, He resides in the hearts that He made alive.

In conclusion, the heavenly messenger says to the women, *"Then go quickly and tell his disciples: 'He has risen from the dead ...'"* (Mt. 28:7). That is our calling and duty as His disciples: to spread the word of a living Savior. To narrate with our mouth and our life: He is not dead, He Lives. And because He lives, we will live as well. Exchange that precious nard perfume that you brought to anoint one that is dead. Instead, carry the living Christ's gospel of resurrection in your heart and mouth! It is far more fragrant than spices. Its aroma should spread through the entire world to give new courage to the broken-hearted and the dying: A fragrance of life to life!

Lord, thank You that You died on the cross for me. I know that there is new life in You. Thank You that I may place my hope in You. Amen.

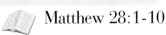 Matthew 28:1-10

WHAT THE RESURRECTION MEANS TO ME

"Why do you look for the living among the dead?"

~ LUKE 24:5 ~

Luther said about the birth of Christ: "Even if Christ was born a thousand times in Bethlehem and not yet in your heart, you will still be lost." In the same vein, we can declare: "Even though Christ rose miraculously from the dead but it means nothing to you personally, then His resurrection is a useless event."

- Christ's resurrection expels all doubt. The resurrection demands responsibility regarding faith. It is the immense assurance that forms the foundation for all other things. Like Thomas' doubt, mine must turn into worshiping assurance: "My Lord and my God." Mary's words of doubt are transformed into: "Rabboni! Master!"
- The resurrection expels all fear. The messenger at the open grave said: "Do not fear!" I do not fear the enemies of the cross; neither sin, nor Satan, nor death. Christ triumphed over them all. I do not fear eternity. Because He lives and is by my side, I no longer fear.
- The resurrection expels loneliness. His faithful followers thought that they had been left lonely and scattered. But the lonely of this world can rejoice, because the resurrected Savior said, *"... And surely I am with you always ..."* (Mt. 28:20).
- The resurrection expels my fear of death: *Even though I walk through the valley of the shadow of death, I will fear no evil, for you are with me; your rod and your staff, they comfort me* (Ps. 23:4). Paul assures us, *"Death has been swallowed up in victory"* (1 Cor. 15:54). I no longer grieve like one without hope.
- The resurrection forces me to testify, *"Then go quickly and tell his disciples ..."* (Mt. 28:7). The men ran back to Jerusalem to spread the good news of His resurrection. The church lives and grows because of those who testify that they have a message from a living and redeeming Christ who has risen from the dead!

Jesus, I glorify You. No grave could keep You prisoner. You give steadfast hope. Amen.

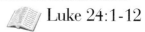 Luke 24:1-12

The mind of sinful man is death, but the mind controlled by the Spirit is life and peace.

~ Romans 8:6 ~

Physical growth is nature's way of allowing your body to develop. Through effort and exercise your body progresses from infant to teenager, from teenager to adult, and then to the wisdom of old age. The natural laws of growth control your development. In the process of growth, some people achieve far more during their lives than others. Their thoughts can inhibit or expedite their progress and performance, but there is nothing that can prevent their development from reaching old age.

If you desire a fully balanced personality and a life of confidence and dignity, you dare not disregard your spiritual nature. Many people ignore this important aspect of their lives, because it cannot be observed or measured like that of your body. As a result, they risk suffering immense loss.

By far the greatest Guide and Advisor that you could find is Jesus Christ. He is the revelation of the living God and therefore has a perfect understanding of the problems that you wrestle with. If you embrace His salvation and sovereignty in your life in an intimate partnership with Him, your life will gain new sense and meaning. It is of vital importance that you continue to yearn for a deeper relationship with Him. Your prayer life will be renewed and your realization of your oneness with the living Christ will become a dynamic and powerful experience that will result in your spiritual growth.

I can do nothing without You. In You I can grow and gain fulfilment. I wish to remain in You always. Amen.

Romans 8:1-17

SPIRITUAL RENEWAL IS ESSENTIAL

Those who trust in the LORD will renew their strength. They will soar on wings like eagles; they will run and not grow weary, they will walk and not be faint.

~ ISAIAH 40:31 ~

On every conceivable level of life people have to take a breather from time to time in order to refresh themselves. Great artists and musicians get dull and jaded unless they make time for relaxation; writers need time away from their computers and typewriters if they want to retain the attention of their readers; learners need holidays; professional sporting stars need to relax from time to time in order to do their best. Just like those mentioned above, if not more so, the Christian worker needs a respite from his labors if he wants to play an effective role in the service of his Master and prevent burnout.

We read in the Bible how often Jesus detached Himself from the masses and withdrew from society so that He could be alone with His Father. It is much more necessary for us to spend time with our heavenly Father. It is in these precious moments, when you spend quiet time with God in prayer, Bible study and meditation, that you will discover the benevolent work of the Holy Spirit in your life. He once again fills the empty reservoirs of your life so that you may be better equipped for service to the Master.

If you become aware that you are entering arid and barren spots in your labors, or if you know that your spiritual life is losing its sparkle, break away from all routine so that you can devote your entire being to becoming quiet in the presence of God. Draw strength from the means of grace that He places at your disposal: Bible study, prayer, meditation, spiritual conversation, and so forth. Then return to the world, fresh and refreshed, bearing testimony of Him with the new strength and energy that you have drawn from the Source.

Lord, fill me with Your Spirit. I plead with You for comfort, strength and guidance – all to Your glory. Amen.

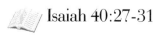 Isaiah 40:27-31

But grow in the grace and knowledge of our Lord and Savior Jesus Christ ...

~ 2 PETER 3:18 ~

If you have embraced the resurrected Christ as your Savior and Redeemer, it is your solemn responsibility to maintain spiritual growth. To be half-heartedly sentimental in this regard, is to court spiritual disaster. In order to have a meaningful spiritual life, you must be disciplined and subject to the will of God. This discipline should not be a burden, but a sincere desire and a cheerful obligation.

Your prayer life should reflect a willingness to pray according to the will of God and not according to the demands of your own emotions. Out of an active and positive prayer life, a definite thinking pattern will develop that will enable you to think spiritually so that you will gradually understand what Paul meant when he said, *"Your attitude should be the same as that of Christ Jesus ... "* (Phil. 2:5).

To grow in the image of Christ is not a spiritual luxury to occupy you in spare moments, but an absolute necessity if you wish to maintain a pulsating faith. Failure to "grow in Christ" always ends in a decline of your spiritual life. You may be able to maintain the pretense of Christlikeness, but if you lack the conviction of a strong and positive inner spirit, inspired and confirmed by the Holy Spirit of God, your faith will collapse. Therefore you must not stagnate spiritually, but progress steadfastly, day and night, by the grace of God.

Lord, help me to remain steadfast in faith. Make me brave, strong and courageous, so that my labors will carry Your blessing. Amen.

2 Peter 3:12-18

SHARE IN THE LIFE OF CHRIST

God, who has called you into fellowship with his Son Jesus Christ our
Lord, is faithful.

~ 1 CORINTHIANS 1:9 ~

God granted you a privilege beyond words. He called upon you to
share in the life of His Son, Jesus the living Christ. Once the full
meaning of this Divine grace has dawned upon you, the implications
are almost too vast to assimilate with our human mind.

To share in the life of Christ opens up immense possibilities for us,
but also huge responsibilities. Linked to such an infinite force and holy
wisdom, is the glorious fact that your understanding of God deepens,
your vision of what your life could be broadens, and you become aware
of the constant presence of Christ in your life.

Such an intimacy with the Master calls for definite responsibilities.
The quality of your life must be in balance with the way in which you
profess your faith. The holy characteristics of God must be revealed in
your daily life by love, unimpeachable honesty, selflessness and the
integrity of your goals. To realize the spirit of Jesus Christ to the best of
your ability, means that you have a vision of what you could achieve in
the service of your Master. You will not be restricted again by secret
fears and doubts, but you will face the future with faith in the power of
the living Christ.

Christ offered Himself to you so that you may share your life with
Him. However, this offer cannot become an effective reality in your life
before it is embraced in faith. You might have long since been aware of
this glorious truth, but until you claim it as your own, you will not
experience the joy and strength of Christ in your spiritual life.

You are the true vine that gives lasting life. Keep me safe, inspire me
and bless me so that I will forever remain fruitful. Amen.

1 Corinthians 1:1-9

DON'T GET IMPATIENT WITH YOURSELF

Patience is better than pride.

~ ECCLESIASTES 7:8 ~

So many of the Master's disciples get impatient with themselves. They instinctively feel that they should make better progress in their spiritual life, and they lament the poverty of their prayer life and their lack of knowledge of the Scriptures. They have a deep but varying desire for a richer experience with the Triune God, but it seems that they will never attain the objectives that they have set for themselves. They yearn to get to know God better and do not realize that this yearning in itself is a prayer that is acceptable to the Father. He understands only too well your desire for deeper and more intimate fellowship with Him, which is expressed in your impatience with yourself.

Anything that is worth achieving takes time to obtain. As an infant you crawled before you could walk. If you play a musical instrument, it took time before you mastered it. It is the same with your spiritual life. Sanctification does not happen in a moment. It is the result of a life lived in harmony with Christ and embracing a disciplined spiritual life.

You can measure your progress from time to time. Spend some quiet time in the presence of God. Allow His Spirit to reveal Himself to you. The result of such a revelation can be both challenging and beneficial. Is Jesus Christ a greater reality today than a few years ago? Is there greater depth in your prayer life? Does the Word of the Lord play an ever-increasing role in your life? These questions will inevitably present themselves to you. Do not get impatient with yourself because your progress on the road of spiritual growth is slow. Take an intimate daily walk with Christ and leave the rest to Him.

Teach me to walk with You in faith and to please You. I know that those who follow You are one with You. Amen.

Ecclesiastes 7:1-10

⊘HE DAWN OF A NEW BEGINNING

He who was seated on the throne said, "I am making everything new!"

~ REVELATION 21:5 ~

⊘f you have given serious thought over the past few days to your spiritual growth and your life with Jesus Christ, you are facing an important decision. Today is a new day in your life; a new opportunity, presented to you by God. Yesterday, with all its disappointments and even despair about yourself, belongs to the past. You now face the future and you look ahead. Do not look back; what is past is past, and is merely a memory. God is giving you a future.

For you as a Christian, the good news is that God, in His infinite grace, is granting you the opportunity to rectify those things that have gone wrong in your life. Learn from your failures and mistakes, from your weaknesses and defeats. Now you have a precious opportunity to start anew. Assured of Christ's forgiving love, you can learn from your past experiences and decide from now on, to live in obedience to the Master's commands and regulations.

Jesus promised not to spurn anyone who comes to Him in sincerity, repenting of his sins. Today you can start anew in your spiritual growth. Turn to Christ and confess your weaknesses and shortcomings to Him. Open your heart for His Spirit to enter and take control of your life. Then face the future with confidence in the joyous knowledge that God is with you. It is extremely important how we handle the future. If we turn our back on this opportunity, we will remain lonely, unhappy people. However, if we allow Christ to make us new, we will handle life with maturity and understanding, and we will experience the peace of God that transcends all understanding.

Lord, You did not deserve to die on the cross for us. You had mercy on us. Embrace this sinner as well. Amen.

Revelation 21:1-8

RENEW YOUR PERSONALITY AS WELL

Therefore, if anyone is in Christ, he is a new creation; the old has gone, the new has come!

~ 2 CORINTHIANS 5:17 ~

Our personalities are the part of us that are observed by others and the criteria on which impressions are formed. When we meet people, they react to our personality as we react to them and favorable or unfavorable opinions are formed. There are relatively few people who take the trouble to create an acceptable and pleasant personality. They may put up a plastic smile and keep up a pleasant front for a special occasion. However, when the fleeting moment has past, they return to their old self.

Many people believe that a personality cannot be changed. This is not in the least true. If this were so, the redeeming love of Christ would have been in vain. Experience has taught us that sinners can change into saints and that unapproachable people can become acceptable when the love of Christ enters their spirit.

When you open your life and your spirit to the Spirit of the living Christ, and His influence is reflected in your life, a transfiguration takes place in your personality and style of living. Your calling as a Christian is not merely to be a "good person" – although, obviously that is what you will be. You will also be totally devoted to your Lord and that recreates your personality.

This will not happen through your own strength, abilities and ingenuity – no matter how hard you try. However, when Christ presents His abiding Spirit, the impossible becomes possible. Then our personality is taken over by Christ and we grow to the likeness of our heavenly Example.

Your love is always with me. Father, pull me closer into Your circle of love every day. I want to remain in You. Amen.

2 Corinthians 5:11-21

REFLECT GOD'S GLORY

Be imitators of God, therefore, as dearly loved children ...

~ EPHESIANS 5:1 ~

A ll of us, in one way or another, need guidance and counselling in order to reach our goals in life. For this, learners look up to their teachers, children trust in their parents, employees are trained by their employers. You seek advice from your friends, or somebody that you admire serves as a role model for you. Deep in the heart and thoughts of man, there is a hidden desire to be like someone else.

God called you, through His mercy, to be His child. Nothing that you might have done, or could still do, will render you worthy of this deed of grace. You can never deserve it. It is simply a deed of love and grace from your heavenly Father. However, there is something that you could do to try and prove your gratitude. That is to try, through the power of the Holy Spirit, modelling your life after the example that Jesus Christ set for us. Never forget that He was also born under, and lived in, humble conditions. He lived and worked just like us and was subject to all the temptations, frustrations, joys and sorrows to which you and I are subject. It is for this reason that He is the perfect Role Model for you and me.

Open your heart and life to the formative influence of the Holy Spirit so that He can take control of your life and manage it in a way that is acceptable to God. In this way, you will display a measure of likeness to Christ that will glorify God.

Lord, transform me into Your image more and more. Transfigure me, so that I may be more and more like You in my conduct, thoughts and words. Amen.

Ephesians 4:25-32

You, however, are controlled not by the sinful nature but by the Spirit, if the Spirit of God lives in you ...

~ ROMANS 8:9 ~

Spiritual maturity has many faces. To be able to see and appreciate the greatness of God and to rejoice in the majesty of His creation, lifts man's spirit above all pettiness, which is the product of a limited and immature outlook on life.

If you cannot look past the grief and pain inflicted upon you by unthinking people; when your lifestyle is stifled at times by a lack of opportunity and confining circumstances; or when you have fallen into a rut from which there seems to be no escape, then it is time for you to have a serious look at the basic reason for your existence.

The direction that you have taken reveals where the emphasis in your life lies. If you seek financial success or social prestige, to the exclusion of more important things in life, you may achieve your objective. But is it enough? Is that why God has given you life? Because you are also a spiritual being, your spirit could never be satisfied with purely material assets. You need a dynamic relationship with the Holy Spirit, because He alone can give you permanent gratification. This intimately personal relationship with God can be attained by a positive faith in the resurrected Christ.

Faith in the living Christ is much more than a fleeting emotion. It is accepting His authority in all aspects of your life. It is choosing to allow His Spirit to reveal Himself through your life. With this acceptance will come definite growth into spiritual maturity and it will give true sense and meaning to your life.

I never want to be separated from You. I wish to experience Your love and be a fruitful vine in Your kingdom. I want to glorify You. Amen.

Romans 8:1-17

THE IMPORTANCE OF AN INNER LIFE

"The good man brings good things out of the good stored up in his heart, and the evil man brings evil things out of the evil stored up in his heart. For out of the overflow of his heart his mouth speaks."

~ LUKE 6:45 ~

One of the most significant things for any person is the quality of your inner life – not that which you outwardly pretend to be. For a while you may be able to maintain a front that is acceptable to others. It seems as though you have a solid and healthy personality and normally you are never short of friends. But the test comes when the storm clouds gather and you must meet the demands imposed upon you. Then a genial personality is insufficient to meet the needs. The more basic part of your personality which, because of your carnality, lies hidden somewhere, will take over, unless you have inner strength and strong spiritual reserves on which you can draw.

Cultivating a practical spiritual life is the most important exercise that one can undertake. It influences every aspect of your life and creates moral stamina which enables you to rise victoriously above inner weaknesses, a lack of self-confidence and other disparaging influences on your inner being.

The basic requirement for a strong spiritual inner life is the right relationship with your heavenly Father. If you live in harmony with God, and if you are aware of the Holy Spirit residing and working in you, you will experience a motivating force in your inner life that will be reflected in your everyday conduct.

Teach me to fix my eyes upon You more and more. I want to devote my whole life to You. Amen.

Luke 6:43-49

His divine power has given us everything we need for life and godliness through our knowledge of him who called us by his own glory and goodness.

~ 2 Peter 1:3 ~

There are many people who express their dissatisfaction with their destiny. Some feel that life is unfair and owes them something. Others again, regard themselves as failures, with the result that they throw in the towel for fear of further failures. Some feel hurt and foster bitterness and grievances in their hearts. Regardless of the reason, these people are inclined to adopt a negative and defeatist attitude towards life and, as a result, they withdraw from society and become lonely people.

The result of this disposition and conduct is obvious: they cease to enjoy life, it becomes a monotonous existence to them without any sense or meaning. They find little to get excited about. As a result, it is not long before they find themselves without any friends, because their attitude towards life alienates people instead of attracting them.

If things are not turning out right for you at this moment, remember that you are a child of God and that He loves you dearly. God, in His mercy, chose you to be His friend and He offers you the life-giving strength of the Holy Spirit to enable you to live life to the full. Do not succumb to negative experiences and influences but, through Jesus Christ, rise above them and live your life the way He intended it to be. Remember what Jesus said, *"... I have come that they may have life, and have it to the full"* (Jn. 10:10).

I am lost in guilt. Only through You may I be born again. I know that You embrace sinners. Amen.

2 Peter 1:1-15

⟶HE CHRISTIAN'S DEEPEST DESIRE

I want to know Christ ...

~ PHILIPPIANS 3:10 ~

⟶ he Christian's path has many byways. Unfortunately, many of the people who find themselves on a specific byway, think that they are on the highway of life and they show little patience or mercy for a fellow-pilgrim who has chosen another path. The binding and unifying force amongst all Christians is their collective love for the Master. It is impossible to be a Christian without knowing Christ and without loving Him dearly. He often taught us that it is difficult to live in isolation. Love, because of its intrinsic nature, rises above all differences of race, color and denomination. Because love is the determining factor in life, it cannot be confined to the limitations of the human mind and experience. It must flow from the Christian in order to be seen, to inspire, to heal and to encourage. It requires courage and wisdom to acknowledge the sovereignty of love and to live it to the full.

Such a love cannot be engendered by human emotion and desire because God is its origin and source. Only those who recognize God as love, can display His love in their lives. A developing and growing Christian faith requires an ever-increasing awareness of God's great love. Because of this great longing of every Christian, regardless of the byway on which he finds himself, our desire must be to know Christ better and to serve Him better in love. This is done through His abiding Spirit. This is the only way in which Divine love could be truly experienced.

If love fills your life, it releases a spiritual energy that could only come from the loving, living, resurrected Christ.

Lord, teach me to be strong and faithful in my love for You and also to love my neighbor. Amen.

Philippians 3:7-16

DISCIPLESHIP REQUIRES DISCIPLINE

Humble yourselves, therefore, under God's mighty hand, that he may lift you up in due time.

~ 1 Peter 5:6 ~

The moment that you become a Christian, you can no longer live to please yourself. Your entire life is then devoted to God and the depth or your devotion determines the quality of your spiritual life. When this truth is realized and embraced, it determines the zeal with which you endeavor to live as God is expecting of you.

Your devotion to God requires a willingness to reach beyond the emotional and sectarian approach to God, and to apply discipline in your spiritual life. Without this discipline, faith cannot grow, and God cannot be effectively served.

For many people, one of the most difficult forms of discipline is to prove their love for God in a practical manner – without emotional demonstrations. It is easy to declare your love for God when the music is soft or when the sermon is inspiring. However, go and live in an unsympathetic environment amongst ungodly people and confirm your love for God *there*. This requires discipleship that reaches far beyond emotion.

Discipline requires you to pray when you do not feel inclined to pray. It is false reasoning which declares that your prayers are only heard by God when you offer them in an atmosphere of prayer. It is precisely when you do not feel like praying, that you should indeed pray. If possible, you should have a fixed time and place to meet with God and nothing should deter you from keeping this appointment with God. The same applies to your study of the Scriptures and meditation in the presence of God. It is through discipline alone that you become a worthy disciple of the Master.

Lord, help me to be devoted to Your work. Help me to be steadfast and strong. Amen.

1 Peter 5:1-11

$\mathcal{I}$T ALL DEPENDS UPON YOU

In the same way, faith by itself, if it is not accompanied by action, is dead.

~ JAMES 2:17 ~

$\mathcal{T}$o be a Christian implies that you accept responsibility for your own life. You may reason that, because you belong to God, He is in control and therefore everything is His responsibility. However, if God is to accomplish anything with your life, He must have your full co-operation.

God the Creator has equipped you with an intellect, not so much in order for you to excel academically, but rather that you should have the correct disposition towards Him and life. A correct and positive disposition is a product of a life lived in obedience to God and a will that is in harmony with His holy will.

The large majority of people yearn for happiness. They work hard in their pursuit of it. Often they pray to God to make them happy. But, regardless of this, they cultivate and maintain their unhealthy patterns of thought and their negative disposition towards life. If you live a self-centered life, caring only about your own interests and remaining blind to the distress of your fellow man, you are ignoring the Scriptural truth that assisting others is a prerequisite for personal happiness. You cannot be truly happy without recognizing and alleviating the distress of those around you. This is best achieved through positive prayer, for their sake, and creative action from your side.

Regardless of the nature of your requests in prayer, you must offer yourself to the Master to use you as He sees fit. In this way you will fulfil your own prayers. Become a partner of the great God of Compassion and experience His enriching influence in your life.

> Help me to set an example to others. Lend me a helping hand so that my conduct will always carry the seal of love. Amen.

James 2:14-26

ᒐIVE ANEW IN A FAMILIAR ENVIRONMENT

... Each man, as responsible to God, should remain in the situation God called him to.

~ I CORINTHIANS 7:24 ~

𝓘f you have recently entered a world of new experiences after being born again, you will be confronted with diverse challenges that you did not previously have to face. One of the most important challenges is to inform your friends and fellow workers of your loyalty and obedience to Jesus Christ. In the past you went along with the group, accepting their standards of behavior, and doing what they were doing. Now, however, you have spiritual obligations and responsibilities. Your friends will notice the change in your life before long.

Some of your friends will not like the changes in your life, and will try everything in their power to lure you back to your earlier lifestyle. Circumstances may become so unpleasant that you will start doubting the wisdom of your new viewpoints. You may even think that if you move to a new environment, you will find it easier to maintain your Christian standpoints and testimony. Have you ever thought of the possibility that your intellectual and spiritual confusion could be an effort by Satan to undermine your newly found faith? In a new environment and under new circumstances, it might even be more difficult to stay true to your convictions.

God often expects a new disciple to remain where he is in order for his positive faith to be a shining light in sinful and negative circumstances. Should the Master wish to keep you in your familiar environment, He will grant you the courage and strength to bear loyal testimony to His love and constant protection.

I know that I may trust in You. You know my circumstances. You transform my sorrow into joy. Amen.

1 Corinthians 7:10-24

ℱIND STRENGTH AND COMFORT IN THE WORD

Open my eyes that I may see wonderful things in your law.
~ Psalm 119:18 ~

Two of the most important components of our spiritual growth are prayer and Bible study. Disillusion and dejection are very common in our times. The ups and downs in the emotional lives of people result in a precarious and unstable existence. Therefore, many people are unhappy, unsure of themselves and depressed. As a result of this, many people tend to have a melancholy outlook on life. Then their plans, conduct and decisions are negatively influenced.

In order for you to "live" and not merely "exist", it is essential to have a positive disposition. When everything goes well, enjoy life and try to remain cheerful. Praise God. If, on the other hand, things do not go well, analyse the circumstances and identify where things went wrong and then try to do something about it.

To achieve this, you will require a strong faith in order to deal with problems, to overcome stumbling blocks and eventually to triumph. Such a faith will come to you through prayer, when you seek the help of the living Christ. But to prevent you from falling prey to discouragement and pessimism, something more is required of you.

Ceaselessly seek in the Scriptures for testimony of the wonderful work of the almighty God. You will find example upon example of the ways in which ordinary people, like you and me, overcame tremendously hostile forces in the Name of the Lord. Draw comfort from the Word and, through the incarnate Word, Jesus Christ, you will be able to triumph over any adversity.

You reveal Yourself in Your Word. It is trustworthy, steadfast and unfailing. Thank You that I may know this Word contains life. Amen.

Psalm 119:9-19

Instead, speaking the truth in love, we will in all things grow up into ...
Christ.

~ Ephesians 4:15 ~

A mistake that people make in their efforts to grow spiritually, is to accept that this life is divided into two separate parts: the spiritual and the materialistic. This gives rise to people being divided into two groups as well: those who try to cultivate a meaningful spiritual life, and those who are inclined to follow the ways of the world. Unfortunately, there is a tendency amongst the former to regard themselves as superior to the latter and to think that they are necessarily the better people.

The moment when a disciple of the Master starts thinking along these lines, he loses contact with reality, his discipleship deteriorates and he becomes an ineffective witness. A spiritual person has a lively interest in people and in what is happening around him. As he grows through the Spirit of God, this experience will be reflected in his daily life. True spirituality is extremely practical. Jesus himself was a very practical Person. For Him, no division existed between the spiritual and the materialistic. For Him, life held a unity that sanctified it. A developing spiritual life should turn the disciple into a balanced and stable person. If you live in the strength of the living Christ, you will be able to understand that life in its totality should be approached from God's point of view and that everything is subject to His sovereignty.

The truth is that you were created in the image of God and you are a spiritual being. To maintain that part of your being is spiritual and the other part materialistic, is to deny your spiritual heritage.

Thank You that I may know that You are always with me. Through every obstacle You will take my hand. Thank You, Lord. Amen.

Ephesians 4:1-16

A SPIRIT OF DISCERNMENT

But you have an anointing from the Holy One, and all of you know the truth.

~ 1 JOHN 2:20 ~

As the years roll past, more and more books are written dealing with every conceivable aspect of the Christian faith. Various theories are favored; changing interpretations are propagated. In many instances in our times, age-old concepts in the Word of God are questioned and rejected. This could be very confusing and disturbing for the average Christian. As a result you run the risk of easily starting to have doubts about your faith.

It is your primary duty to develop a personal relationship with the living Christ. The experience of people and the guidance of writers may be a source of help, but it is essential for you to know Christ personally, not only to know "about" Him. By following His example and living according to His commands, by spending precious time in His presence, and through intelligent and faithful study of the truths contained in His Word, you will experience the resurrected Savior abiding with you and, through His Holy Spirit, actively at work in your life.

The more sensitive you become to the stirrings of the Holy Spirit in your life, the more He will guide you and enlighten you about the whole truth. In this way you will know instinctively which doctrines of which writers are authentic; the Holy Spirit will grant you discernment. This is an important aspect of your growth towards spiritual maturity.

Strengthen me in faith, oh Lord. Fill me with enthusiasm and passion so that I may proclaim the peace of Jesus. Amen.

1 John 2:18-27

For this reason I remind you to fan into flame the gift of God, which is in you through the laying on of my hands.

~ 2 TIMOTHY 1:6 ~

A major stumbling block in spiritual growth is complacency. When you believe that you have reached the point where there is nothing more for you to learn about the Master and His doctrines, you have reached a dangerous cul-de-sac that always ends in frustration and spiritual impoverishment.

The life of a Christian is not a static experience, but a constant development in spiritual awareness that, from day to day, God becomes an increasing reality in your existence. Referring constantly to your conversion and rebirth, while lacking an increasing awareness of the presence of the living Master during the years that followed, is a denial of the effectiveness of that experience. Conversion is a process. The seeking disciple finds great satisfaction in making Christ the Lord and Master of his life. However, at the same time, he has a burning desire to know more about Him every day and to live nearer to Him. This forces him to study the Scriptures and to analyze the lives of those who walked the path of Christ before him. More than anything else, this quest drives him increasingly closer to the Lord.

If you have not yet experienced this desire, it could be that you have become complacent and do not react to the challenge of Jesus. This is the death-knell for spiritual growth. Plead with the Holy Ghost to once again fan the flame in your life so that you may experience a period of new spiritual growth.

You are my power and my strength. With Your armor I can remain steadfast against Satan's cunning. Amen.

2 Timothy 1:3-18

REVIVE YOUR FAITH

He who has the Son has life; he who does not have the Son of God
does not have life.

~ 1 JOHN 5:12 ~

O ne often hears about people who are deeply involved in church
matters, but their spiritual life has lost its momentum The spark
is gone from their spiritual life and that they feel empty and lacking in
dynamic faith. Unless something active is done about this, the greatest
inherent danger is that these people could be permanently lost to the
cause of the church and the Lord. They seek other ways of fulfilment
and more often than not, this results in spiritual adversity.

Jesus came to this world so that you and I may live "life" in all its
fullness. As part of His Divine mission, He died and rose from the dead
so that fear, sin and death would be conquered. In addition, He made
us a promise of eternal life. In order to turn His promise into practical
reality, Jesus proffers the Holy Spirit to all who believe in Him and who
embrace Him as their Savior and Redeemer.

If your faith has reached a low or if you are serious in your intention
to prevent your spiritual life from stagnating, then now is the time to
open your heart anew to Christ and to ask Him once again to take
control of your life – spirit, soul and body. This will require subjecting
yourself to the will of the Master. In turn, He will transfigure you into
a new person. And when He once again resides in you through His
Holy Spirit, you will experience self-confidence, joy and peace – all of
which are the result of an intimate and personal relationship with God.

Nothing can separate me from You. You always abide with me through
Your Spirit. Lord, help me to remember that always. Amen.

1 John 5:6-15

WHEN GOD LIVES IN YOU

If anyone acknowledges that Jesus is the Son of God, God lives in him and he in God.

~ 1 JOHN 4:15 ~

The simple doctrines of Jesus Christ have enormous power. People from all walks of life experience their impact on their lives. Theologians may debate the various guidelines of Christ's doctrines and, in doing so, cause confusion in the mind and spirit of ordinary people. However, if you acknowledge and embrace the Deity of Christ, you will have a force in your life like you have never experienced before. Such an acknowledgement, which is founded on the Scriptures, gives you energy, strength and inner life. Just by stating: "Christ is the Lord" causes that force to sparkle in your life.

The miraculous truth is that you will not live alone with God, but that He will live in you. This is the most significant and amazing experience that you will ever witness, because it will mark a complete revolution in your existence. Your disposition towards people and circumstances changes, you notice the beauty of life instead of staring yourself blind against its dreariness. Your objectives are creative and you work positively towards them. Your entire life becomes a pilgrimage to an ever growing relationship with God.

Acknowledging the Deity and Sovereignty of Christ results in such far-reaching consequences that you will stand amazed each day about that which God has achieved in your life.

I wish to celebrate Your strength. Make me victorious in battle through Your Spirit. Amen.

1 John 4:7-21

GOD ENABLES YOU TO CONTROL YOUR THOUGHTS

> You, LORD, give perfect peace to those who keep their purpose firm
> and put their trust in you.
>
> ~ ISAIAH 26:3 ~

Your thoughts are servant to you. Total control of your thoughts is possible if you do not give wrong thoughts free reign. Your thoughts influence your deeds because that which you think and believe is the cause of your circumstances. It is therefore imperative to discipline your thoughts in order to have a positive and constructive disposition towards life.

Behind every thought lies the power of desire. That which you think, motivates your deeds and reactions in life. If there is conflict between your emotions and your common logic, your emotions will usually get the upper hand. It is therefore of vital importance to rid yourself of destructive emotions that result in mental deterioration. Replace them with positive and creative thoughts.

The greatest force in a healthy emotional life is allowing the Holy Spirit to take control of your thoughts. Trust in God and live in harmony with Him. Then your life will stabilize, in spite of anxieties, problems and temptations surrounding you. If your thoughts are concentrated on God, He will enable you to approach life with serenity and trust, and your emotions will increasingly be subject to the sovereignty of the Holy Spirit.

You can, through the strength which Christ grants you, select your thoughts and, in doing so, experience the peace of God. There will be moments of disruption when evil thoughts are trying to re-establish themselves. But while you are focusing on the benevolence and grace of God, you will receive confirmation that the Master is in control of your thoughts; and then there is nothing that can destroy your peace.

You are my only Savior. Help me to trust in God as my shield against the Evil One. Amen.

Isaiah 26:1-15

How can I serve God?

Your love has given me great joy and encouragement, because you, brother, have refreshed the hearts of the saints.

~ Philemon verse 7 ~

There are many people who fervently desire to serve the Lord, but they cannot think of a way to do so. As a result they experience a vacuum in their spiritual life. They get frustrated and complain that they remain unfulfilled. They seek in vain for ways to bear testimony to the Lord and to serve Him, but every search ends in a cul-de-sac. In their disappointment, they withdraw more and more, until they, in their opinion, wave a lost cause goodbye.

Every disciple of Jesus the living Christ has a capacity for love. There is no emotion that is more important to serve the Master with than to share His love with others. Love can comfort, save those who are lost, and lend hope to those who need it. It can break down barriers, build bridges, establish relationships and heal wounds. As Paul states: Love is the greatest.

If you are sincerely looking for a way to serve the Lord, why don't you start to love others in His name! A telephone call, a letter or a visit to somebody who is in distress, will provide unprecedented joy and comfort. Even more important, it will lend a feeling of fulfilment to your life – while you serve the Master.

Lord, grant that I may be the manifestation of Your love for all those around me to see. Amen.

Philemon verses 4-22

○HE DISCIPLINE OF SERVICE

"... We too will serve the LORD, because he is our God."

~ JOSHUA 24:18 ~

○ he most important moment of your life is when you are born again. Whether it meant emotional ecstasy or quiet reassurance, you were filled with that wonderful, indescribable feeling of peace that could only come from Jesus, the One to whom you have surrendered your life. The holiness of that moment makes you naturally inclined to place yourself at the service of the Master. At that moment, no sacrifice seems too big for you.

You must, however, be prepared for the afterglow of this experience. Shortly on the heels of the joy of being born, moments of doubt and uncertainty will follow. The more you get involved with the activities of the church, the more things there will be to disagree with. In all probability you will experience disillusionment and even discouragement. In this way, your faith will be put to the test and you could be hurt.

All these things form part of the devil's armory. He continually bombards the Christian with it in the hope that his faith will weaken and his testimony to God be silenced. To counter this, you must hold on steadfastly to the promises of Jesus, that His grace will be sufficient for you at all times (cf. 2 Cor. 12:9). Discipline yourself to look up to Jesus – the Author and Perfecter of your faith. Trust in Him at all times and not on man. He will lead you from temptation onto His eternal path of devotion. Give your life to Him once more and devote yourself once again to His glorious service.

Strengthen me through Your power, Lord. Grant that I may remain steadfast against sin and that I will be honorable in my conduct. Amen.

Joshua 24:13-24

☉HE INFLUENCE OF THE HOLY SPIRIT

Live by the Spirit, and you will not gratify the desires of the sinful nature.

~ GALATIANS 5:16 ~

☉f they are totally honest with themselves, most Christians will acknowledge that they experience problems living in obedience to the commands of the Master. Some go through barren patches of the spirit and struggle with the temptation to form a compromise with the sinful world. Many simply give up while their faith weakens. They give in to despair regarding the situation in which they find themselves. When others urge them to hold on to their faith, they disregard the appeal by stating that they find it an impossible task.

Don't forget that Jesus was exposed to immense temptations. There were moments, like shortly before His capture and crucifixion, when a compromise of His principles would have been greatly advantageous to His human welfare. If He had given in, He would have been spared the horror of the cross, but He would have robbed Himself of the glory of the resurrection, and the world of salvation.

Just as Jesus drew His strength from the Spirit of God, He proffers His Holy Spirit to you to enable you to triumph over temptation and to live the way in which He wants you to live. Open your life to the work of the Holy Spirit and remain sensitive and obedient to Him at all times. He will guide you in the justness of God. His influence will radically change your life for the better.

Oh, Spirit and Creator, grant me Your blessing. Amen.

Galatians 5:13-26

ALLOW YOUR ENEMIES TO HELP

YOU GROW SPIRITUALLY

"But I tell you, Love your enemies and pray for those who persecute you."

$\sim$ MATTHEW 5:44 $\sim$

Blessed is the person who has no enemies! Many of the Master's disciples are disturbed by the thought that, regardless of their efforts to spread good nature and love, they still have enemies. It is precisely their testimony to Christ that could cause intense hostility.

Man's natural reaction towards someone who dislikes him is to pay such a person back in kind by disliking him in turn. If you do this, you cause a vicious circle that could only be broken by forgiveness and love. It is under such circumstances that a living Christian experience can restore a balanced outlook on life.

If you have an enemy, you are confronted with a challenge to your faith. You can try to ignore him, or you can take revenge by making public damaging facts about him that will harm him. However, it will be better by far to act towards him according to Christ's commands.

Your first obligation is to erase all hatred and bitterness from your heart. It may seem difficult, but if you open yourself to the influence of the Holy Spirit, you will achieve that which seems impossible. If your bitterness is under control, pray for your enemy. Prayer has healing and salving qualities that will enrich your own spirit.

An enemy, who is treated according to Christ's commands, enables you to develop into spiritual maturity. Should your enemy become your friend, you have achieved a resounding victory for the cause of the King of the Church.

I plead guilty before You, Lord. Give me strength to actively display my love for You and for my neighbor. Amen.

Matthew 5:43-48

Your attitude should be the same as that of Christ Jesus.

~ Philippians 2:5 ~

Different denominations depict the challenges of Christianity according to their specific interpretations of His message, therefore it is extremely difficult to understand what Christ's challenges to His followers really entailed.

However, one thing we know, those who call themselves Christians and walk in His fellowship, must grow in the knowledge and grace of their Lord and Master so that they can become like Him. Any Christian church that is satisfied with less, has an incomplete gospel.

To walk in fellowship with the living Christ, and to grow in His grace and knowledge, requires spiritual and mental discipline. You do not need to be a brilliant student, but you must utilize your mind to the best of your ability and be devoted to the service of your Master. Through this devotion your thoughts must be free of fear, bitterness, hate, greed, pride and other destructive forces.

If you feel inadequate to implement these high standards in your own life, you must, in your quiet time with God, recall all the wonderful promises of the Scriptures. The Bible encourages disciples to maintain and develop Jesus' attitudes towards life. This means that you should also take note of His approach to human relationship problems in order to share in His wisdom. You must declare yourself willing to follow His guidance unconditionally.

If these challenges sound too theoretical, remember that the Lord has promised His abiding Spirit to all of those who ask for it. Do you accept this challenge?

You are my Comfort, God. Guide me, direct me and teach me. Amen.

Philippians 2:1-11

DO YOU PURSUE PERFECTION?

"I am God Almighty; walk before me and be blameless."

~ GENESIS 17:1 ~

Throughout the world today, the emphasis is on perfection and excellence. In the arts and sciences, in the business world and in education, everyone is pursuing perfect methods and machines in the name of progress. In some cases, man has become so obsessed with the necessity for perfection in material objects, that he has allowed social and spiritual standards to decline to a disturbing extent, or to be dismissed altogether.

The beauty of God's creation is marred by pollution and the waste of machinery and prodigal lifestyles. Abominable weapons are manufactured, while one nation seeks dominance over all the others. Personal moral standards are often of secondary importance to avarice. That is the price of progress.

Even spiritually, there are negative sides of perfection. Dr Andrew Murray justifiably stated, "Perfection has defeated thousands, but imperfection tens of thousands!" There is only one perfect life that is worthwhile, and that is the life that the living Christ proffers His followers. Nothing else can ever give you true fulfilment and satisfaction, because life in Christ is eternal and constant. In comparison, all other forms of life are states of misery, imperfection and insufficiency. There simply is no substitute for a Christian life.

Regardless of the nature of your lifestyle, and regardless of the level of life that you function on, if you sincerely pursue perfection and sanctification, embrace God as your Guide in your undertaking. Dedicate everything that you do to Him; stay within His holy will in all your undertakings, and maintain the standards set by Jesus. Then you will achieve a degree of perfection far beyond anything you could imagine.

Oh, perfect Holiness, You are the Lord and Ruler of my life. Lend me a helping hand to devote my life and heart to You. Amen.

Genesis 17:1-8

July

Praise be to the God and Father of our Lord Jesus Christ, who has blessed us in the heavenly realms with every spiritual blessing in Christ.

~ Ephesians 1:3 ~

Prayer

ETERNAL GOD OF LOVE AND MERCY,

We come to You pleading for Your vital blessing: we, as little earth-bound people, call it "happiness". But what we really want is to be blessed by You; that You will grant us true, lasting happiness that is not dependent on our circumstances.

Thank You that You promised Your blessing to Your children so that, at midnight in captivity, we can sing songs of praise to Your glory; so that we can regard ourselves as happy, regardless of a thorn in the flesh; so that we may know happiness in the faithful performance of our duties. Holy Spirit of God, come and teach us what true happiness is and that it cannot be found anywhere but in obedience to our Lord and Master.

Thank You, Lord Jesus, that the happiness that You grant us, not only has bearing on a hazy great beyond, but also on the "now" and the "here" of every day.

We thank You, Father, for the promise of blessing from Your Word: "The LORD bless you and keep you; the LORD make his face shine upon you and be gracious to you; the LORD turn his face towards you and give you peace" (Numbers 6:24-26).

We pray this in the Name of our benedictory Savior and Redeemer, Jesus our Lord.

Amen

ℐESUS, THE SOURCE OF ALL TRUE HAPPINESS

"Hosanna! Blessed is he who comes in the name of the Lord! Blessed is the coming kingdom of our father David!"

~ Mark 11:9-10 ~

ℐ esus is the source of all true happiness or blessing. To be blessed, we must know Jesus as our personal Savior and Redeemer; we must devote our lives to Him; we must be obedient to His will under all circumstances. Without Jesus there will be no happiness or blessing awaiting us. The Holy Spirit wants to cleanse and sanctify our expectations, so that we may be of service to Christ and His kingdom.

Our expectations regarding blessing, and God's way of providing it, often differ widely. Through the ages, this has presented man with a problem: Adam and Eve, the people of Israel, and even the disciples searched for a worldly kingdom while Christ came to build a heavenly one. The same mistake could manifest in our lives. We are selfish about happiness because we want to be cleverer than God Himself.

We all search for happiness and we want to personally determine the nature and detail thereof. Then we run the risk of missing Christ's blessing. Christ's happiness is a "singular happiness", a happiness that is different, a happiness in Christ. Our happiness as humans often depends upon "chances" or "luck": a sudden and unexpected change in our condition; poverty is suddenly turned into affluence; sorrow is changed into joy; obscurity is elevated to fame, status and strength. The one moment we have nothing, and then, suddenly, we have wealth and abundance. This easily results in materialism. We are like someone winning a prize and not knowing what to do with it.

Human happiness is something that life can offer, and then, just as suddenly, take away again. Man, in his short-sightedness, calls it "happiness" when things are in his favor for a while. But that is not what God's happiness or blessing means.

> Lord Jesus, I praise Your glorious Name, for You are the source of all my happiness because You delivered me and made me a child of God. Amen.

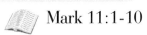 Mark 11:1-10

ℋApppiness in Christ

He who has clean hands and a pure heart, who does not lift up his soul to an idol or swear by what is false. He will receive blessing from the Lord and vindication from God his Savior.

~ Psalm 24:4-5 ~

Christ's happiness, blessing and joy are indestructible (cf. Jn. 16:22). Christ's happiness is a blessing, even when we are in pain. It is a happiness that cannot be erased by sorrow, loss, disappointment or failure. It is a happiness that still sees a rainbow through your tears. It is something that nothing in life or death could deprive us of.

Christ's happiness is born from an intimate walk with God: today, through the dark night, tomorrow and every day. It is like the depth of the ocean that surges and seethes above, where waves toss and break, causing rough waters. However, deep underneath, it is quiet and calm. It is like the little bird that builds its nest on the rocky ledge under the thundering roar of the waterfall and, in the midst of the storm, serenely sits on its nest, hatching its little eggs.

Christ's happiness does not necessarily coincide with our external circumstances. It is a deep joy that is everlasting and steadfast. It is furthermore not a human feat that we achieve through our own excellence or could cultivate through effort. It is a gift of God in our lives, through the work of the Holy Spirit, which is the channel God uses to let it flow into our lives. If we study the Beatitudes of Christ, we will discover the secret of true happiness. The Holy Spirit will guide us to be obedient to the demands of Christ, so that His happiness and blessing will become our portion.

Pray that the Holy Spirit will clearly lead us and that He will inspire us so that we will yearn for the "happiness" and "blessing" of Christ.

Loving Master, thank You that the happiness that You bestow is steadfast and indestructible, unlike the temporary and transient happiness of the world. Amen.

Psalm 24:1-10

THE BLESSING OF DEPENDENCE

"Blessed are the poor in spirit, for theirs is the kingdom of heaven."
~ MATTHEW 5:3 ~

This is possibly the most important of all the Beatitudes, because it is the unavoidable condition for the blessing that follows all the others. The main idea is that our unconditional surrender to God's will brings us untold happiness and blessing. This is not about poverty or wealth. It is about our relationship with God.

When we trust in God completely, worldly possessions have lesser value and we are increasingly bound to God and His kingdom. We pray, "Your kingdom come; Your will be done." If God's will is done in my life, His kingdom has entered my heart. In plain language this Beatitude tells us, "Blessed is the man who realizes his own absolute impotence, who has placed his trust completely in God and who is so obedient to God that he could become a citizen of God's kingdom." The first Beatitude is therefore the summation of the entire Sermon on the Mount.

Jesus is the Teacher and He is the perfect Example. He humbled Himself. He knows that God has handed everything over to Him, but He gets up from the table and washes the feet of His disciples. The world says, "Obtain everything you can and hold on to what you have!" The Christian disciple says, "He must become more and I must become less." The only people who are without hope, are those who are complacent and smug; who think that they have no need for God. They pay a terrible price and miss out on the blessing of God. Therefore, the child of God prays evermore, "Teach us to be small before You in our own eyes, oh Lord, deeply aware of our inability to sincerely glorify Your Name, make us humble and still, to live according to Your will" (Hymn 259:1).

Thank You, Lord Jesus, that I have the privilege to be dependent upon You, because there is no other anchor in life that could make us feel safer. Amen.

Matthew 5:1-12

◯HE BLESSING OF DEPENDENCE (2)

But those who hope in the LORD will renew their strength. They will soar on wings like eagles; they will run and not grow weary, they will walk and not be faint.

~ ISAIAH 40:31 ~

O f whom does Jesus speak when He says, "Blessed are those who know how dependent they are on God"? Those who desperately battle to find God. They are distraught with themselves and their lives. Theirs could be any need: spiritual bankruptcy; economic poverty; poor health; unexpected sorrow and suffering; failed ideals, or anything else that makes one plaintively dependent upon God. It is related to our real stresses and strains, as well as to our problems; those things that drive us to God and cause us to plead for His mercy and blessing.

One can handle one's desperation with oneself in different ways. You can call on people for help and possibly find temporary relief there. However, complete satisfaction you will not find. You can attempt to solve your own problems or poverty, only to find yourself drifting further away from God. Or you can take your poverty and go and stand at God's door like a beggar without making demands, because we know that we deserve nothing. That is the first step that we must take to share in the blessing of God.

It is very difficult for modern man to be dependent. Independence, self-reliance and self-sufficiency mean so infinitely much to us. However, this independence is an illusion. It is a great lie that Satan has placed in our hearts. Only think of Jesus' parable of the rich fool (cf. Lk. 12:13-21). This man's sin was not the fact that he was rich, but that he had left God out of his calculations.

To chase after independence from God in your life, is to waste your energy on a mirage in the desert, and it is the height of folly.

Holy Spirit of God, through Your mercy, keep me safely anchored in Jesus Christ, upon whom I am so totally dependent. Amen.

Isaiah 40:27-31

"And I'll say to myself, 'You have plenty of good things laid up for many years. Take life easy; eat, drink and be merry...'"

~ Luke 12:19-20 ~

We are all deeply dependent upon God: that is a given fact. But many people do not want to hear of it. Therefore, Christ says, "Blessed are those who know ..." The Holy Spirit enters our lives when we stop running away from this truth; when we realize that our happiness does not depend upon our own insignificant efforts and achievements, but upon God and God alone.

Could there be any "happiness" when you surrender control of your own life? Christ says, "Yes!" There is an extraordinary happiness in it that touches your life bounteously and blesses it abundantly. A kind of happiness that enables you to gain the kingdom of God. It is not boisterous and sensational, not as blinding and shining like the tinsel of the worldly kingdom, but it is indeed a deep, veritable, quiet and sacrosanct happiness that brings peace to your life.

It is to be secure in God. To be assured that Somebody loves you and cares about you. That He holds you with a strong hand, a hand with nail-marks which bear witness to His immense love for you. Man only discovers true happiness when he becomes completely dependent upon Christ. When you can voice the same sentiments as Christ, "Yet not as I will, but as you will". It is like taking a blank sheet of paper, placing your signature at the bottom, and saying to Christ, "Please fill in Your will for my life, Lord!"

Through dependence on Christ, the Holy Spirit guides us to true happiness and blessing. This is the result of unconditional surrender to Christ and His will for your life. The essence of sin is selfishness and self-righteousness. The essence of salvation is self-surrender and devotion; total dependence on God. May you, through the work of the Holy Spirit, share in that happiness and blessing.

Help me, Lord Jesus, to store up treasures for myself in heaven where moth and rust do not destroy. Amen.

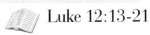 Luke 12:13-21

⑦HE BLESSING OF A BROKEN HEART

"Blessed are those who mourn, for they will be comforted."

~ MATTHEW 5:4 ~

⑦ here was a young man who was trying to establish himself as a farmer. He worked hard, and eventually invested everything that he owned in a beautiful peach orchard. Then, in his peak year, a devastating hailstorm destroyed his entire orchard. He went and spoke to his minister about the bitterness and sorrow in his heart that he found difficult to handle. The minister's reply gives us some understanding of God's holy purpose with the mystery of sorrow and heartbreak, "My young friend, God loves you much more than your peaches. He knows that peaches fare much better without hail. However, it is impossible to cultivate better people without trials, tribulations and sorrow. His purpose is to cultivate people who believe, not beautiful peaches." The young man started over again and worked zealously to make a resounding success of his farming operations.

God has a purpose with all suffering and sorrow. He wants to lead us through to the other side as better people. Who can understand sorrow and suffering better than Jesus himself? Is there need or want in your home? He had no place to lay His head. Have your friends disappointed you? His friends denied and betrayed Him. In prayer, do you grapple with a sorrow that you cannot handle? In Gethsemane, He fought a bloody battle. Do you weep for someone dear that has died? He wept at the graveside of His friend Lazarus. Do you sometimes feel forsaken? On the cross, He had to sob in Godforsakenness.

However, sorrow and grief remain a grim reality and a problem in our lives. Therefore, it is comforting to know that God is involved in our sorrow through Jesus Christ and the Holy Spirit. God's own Son drank the cup of sorrows that His Father had poured for Him to the lees. Therefore, He has sent the Holy Spirit to be our Comforter.

I glorify and praise You, Heavenly Comforter, that You press me against Your heart when I mourn – not like one without hope, but like a child of the Almighty. Amen.

Isaiah 53:1-3

THE BLESSING OF A BROKEN HEART (2)

My God, my God, why have you forsaken me? Why are you so far from saving me, so far from the words of my groaning?

~ PSALM 22:1 ~

An anonymous English poet wrote:

I walked a mile with pleasure; she chattered all the way,
but left me none the wiser for all she had to say.
I walked a mile with sorrow, and ne'er a word said she,
but O, the things I learned from her, when sorrow walked with me!

It is one of life's real truths that one looks for the stars in the darkest night and one is driven to God by sorrow. There is an ancient Arabic proverb that states, "If you walk in sunshine every day, you later live in a desert." There are certain fruits that need rain to grow; and there is spiritual growth that we can only learn through sorrow.

Sorrow can do two essential things for us: like nothing else in the world, it can show us the goodness of our fellow man; and like nothing else in the world, it can teach us about the comfort and love of God. In our moments of sorrow, many of us discover our fellow men and our God, as we never have before.

It is possible that we can live on the surface for years and then, suddenly, we are driven to the dark depths of life through sorrow. If we accept this with the right attitude, new beauty and strength are born in our hearts. Christ taught us this, so that in our sorrow, we will still follow God in faith and obedience.

Thank You, Spirit of Grace, that You comfort us when our hearts are broken and for guiding us once again towards the love of God. Amen.

 Psalm 22:1-11

⟨T⟩HE BLESSING OF A BROKEN HEART (3)

"Blessed are those who mourn, for they will be comforted."

~ MATTHEW 5:4 ~

C ould there be a human heart in the whole wide world that could hear this Beatitude without being touched? A promise of comfort finds a response in the heart of every person. There is so much sorrow and grief amongst people on this earth, that one instinctively listens to the voice that brings a message of comfort to the broken heart. On our pilgrimage, we meet so many Marahs. This world is not called a vale of tears without reason. There is more than enough pain, sorrow and grief to verify this.

We walk down a cheerful street with its busy traffic and, suddenly, we stand in front of the closed windows of a house where people live with wounded hearts, filled with sorrow and pain. We hear about people who still steered the plough with a healthy hand yesterday, without looking back; today in a fraction of a second their health has been impaired. Suddenly their lifeboat was torn to shreds by storm winds and they whisper that they have become a wreck on the beach of life.

Then there is a dark procession of ailments and disasters; of famine and poverty; of trouble and anxiety. There is truly no home without its cross and no heart without its sorrow. Do not forget either the quiet sorrow of many a heart of which the world bears no knowledge and which often weighs doubly heavy because it cannot be shared with anyone. There is so much hidden sorrow that one carries in the company of your friends, trying to conceal it behind a mask of laughter, without ever really succeeding.

The blessed words of Jesus are like balm for the melancholy heart and offer us new hope and peace. It is a flood of sound of heavenly music to hear the Master say, *"Blessed are those who mourn, for they will be comforted."*

In our sorrow, Heavenly Father, we know that You are very close to us in Your comforting love. Amen.

Psalm 61:1-9

When Jesus saw (Mary) weeping, and the Jews who had come along with her also weeping, he was deeply moved in spirit and troubled.

~ JOHN 11:33 ~

ᴛhere is so much hidden sorrow in our dismal world, sorrow that one tries to conceal in the company of your friends, without really succeeding. There is the affliction of dependency on some habit that is hard to break and that is denigrating your life or the life of a loved one. There is the grief of a shattered marriage, or the sorrow of estrangement of children who have rebelliously and disobediently left the parental home. Then there is the hidden sorrow that you dare not discuss with anyone because there is shame attached to it. In the company of others, you rather cover it softly with a cloak of love. Nobody is allowed to know about it and you must carry it alone.

There are the people in mourning. What sad heart may be beating under the mourning clothes? Relentlessly death takes your dearest away from you. Death cannot be ransomed; he cannot even be chased away through prayer. He leaves your heart empty, your home empty, and the world around you empty. There comes a day in each life when we sit in the solitude of our private sanctum, with red, swollen eyes, weeping for a loved one. It is therefore small wonder that all teary eyes, at one time or another, are lifted to Jesus, the Comforter. So much the more because the Gospels sketch Him where He gathered all the sick, the distressed, the seekers and the outcast around Him. He was always willing to pour balm on their wounds and to pay individual attention to them.

It is therefore essential that we will, at all times, know the path to His Throne of Grace, so that we may share in His comfort and blessing; because we do not know Him only in times of sorrow, but we live in daily fellowship with Him.

Spirit of God, You also taught me the path to the Throne of Grace when I mourn. Thank You, my God and Father, that You comfort broken hearts.

John 11:33-44

$\bigcirc$HE BLESSING OF A BROKEN HEART (5)

Comfort, comfort my people, says your God. Speak tenderly to Jerusalem, and proclaim to her that her hard service has been completed, that her sin has been paid for, that she has received from the LORD's hand double for all her sins.

~ ISAIAH 40:1-2 ~

$\bigcirc$he greatest of all human grief is that which manifests through our sins. Christ carried even that for us in His body. Grieving about sins includes many things: anxiety about our betrayal of the living God; our shallowness, disobedience and unwillingness to serve Him; our lack of holiness; our refusal to subject ourselves to His holy will; our devotedness to our worldly possessions, and many more abominable sins.

However, when Christ speaks of comfort, that judgment places us in the midst of the Gospel of Grace. Our sole comfort in life and in death is that we belong to Jesus our Savior. Christ is the Comfort for all who have learnt through grace to grieve about their sins and who steadfastly know that, through repentance and remission of sins, they belong to Him. The bitter fountain of Marah reminds us of the fountain of life from which so much bitterness wells up into life. God showed Moses a piece of wood which made the bitter water sweet. That piece of wood is to us a symbol of the cross: through the bitter cursed tree the source of our sin and sorrow is healed. It becomes a "wonder tree" to which we owe our eternal Comfort in life and in death.

On this tree He carried *our* sins in His body. On this tree He fully becomes our Comforter, Savior and Redeemer. Therefore we rejoice:

Savior, You're the center and furthermost flight of our desire
Through forsakenness and fear You lead us back to God.
Through Your love You evoke love and teach us to love our neighbor
and cultivate in us the joy of a new and meaningful life (Hymn 130:3).

I stand in wonder before You, my Savior, that You have delivered me from the sorrow of sin. I glorify Your Name! Amen.

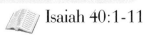 Isaiah 40:1-11

"Blessed are those who mourn, for they will be comforted."

~ MATTHEW 5:4 ~

⊘ f this comfort fades when you walk out of your quiet time with God into life; if you once again stumble in doubting sadness and sorrow; if you have lost your heavenly comfort, remember that He, the Great Comforter and Friend, holds your hand firmly in His. You have a Mediator who not only died on the cross for you, but who has also risen from the dead and ascended to heaven where, at the throne of the Father, He intercedes for your comfort.

This is how Christ comforts us in our temporary ordeals. He never leaves us alone in anxiety and distress, in difficulty and sorrow. He is with you in the fiery oven, in the depth of the ocean, in the valley of the shadow of death. He is with you always, till the end of the world.

Sometimes He completely removes the bitter cup: the sick are healed; the cross is taken from your shoulders; the thorn is removed from your flesh and the burden is lightened. Another time you face Marah: the burden remains heavy; the water in the cup of bitterness remains bitter; but through His mercy He takes the bitterness from it. Then you will be able to drink willingly from the cup that the Father has poured for you. And remember: not far from Marah, there is Elim with its fountains and palm trees.

Then you realize: it is not what you lose in the course of life, but what you have retained through grace that really matters. Marah is merely the transit gate to the heavenly Elim. Simply trust in Him who pours our cups for us and hands them with a loving hand to us to drink. It is He who said, "Blessed are those who mourn, for they will be comforted."

Jesus, Man of Sorrows, You have drunk Your cup of bitterness to the lees. Help me to do the same. Amen.

Matthew 5:3-12

❍HE BLESSING OF MEEKNESS

"Blessed are the meek, for they will inherit the earth."

~ MATTHEW 5:5 ~

❍ eekness means friendliness and generosity in your interaction with others. The dictionary defines it as follows: "A gentle disposition, meek, good-natured." It is not a characteristic that people of our time get excited about. The word has a connotation that, in general, causes people to react negatively rather than positively. It causes people to state derisively, "He is a gentle soul." By implication they mean that the person is too soft; almost spineless, spiritless and spunkless.

People of our time think that meekness does not pay; not if you want to get somewhere in life. The people of our time believe that nice guys come second. The credo of our time is, "I must get somewhere in life. How I get there, is of no real importance. I must assert myself: on the sporting field, at school or at university, in the business world, in the political arena and, alas, also in the church and in religion!"

The catchword of our time is "self-assertiveness". Polish your own self-image. Live according to the law of the jungle: only the strongest will survive. It is placing yourself and your own interests foremost. At its core it is a denial of God and His omnipotence. You believe that you can do everything yourself. "It is I alone against the whole world, therefore I must take care of myself, nobody else would want to do it for me." In this way we assert ourselves against the whole world, even against God.

Our sinful nature, inclines us towards self-assertion and arrogance. We are the descendants of Adam and Eve who, even in paradise, asserted themselves against God. And now Jesus comes and teaches us exactly the opposite approach to life. He speaks of the "happiness" of the meek and that they will inherit the earth. Come and listen attentively to what the Master wants to teach us.

Lord Jesus, I wish to learn the virtue of meekness from You. Stand by me in my moments of weakness. Amen.

Isaiah 53:1-12

"Blessed are the meek, for they will inherit the earth."

~ MATTHEW 5:5 ~

With all these Beatitudes Christ requires a positive mind-shift and a renewal of our thoughts. He Himself is the Prototype of all the meek. Who has ever been as high and powerful, and at the same time as humble as Jesus? He rides into Jerusalem on a donkey; He washes the feet of His disciples; He touches lepers; He talks to prostitutes about a better life. His meekness was not by any means a weakness, but Divine power. This Jesus does not demand of us self-assertiveness, but meekness.

What does Jesus mean when He pronounces this benediction? There is a notable similarity between the first and the third Beatitudes of the Sermon on the Mount. "Blessed are the poor in spirit," demands of us absolute humbleness towards God. "Blessed are the meek," demands of us humility towards our fellow men. It is a deep-seated and sincere selflessness. Self interest is not of vital importance to gentle people.

We find the classic example of this in Genesis 13, where Abraham allows Lot to choose a part of the land and then does not get upset when Lot, in his selfishness, chooses the best land. He does not feel aggrieved and, through his meekness, he is spared Sodom and Gomorrah.

In the school of meekness we learn to patiently carry the grief people cause us, without calling for revenge; to forgive every injustice done to us and to return good for evil and triumph over evil with good. In this we have the immortal example of our Savior himself.

Are you willing, in following Jesus Christ, to learn in meekness from day to day?

Holy Jesus, You have taught us that meekness is not by any means a weakness. Help me to patiently carry the grief people cause me. Amen.

Isaiah 53:1-12

$\mathcal{O}$HE BLESSING OF MEEKNESS (3)

"Now that I, your Lord and Teacher, have washed your feet, you also should wash one another's feet."

~ JOHN 13:14 ~

$\mathcal{O}$ here is a half-forgotten Christian legend that tells how the angels in heaven were touched by the piety, meekness and devotion of one of Christ's surrendered children on earth. Everywhere he went, he displayed the disposition of Jesus. The angels then came down to earth to investigate the secret of his meekness and powerful testimony.

They were so impressed with his life, that they offered him the gift of miracles. Through touching the sick, he would be able to heal them and resurrect them from the dead. However, he declined the offer, saying that only God can heal the sick and resurrect the dead.

Then they offered him the special power to convince sinners to show remorse and come to repentance. Thereafter they offered him the strength to be a model person and to appeal to people with his way of life. "No," he says, "if people come to me, I might just take them away from God."

In surprise the angels then asked him, "What is it that you want then? What can we do for you?"

His reply spoke volumes, "Only the grace of God so that I may be meek and do good to people without being aware of it myself."

Then the angels decided that wherever he might cast his shadow, and where he could not see it, it would heal the sick, it would heal broken hearts and it would wipe away tears.

That is the benediction that God's meek receive.

God our Father, grant me the grace to be meek and to do good to people, regardless of who they are. Amen.

John 13:1-17

"Blessed are the meek, for they will inherit the earth."

$\sim$ MATTHEW 5:5 $\sim$

Meekness speaks of contentment with your circumstances. This is in stark contrast to a life of greed. Greedy people are the "takers" in life who, with clenched fists and white knuckles, cling desperately to everything that they can draw from life. The former are the "givers" who, through the grace of God, always ask what they could give of their most precious, their best and their most pure. They are the people who give of themselves, and through their eyes God smiles down on this world. They understand something of the suffering of the world and do not want to contribute to this suffering through their deeds.

Like the haughty, the meek also hope for a new world. Who will inherit this new earth? The Master emphasizes that the meek will do so. Indeed, the world does not belong to the brutal, but to the meek. The new earth will also belong to them; this is the blessing that God promises here.

Where does this meekness originate? How does it manifest itself in the lives of people? What is the secret to this "singular happiness"? Those whose lives are completely in the hands of God, receive this benediction. Then you will be gentle and friendly, selfless and uncomplaining. The meek person knows that the omnipotent God is by his side and that He will take care of him in His kingdom. In this we are guided by the Holy Spirit. He leads us to experience God's kingdom here and now, but also in the great beyond when we will be with God.

The kingdom of God, the new earth, will comprise meek people. Will you feel at home there? Let us pray that God, through His Holy Spirit, will lead us to true meekness.

> Merciful God, I surrender my life completely to You, so that I may receive meekness, which is a gift of grace.

Revelation 21:1-8

⊖HE BLESSING OF A HUNGRY HEART

"Blessed are those who hunger and thirst for righteousness, for they will be filled."

~ Matthew 5:6 ~

ew of us really know what it means to be "hungry" and "thirsty". The people, whom Jesus addresses here, knew it well, because they were particularly poor. Jesus had to give them bread to eat. They also knew thirst in its worst form. In the desert and wasteland in which they lived, water was a sought-after commodity. Water was sold as "a gift from God". The hunger of these people could not be stilled with refreshments, served during morning tea.

It was often the thirst and hunger of the dying these people knew. That is why Jesus so often speaks of the "bread of life" and the "water of life". He comes to us with a serious question and a major challenge: "How intense is your desire for justice? As intense as the dying needing water and bread? How much would you really like to do that which is right before God? How intense is your desire for justice?" *As a deer pants for streams of water, so my soul pants for you, O God. My soul thirsts for God, for the living God ...* (Ps. 42:1-2). Can you sincerely echo the psalmist?

Many of us have beautiful ideals regarding our relationship with God, but when the moment of decision is upon us, we are not willing to make the necessary effort. Like Felix, we say, ... *"That's enough for now! You may leave. When I find it convenient, I will send for you"* (Acts 24:25). It would make a world of difference if we would "hunger" and "thirst" for what is right before God.

Here is our comfort: it is not only in the "achieving", but especially in the "desire" that God will grant satiation. We must be willing to strive for what is right. It is a sin not to try. For those who sincerely try, God *will* grant satiation.

Heavenly Father, You are aware of my hunger and thirst for righteousness. With You alone my hunger is satisfied and my thirst quenched. Do it for me for the sake of Your grace. Amen.

John 4:1-14

"Blessed are those who hunger and thirst for righteousness, for they will be filled."

~ MATTHEW 5:6 ~

𝒟avid wanted to build the temple in Jerusalem to the glory of God, but God never allowed him to do so. However, God comforts him by commending this holy desire in his heart. Our text for the day speaks of "hunger and thirst for righteousness". Those who have this desire, will be satisfied by God.

Mention is made here of what is righteous before God. It is remorse, confession, rebirth, repentance, sanctification and spiritual growth. (See Jn. 3.) God does not want us to remain unchanged year after year. The hunger and thirst for righteousness is the sum-total of all the Christian virtues.

All people yearn for "happiness". The devoted Christian yearns for righteousness. First and foremost, this includes an awareness of one's own sins and unworthiness; a holy sadness about it, and confession thereof. Christ speaks of the desire for a pure heart (cf. Ps. 51). Where do we find the bread and water for which we yearn? The Holy Spirit leads us to Christ who is the bread and water of life. The food that He provides prevents us from ever being hungry or thirsty again.

This Beatitude is an invitation to the supper of the Lamb. Christ says, *Here I am! I stand at the door and knock. If anyone hears my voice and opens the door, I will go in and eat with him, and he with me* (Rev. 3:20). It is at God's supper where we are finally satiated. The Holy Spirit delivers the invitation to us. The price for the supper has already been paid at Golgotha. We only need to hunger and thirst for righteousness. The host is Jesus Christ Himself and the supper lasts from now into eternity.

Will you partake of that supper and will you be satiated? Or do you prefer to stand outside and remain hungry and thirsty forever?

> Holy Spirit, thank You for leading me to the bread and water of God, so that I may never again experience spiritual hunger or thirst. Amen.

 Psalm 42:1-12

⊘HE BLESSING OF A CARING HEART

"Blessed are the merciful, for they will be shown mercy."

~ MATTHEW 5:7 ~

⊘his Beatitude teaches us that the Gospel is about "people". There are those who maintain that church people are Bible-dazed about mercy. However, this is to belittle one of the most powerful doctrines of Jesus the living Christ. He gave His life because He cares about "people" and He expects His followers to care as well. This principle interweaves all Jesus' doctrines.

Mercy has been described as getting beneath someone else's skin and identifying with him to such an extent that you see through his eyes, hear with his ears, think with his mind and feel through his feelings. It is to personally care about another's distress and to show understanding for the circumstances of others. It is to carry each other's burden. Jesus came to do precisely that for us: He came to share in our distress. Therefore, He has the right to tell the parable that we read in Luke today and to put the demands it contains to us. This parable tells us about three kinds of people: Takers, Hoarders and Givers.

The highwaymen were the Takers. Their philosophy is: "Everything that is yours, is mine; I take it!" They rob the innocent traveller and walk callously away from the scene with their loot. They are not always your enemies. Sometimes they are your supposed friends who take everything that they can get from you and then leave you to your fate. This was the case with the supposed friends of the prodigal son. These people are only interested in what they can obtain for their own selfish purposes. They are devious and violent. We even find Takers in marriage: people who only take and never give; who always break and never repair. We also find them amongst children and young people who always expect life to revolve around them and their needs. These Takers have not even begun to understand what mercy is all about.

Lord Jesus, grant me a caring heart such as You had for sinners and publicans, prostitutes and outcasts, so that I can do Your work in this world. Amen.

Luke 10:25-37

"Blessed are the merciful, for they will be shown mercy."
~ Matthew 5:7 ~

⟨I⟩t came to pass that a priest and a Levite also came along that road, and upon seeing the man, they passed by "on the other side". These people are the Hoarders in life. Their philosophy of life is, "Everything that is mine, is mine. I keep it." They cling desperately to their status, their prestige and their possessions. They only gather for themselves, without a thought to their fellow men in need. They do not know what you are talking about when you maintain, "It is more blessed to give than to receive."

They are the people with callous hearts of iron, who never notice the misery around them, because they do no want to see it. They refuse to get involved. They close their ears and harden their hearts for fear that their sympathy might cost them something. They are like the rich fool in the Scriptures, forgetting that man's shroud does not have any pockets.

But a Samaritan came upon the wounded man and felt deeply sorry for him. Here we have to do with the Givers in life: people who always practice mercy and display Christian love. Their philosophy of life is: "Everything that is mine, is yours. I give it." The Samaritan was the despised who probably had first-hand experience of being beaten and robbed. Not only does he give of his money and his possessions, but also of his time, his sympathy and his comfort. He gives unconditionally, without asking whether it has been deserved. How does one succeed in living like that? Through the guidance of the Holy Spirit and the example of Jesus Christ. Jesus did not ask whether we deserved salvation, but He was urged by love.

The undeserved miracle is that, when we show mercy, God will also have mercy on us.

Lord Jesus, You had mercy on me when I did not deserve it. Help me to do the same for my fellow man. Amen.

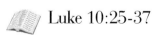 Luke 10:25-37

ℭHE BLESSING OF A PURE HEART

"Blessed are the pure in heart, for they will see God."

~ MATTHEW 5:8 ~

ℭ oday we pause at the "singular happiness" of those who are pure in heart. What does "heart" mean in spiritual terms? It is the core and most profound point of my life; the most concealed part of my whole being. Because it is "concealed", it could be an ugly place: an impure fountain from which bitter and poisonous water is welling up. Justifiably, we can confess, "The deeper we attempt to dig, the more decay faces us."

This is not only true of the heart that has not been born again: the transfiguration of our sinful heart does not take place in an instant. Think about David, the man who wrote Psalm 51. Nobody would have questioned his faith in God. Nevertheless, he goes lamentably beyond the limit with Bathsheba. In his deepest being he was a "man after God's heart". Yet, he succumbs to temptation. A pious heart is by far not a pure or holy heart yet.

David is not reduced to despair or self-pity. He seeks sanctuary with God with an urgent supplication on his lips, *Cleanse me with hyssop, and I will be clean; wash me, and I will be whiter than snow* (Ps. 51:7). The pious heart knows its own impurity, but also knows how to pray earnestly for purification and forgiveness from his God.

In Biblical times, "cleansing" pertained to leprosy. When a person was healed from leprosy, he was declared pure by the priest. This was accompanied by an impressive ceremony. A pure bird was slaughtered over an earthenware pot with boiling water, so that the blood mixed with the water. Then the priest took a branch of hyssop leaves, dipped it in the pot like a brush, and sprinkled the leper seven times with this purification remedy that was instituted by God himself. It is to this that David alludes when he prays for cleansing.

Holy Spirit, You who lead us on to truth, grant me a pure heart so that I may stand before God with confidence. Amen.

Psalm 51:1-15

"Blessed are the pure in heart, for they will see God."

~ MATTHEW 5:8 ~

It is specifically for a pure heart that David prays so fervently in Psalm 51:7: *Cleanse me with hyssop, and I will be clean; wash me, and I will be whiter than snow.* "Whiter than snow." Whiteness comes in varying degrees, but the whiteness of snow is blinding and pure as the sun. Nothing on earth can compare with it. You knew that God forgives, but not like this! So completely, totally and absolutely!

Those of us who are familiar with snow, who have experienced it in winter, will know. First, there is only the earth: dark, black, polluted. Then it starts drifting down from heaven and all the dirt and black become miraculously white. All the unsightliness is covered with a pure white mantle of snow. Wherever you look, there is only the blinding white of the snow.

Christ's justness is like that. It gently descends on you and covers the leprosy of your sin. Your life is cleansed and purified: heart, soul, thoughts, speech and deeds. Everything is cleansed under the purifying justness of the living Christ: *... the blood of Jesus, his Son, purifies us from all sin* (1 Jn. 1:7). According to our knowledge, we are pitch-black sinners, but God sees us in His Son and judges us according to His holiness a being whiter than snow. Then we state with Tennyson: "My strength is like the strength of ten, because my heart is pure."

Therefore, look away from yourself. Place your hope and faith in Jesus Christ. His justness is abundant like the snow: covering all and making you whiter than snow. And what will you see when you are pure in heart? You will see God in all His splendor, majesty and glory.

Spirit of Grace, take all the dirty sin from my life and wash me so that I may be whiter than snow. Amen.

Psalm 51:1-15

⊘HE BLESSING OF A PURE HEART (3)

"Blessed are the pure in heart, for they will see God."

~ MATTHEW 5:8 ~

David confesses to God that he is leprous with sin. He is unworthy to be allowed to sojourn in the presence of God, as lepers had to stay outside the city. He yearns for God to purify him and free him from sin. We cannot merely shrug our shoulders and say, "All men are but sinners!" This is not about "all men" but about my personal relationship with the living God. It is about my own heart where there should be a burning desire to be allowed once again into the presence of the holy God.

Look at the leper as he wanders around in the open: he longs for his home, his people, the temple of his God. But he is leprous ... In the same way, we wander around in our sinful ways while longing for God, for His forgiveness, for His purification. Together with Paul we sigh, *What a wretched man I am! Who will rescue me from this body of death?* (Rom. 7:24). The pious heart not only knows its own impurity, but it also prays fervently for forgiveness: *Cleanse me with hyssop, and I will be clean ...* (Ps. 51:7).

When I discover the wretchedness of my own sin, it drives me to God. With my whole heart I seek purification through the blood of the Lamb. I am desperate in my own guilt; I do not know the extent of my sins and I cannot erase or forgive them myself; I cannot heal my own leprosy. Where do I flee in my distress? To Christ! Just give me Christ or I will die of my leprosy. And then the miracle happens: God forgives my sin for the sake of Christ. He is the Eternal Rock, cleaved for me, who took my sin and impurity on Him in order for me to be free of it so I can see and worship God in His glory.

Holy Jesus, You who were clean and pure when You walked this earth, wash me in Your precious blood so that I may become pure. Amen.

Psalm 51:1-15

"Blessed are the peacemakers, for they will be called sons of God."
~ MATTHEW 5:9 ~

God is a God of peace. Jesus Christ is known as the Prince of Peace. With the birth of Christ, the angels sang, "Peace on earth". Now Jesus tells us that those who live to make peace will be called sons of God. The work of the Holy Spirit makes peacemakers out of us.

The condition of being a peacemaker is that you will live in peace with God, with yourself and with your fellow man. Then you will know a personal, unworldly and quiet happiness. Peace is one of the most glorious fruits of the Holy Spirit, and only those who are guided by the Spirit are truly children of God. To be a peacemaker is an active virtue. The peacemaker does not seclude himself in a monastery and ponder over peace. He goes out into the world, lays himself open and works actively and positively towards peace.

What do we understand from the word "peacemaker"? It requires that I contribute to my fellow man's advantage. This peace does not come through escapism, but through wrestling with and triumphing over problems. The road to peace often passes through conflict. It is not passive, but resoundingly active.

These people are blessed, because they do God's work here on earth. They are blessed because they make the world a better place to live and work in; because they are continuously busy taking out weeds and planting fragrant flowers. Even in my own life, the age-old battle rages on: the flesh is locked in combat with the spirit. The good that I want to do I do not do, and the evil that I do not want to do, I do (cf. Rom. 7:15). However, Jesus Christ grants me victory and peace in myself. Many people are locked in a personal civil war. Fortunate are those who find inner peace, because their lives belong to God and they are at peace with God and with themselves. This is the point of departure for becoming a peacemaker for God.

Eternal God, grant me peace with You, with my fellow men and with myself, so that I may be called your child. Amen.

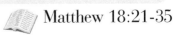 Matthew 18:21-35

THE BLESSING OF A PEACEMAKER (2)

"Blessed are the peacemakers, for they will be called sons of God."

~ MATTHEW 5:9 ~

Peacemakers are those who create healthy relationships between people. Unfortunately, there are many people who are the center of conflict, trouble and bitterness. They seem to be the cause of strife and discord. We find them in every community, family and church. They sow the seeds of dissension, misunderstanding and mistrust. They are indeed children of Satan and they do his work.

There are fortunately also those people in whose presence bitterness, hate and the inability to forgive simply cannot survive. People who build bridges in communities between races, between groups. They heal bitterness and make the world a better place. They are children of God and the world will unmistakably recognize them as such. God's peacemakers are at peace with all people. It is about the restoration and mending of the entire world. Therefore, it is peace at a risk: it includes peace with your enemies and persecutors. Matthew 5:23-26 describes reconciliation with someone who "has something against you". That is the litmus test for being a child of God. We must create a positive living space in which all people can live and work in peace.

There are fraudulent manifestations of peace; an attenuation of the real thing with which people satisfy and comfort themselves. To live in peace with my friends is easy, but what about my enemies? In commerce, in politics and in the sporting arena is where peacemakers are needed. Peacemakers must not only be passive people. There is a fundamental difference between a "dead" sea and a "tranquil" sea. Peacemakers are willing to venture something so that they can perform a deed of peace for the sake of Christ.

To be a peacemaker is not a pious ideal or an unreachable dream. In Christ, it is an achievable reality through the Holy Spirit. Then the world will know that we are children of God.

Holy Spirit of God, enable me, for the sake of Jesus, my Lord, to be a peacemaker in this world. Amen.

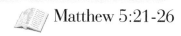 Matthew 5:21-26

HAPPINESS THROUGH PERSECUTION?

"Blessed are you when people insult you, persecute you and falsely say all kinds of evil against you because of me."

~ MATTHEW 5:11 ~

The Gospel of Jesus Christ is unimpeachable and blatantly honest. It speaks of persecution, insult, cross-bearing and suffering. It is not said without reason that the blood of the martyrs was the seed of the church. Christ does not mislead us. He did not come to make life comfortable for us, but to save us for Himself and for eternal life.

Reflect for a moment upon the people to whom Jesus speaks here. A new faith was washing like a powerful wave over the world. For the people who embraced this faith, their Christlikeness would mean disruption and suffering in virtually all areas of their lives. In their daily work they would have to refuse to build a temple for an idol; a tailor would have to refuse making clothes for an unconverted priest. They would have to choose between being loyal to the world or being loyal to Christ.

It also changed their social lives. They would no longer be able to attend feasts in heathen temples. Festive sacrifices to idols would have to stop. But they were willing to isolate themselves from their normal social lives and be faithful to Christ. Their home life would change radically. One member of the family becomes a Christian and the entire family is affected. Irreconcilable divisions develop. They would also have to endure physical suffering: they were taken captive and suffered pain and torture. It was a time of vehement persecution and Christ knew that they would need comfort in the battle. Hence, this promise of "singular happiness" in persecution.

Jesus, Man of Sorrows, grant me the grace to take up my cross without murmur and to carry it, following in Your footsteps. Amen.

Revelation 7:9-17

HAPPINESS THROUGH PERSECUTION? (2)

"Blessed are you when people insult you, persecute you and falsely say all kinds of evil against you because of me."

~ MATTHEW 5:11 ~

What does Jesus mean when He speaks about false rumors and insults? The early Christians were accused in various ways. For example, the rumor was spread that they practiced cannibalism because of these words heard at communion: "This is My body; this is My blood". They were accused of immoral practices because of their *agape* or festival of love. They were branded as agitators and revolutionists because they spoke of the "Second Coming" and the "hour of fulfilment".

They were also politically opposed. The Roman government feared them because they spoke about a Messiah or Savior and because they refused to worship the emperor as a god. The action taken against them was so bloodthirsty that there were no longer enough trees around Jerusalem to make the crosses to which they were nailed. It is these people that Jesus speaks to about the "happiness" and "blessing" of the bloodstained path. We are called upon as Christians to take up our cross and follow Christ. We are to be willing to be faithful to Him until death. To take up our cross also shows that we would walk the path of the prophets and martyrs should this be required. We not only share in Christ's victory, but also in His suffering. This is a glorious privilege.

It is also heartening to our fellow believers. They do not stand alone in battle because Christians support one another. Remember that nobody suffers in vain, because Christ proclaims that it brings us untold happiness. He is by our side and will not forsake or fail us. Suffering is inevitable, because Christians are the conscience of the world. We can endure only with the help of the Holy Spirit. Then we receive a double reward: joy on earth and the crown of victory in heaven.

Holy Jesus, make me worthy of the cross that You place on my shoulders and let me bear it conscientiously for the sake of Your Name. Amen.

Matthew 5:3-12

Now when (Jesus) saw the crowds, he went up on a mountainside and sat down. His disciples came to him, and he began to teach them.

~ MATTHEW 5:1-2 ~

During the past month, like the disciples and the crowds of old, we have sat at the feet of the Master and heard what true happiness and blessing are, and what they are not. To discover this "singular happiness" and to make it our own, the Holy Spirit led us through eight gates:
- The gate of the realization of how dependent I am on God.
- The gate of the broken heart that mourns.
- The gate of meekness.
- The gate of the hungry heart thirsting for God's righteousness.
- The gate to mercy.
- The gate of a pure heart.
- The gate of being a peacemaker.
- The gate of happiness through persecution.

The Holy Spirit teaches God's children that true happiness may be found nowhere else but in faithful obedience to Christ. He is our King. Every Beatitude is therefore also a special fruit from the Holy Spirit.

Matthew 5:1-16 reflects the ideal character of the Christian. It is Christ's "Manifesto". It is the essence of everything that Jesus has taught us, but also of what He was in Himself. This is our comfort in life and in death: I belong inextricably to Jesus and the Holy Spirit helps me to be like Jesus. Our religion is not a system of ideas about Jesus Christ. *It is Jesus Christ!* To believe in Him does not entail knowing a confession by heart or belonging to a church. It is to have a holy, omnipotent and loving Master whom we will follow blindly. He makes us what God intended us to be.

Heavenly Teacher, how glorious to sit at Your feet and learn from You how to live. Touch my mind and my heart benevolently with Your doctrines. Amen.

Matthew 5:1-12

At the feet of the Master (2)

Now when (Jesus) saw the crowds, he went up on a mountainside and sat down. His disciples came to him, and he began to teach them.

~ Matthew 5:1-2 ~

M atthew is the teaching Gospel. It introduces Jesus to us as the Great Teacher. The crowds flocked around Jesus. Like the rabbis of that time, He sat down to teach them. The Sermon on the Mount presents the essence of Jesus' doctrines. Not only does He want us to take note of God's saving grace, but also of His transfiguring grace; His forgiving grace.

The benedictions of the Beatitudes are Christian dispositions. With these Jesus penetrates the inner person and He raises the issue of motives. C.H. Dodd says, "The ethics of the Sermon on the Mount are the absolute ethics of the kingdom of God." Jesus pleads for a change in our thoughts regarding the kingdom of God.

In summarizing the Sermon on the Mount, Dr Richard C. Halverson says, "The path of the kingdom of God is an antithesis of our current culture." Jesus says, "Blessed are the poor in spirit," but we say, "Fortunate are the achievers." Jesus says, "Blessed are the meek," but we say, "Fortunate are the powerful." Jesus says, "Blessed are the meek," but we say, "Fortunate are the manipulators." Jesus says, "Blessed are those who hunger and thirst for righteousness," but we say, "Fortunate are the revolutionaries." Jesus says, "Blessed are the pure in heart", but we say, "Fortunate are those who have no inhibitions." Jesus says, "Blessed are the peacemakers," but we say, "Fortunate are the strong who persist with their point of view." Jesus says, "Blessed are those who are persecuted," but we say, "Fortunate are those who set their sails to every wind." Jesus fearlessly challenges the selfishness that determines so much of our social behavior.

I praise and thank You, Lord Jesus, that I could sit at Your feet this month and learn from You through the work of the Holy Spirit in me. Amen.

Matthew 5:1-12

"You are the salt of the earth. But if the salt loses its saltiness, how can it be made salty again? ... You are the light of the world. A city on a hill cannot be hidden."

~ Mᴀᴛᴛʜᴇᴡ 5:13-14 ~

Jesus follows up the Beatitudes with two directives or symbols for His disciples to follow: salt and light. Both are meaningful; both render a vital service in man's life. The Romans of Jesus' time had a proverb that goes, "There is nothing more useful than sun and salt." Jesus uses these symbols as characteristics of the people of His kingdom in the community where they live and work. The symbols refer to the far-reaching and preservative influence of the Christian in the world and to the influence or testimony that the Christian shares with his Master.

"You are the salt of the earth" implies three specifical things: purity, preservation and aroma. For the Romans, salt symbolised purity. Roman soldiers were often paid in salt. Jesus uses the symbol of salt for the cleansing influence that the Christian carries into the community.

However, salt also served a preservative function before there were fridges. Hence, Jesus warns against salt that has lost its flavor (cf. Lk. 14:34-35). Meat goes off unless it has been salted. In similar fashion, a disciple of Christ should be a preserving factor in society.

Salt sacrifices itself in the service of the object that has to be salted and preserved. Here also, there is a deep symbolic meaning. If salt is correctly used in food, then salt cannot be tasted, but the aroma of the food tastes more authentic – as it should. As salt makes food more tasty, the disciple, as the salt of the earth, must make the world more authentic, as God intended it to be. We must make community life a place of abundant blessing for humanity. Then we, His children, are the salt of the earth.

Help me, oh Spirit of God, to become the salt of the earth through Your grace, so that Christ may be glorified through my life. Amen.

 Matthew 5:13-16

Two directives or symbols (2)

"You are the light of the world ..."

~ Matthew 5:14 ~

L ight is a symbol of brightness and openness that does not want to be covered. It is also comparable to the happiness, blessing and joy that are expressed in the Beatitudes. There is nothing secret about the Christian's devotion or his way of life. The disciple is described as the light of the world, an influence of openness and honesty, of acceptance and love.

This is not a call for monastic seclusion or a withdrawal from life, but it is a call that manifests the joy of fellowship with God, as well as a testimony against a world on the road to perdition. The disciple may not hide or conceal himself, but he should live and work in such a way that his influence can be seen and felt.

While light has to be seen and has to serve as a guide to travellers, the basic function of light is to be of service. The disciples of Jesus are lights in this dark world who do not draw attention to themselves, but who show the path to God's heart. They get their light from the Light of the world and are therefore reflected light. Jesus emphasizes this service by using two illustrations: the city on the hill and the lamp on the stand.

The light expels the darkness simply by being present. It serves no purpose to constantly curse the darkness; you should rather light a small candle and drive the darkness out. The motive is to light up the path to God for others so that they glorify God when they see our good works. We must live openly in the midst of the world so that the light may be seen: testimony of the kingdom and regency of Jesus Christ.

Make it possible, oh Lord Jesus, that I may be ignited by Your light, so that I can make a contribution to spread light in this dark world. Amen.

Luke 14:25-33

So is my word that goes out from my mouth: It will not return to me empty, but will accomplish what I desire and achieve the purpose for which I sent it.

~ ISAIAH 55:11 ~

Oh Lord, my God, I glorify and praise Your holy Name. Your love knows no boundaries! I thank You that I have meditated on Your promises of benediction this month. May Your precious words become part of my thoughts, life and conduct.

Let me never forget how dependent I am upon You. I will always hold firmly onto Your hand and so inherit Your kingdom.

I glorify You for comforting me when I am in mourning, so that I may always see a rainbow through my tears. Keep me meek so that I will not attempt to aggressively assert myself.

Thank you for the hunger and thirsting after righteousness that You have placed in my soul, so that I may be positive and do good each day.

Stand by me through the Holy Spirit, so that I will always have a warm heart for others, so that I may perform the true service of love, in Your Name and to Your glory. In this way, I will not fail to find Your mercy.

Create in me a pure heart, oh God, so that my eyes may see Your glory. I so sincerely want to be called Your child. Enable me to be a peacemaker.

It is difficult to suffer persecution, oh Master, therefore, enable me to accept it in humbleness so that I may receive Your reward with gratitude.

Lord, my God and Father, make me the salt of the earth and a light of the world in Your service, so that Your name may be glorified by my life and conduct.

I ask for all this through the blood of Jesus, my Savior and Redeemer. Amen.

August

God has said, "Never will I leave you; never will I forsake you."

~ Hebrew 13:5 ~

Prayer

Almighty God and loving Father, every day we are surrounded by uncertainty about many things: about our health, our family, our work, our finances, our future, and even about our relationship with You.

Thank You that Your Holy Spirit came to teach us to say: "I know for certain that Jesus lives!" That He redeemed me and made me His child; that, in His hands, I am safe, for time and eternity. Lord, You alone know how doubt still sometimes festers; how my trust in God is often tested and how dearly I want to believe like the faith heroes of old.

Thank You for coming to the aid of my weak faith time and again. Preserve me from resigning myself to religious uncertainty.

Thank You that I may seek refuge in You to receive the power of faith.

Lord, take my hand before I stumble, so that I, like Peter, may say in faith, "My Lord and my God."

I thank You for all the means of grace that You place at my disposal to strengthen my faith: the sacraments of Baptism and Communion; the Bible and prayer, worshiping in church and fellowship in faith; faithful friends who intercede with You that my faith will not falter.

Thank you for being the same merciful God, today and for eternity. I prayer in the Name of Jesus Christ, with thanksgiving.

Amen

"I Know for certain!"

The Lord is my shepherd, I shall not be in want.

~ Psalm 23:1 ~

Those of us who inextricably belong to the Lord know we are safe and secure. We know for certain that the Lord is our Shepherd and therefore we do not face the future with fear. Our Shepherd is there already and He will walk before us every day, leading us to our eternal destination.

Do you, by any chance, feel unsure about the path you have to take? Remember, He is the Good Shepherd. *Whether you turn to the right or to the left, your ears will hear a voice behind you, saying, "This is the way; walk in it"* (Is. 30:21). Your Shepherd will guide you, if only you will willingly follow His guidance. Do you sometimes feel that you need spiritual food and strength? The Lord will provide an abundant feast of good things. He is our heavenly manna, the bread and water of life.

Sometimes we have doubts about the future. We wonder whether we will have enough to provide for our essential needs. With childlike certainty, the psalmist then tells us, "I shall not be in want." I shall not be "in want" of anything that I truly need and which, according to the will of God, is good for me. For every phase of life, every circumstance in which we may find ourselves, we truly do not need to fear. He will certainly be there to carry us through.

We can rest in peace and face the unknown future with the words, "The Lord is my Shepherd, I shall not be in want." He will hear when you call, because His love remains unchanged. Praise His holy Name. I know for certain that He is the Good Shepherd and that He will provide.

Lord God, it is a glorious reassurance to me that You are my Shepherd and that in Your hands I am safe and secure. Amen.

Psalm 23:1-6

"I Know for certain!"

Now we see but a poor reflection as in a mirror; then we shall see face to face ...

~ 1 Corinthians 13:12 ~

"Now" and "then" are two little words with profound meaning. They conjure images of glaring contrast. When we study them closely, we might discover the wisdom of some of the events in our lives. If we look ahead to "then", it might be easier for us to accept the "now" and to make peace with our circumstances.

While we are in this life "now", we are called upon to contend with many situations. For the moment, they look dark and problematic to us. Time and again things happen to us that we cannot understand, and these patches of shadow and trepidation can disturb and sour our happiness, as well as our fellowship with our Lord. But how blessed and happy will we be when we remember both sides of His promise: "now" is a mirror and a poor reflection, but "then" I will see face to face – in all the glory that God has prepared for His children.

Even if the image is now a poor reflection and lacks clarity, we have the glorious comfort that one day we will come face to face with our Lord. When we see Him then, we will discover how often His love and grace shielded us from disasters and dangers. I can know for certain that what we will experience "then" will be so much better than "now".

I thank You, my Lord and my God, that You have ordained my life in such a wonderful way and that Your love and grace guide me from day to day. With this blessed assurance I praise and glorify You all my life. Amen.

1 Corinthians 13:1-13

"I KNOW FOR CERTAIN!"

He makes me lie down in green pastures, he leads me beside quiet waters.

~ PSALM 23:2 ~

It is a blessed assurance to know that you are guided, from day to day, by an omnipotent and loving God. The Lord does not promise that all the pastures will always be green: sometimes they are barren and sterile and desolate. He has also not promised that the waters will always be tranquil: sometimes the waves break turbulently over us and the sky above is covered with ominous storm clouds. But the promise is that He, in His time, will bring us to green pastures and quiet waters. If we put our childlike and unconditional trust in Him, we may rest assured in the knowledge that He will guide us in our everyday lives.

We cannot be guided by someone who is far away and detached. We must stay close to the Shepherd in order to be guided by Him. Often we experience difficult and incomprehensible times, sometimes even storm and stress. However, if we stay close to the Lord, we will become aware of the tranquillity surrounding us. We dare not, like the prodigal son, wander about in the faraway country of estrangement from the House of the Father. The Father is always waiting to run to meet us and to let us take our place at the banquet.

Regardless of how stormy and unpredictable the circumstances of our lives may be, our spirit will be quiet and peaceful if we allow Him to be our Governor. Then we can state with assurance, *"He makes me lie down in green pastures, he leads me beside quiet waters."* I know for certain: He is my Shepherd, my Friend, my Governor and my Guide. Praise the Lord, oh my soul; all my inmost being, praise His Holy Name!

Lord Jesus, Shepherd of my life, thank You that I may be safe and secure in Your care. Help me to accept Your guidance at all times. Amen.

Psalm 23:1-6

"I Know for certain!"

I can do everything through him who gives me strength.

$\sim$ Philippians 4:13 $\sim$

"Apart from me you can do nothing."

$\sim$ John 15:5 $\sim$

Paul learnt life's great lesson of acceptance of his circumstances. It was, however, an active acceptance unlike that of the Stoics. To achieve stability, the Stoics rooted out from their hearts all desires, love, emotions and caring for others and called it "at peace with thyself". Paul, on the other hand, learned peace through a positive act of his own will that was in line with the will of God. He says, "I can do everything" and then significantly adds, "through Him who gives me strength." He is imbued with the strength of the omnipotent Christ. The Stoic's peace is achieved through his own human efforts; for Paul peace was a gift from Christ. Whether he had all or nothing was immaterial to him, because He knew with certainty that he had a Savior.

It is an untold blessing when we realize our own weakness and find acceptance in the omnipotence of God. We need to empty ourselves so that we may be filled by Christ. In this relationship we are filled by Him and we will come to recognize His strength working through us. Often we face a difficult task that seems impossible. If we depend on our own strength or intellect, it will easily become too much for us. If we know that it is the will of Christ for us to perform a certain task, we can, with boldness, request the help of the Lord, in the unfailing knowledge that His strength is revealed precisely when we are weak (cf. 2 Cor. 12:9).

Regardless of what problems loom before us, let us remember Christ's promise as voiced by the apostle, "I can do everything through Him who gives me strength."

Thank You, Wondrous Lord Jesus, for Your promise that through You we can do everything. Let me never again complain about my weakness. Amen.

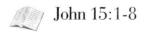 John 15:1-8

"I KNOW FOR CERTAIN!"

"... Yet not my will, but yours be done."

~ LUKE 22:42 ~

It is a privilege and an untold blessing to be able to say like our Master, "Yet not my will, but Yours be done." There are so many things that could happen to us, many disappointments come upon us unexpectedly, many ordeals cross our path in life. Often we cannot see the sense or meaning in them. Sometimes these are major troubles and sometimes minor irritations. However, we must confront and handle them all.

The Lord's love for us is endlessly tender and positive. His caring for us never ends. He assures us, ... *"Never will I leave you; never will I forsake you"* (Heb. 13:5). His thoughts for us are always to our ultimate benefit. He wants us to trust where we cannot see. It is not a reckless leap in the dark, but sincere trust and faith that says, "I know for certain that God's will is best for me." This kind of faith leaves the choice up to God, with the words that His Son taught us, "Your will be done!" Then we will experience the blessed reality of His peace flowing through us and touching our innermost being, so that we will spread joy around us and to others.

Our faithful prayer every day must simply be, "Your will be done!" This is the only way in which we can get to know His peace here on earth. We must trust in Him through grace, until we meet Him face to face. Then we will understand how His perfect will functions: always for our own good and to our benefit, even though it does not immediately appear so. It is a wonderful privilege to be able to testify that our will is voluntarily subject to God's perfect will.

Eternal God and Father, thank You for sending Your Son to come and teach me what it means to let Your will be done in my life. Let Your Spirit assist me in this. Amen

Luke 22:39-46

"I Know for certain!"

But the pot he was shaping from the clay was marred in his hands; so the potter formed it into another pot, shaping it as seemed best to him.

~ JEREMIAH 18:4 ~

For those who want to discover it, there is an exceptional truth hidden in our text for the day. The pot that the potter was shaping, was "marred in his hand". The bystanders, as well as the pot (if it could think rationally) would have been surprized by this. Why did he allow this particular one to be marred? While the spectators were still watching in amazement, the potter "formed it into another pot, shaping it as seemed best to him". Do not misread the words, "as seemed best to him". If it seemed best to him, it had to be something splendid without any imperfections. This is how it is with our lives.

From this comparison between the potter and God, Jeremiah learns that God is slow to anger. As the potter patiently busies himself with shaping the clay, God busies Himself with us. However, we must not regard His patience as an inability to punish. If the object remains marred, the potter can crush it. Even if the punishment is not yet visible, God is already in the process of deciding the fate of His people (cf. Jer. 18:11).

The heavenly Potter shapes many objects and sometimes we see some that have been marred in one way or another. People find it difficult to understand such a situation and cannot see that the hand of the Master Potter is at work in our lives. Maybe we do not yet see the completed, recreated product, but one day, when we are all home with the Potter, we will not only see the recreated objects "as seemed best to him", but we will also understand the reason for failure.

"Do only Your will, oh Lord, with me, You the Potter and I the clay." Amen. (Hall. 286:1)

Jeremiah 18:1-10

"I KNOW FOR CERTAIN!"

"He will never leave you nor forsake you."

~ DEUTERONOMY 31:6 ~

M oses did not enter the Promised Land; the Lord took him away to the Promised Land of heaven. Joshua was appointed as Moses' successor and he received the blessed assurance that God will never leave him nor forsake him. Joshua did what Moses was not allowed to do: lead the people into the Promised Land with the promise that God will be by his side in all circumstances.

It is to good to know someone who is reliable and to whom we may turn at any time. Someone who is always the same and ready to help at all times. You probably have a number of friends like this and yet there are times when our friends do not totally live up to our expectations. It may be precisely the friend whom we trust most who disappoints us; possibly because of his inability to meet our urgent needs.

It is so reassuringly different with our Lord and Master. If you need comfort in an upsetting situation, the Lord will guarantee you that. If you need guidance in a confusing situation, the Lord will grant you that. If you need inspiration for a difficult task or decision, the Lord will guide you, if you allow Him to do so.

Are you tired, troubled or confused? Does the road ahead seem to be strewn with problems, concerns and troubles? Ask the Lord to help you and you will discover the truth of His Word as it is written in our text for the day. He will grant you peace and joy in abundance. If you ask Him, you will discover that the Lord is as faithful as He has promised in His Word.

God our Father, thank You that I have the assurance that You will never fail me nor forsake me. Forgive me for the times when I failed and disappointed You. Amen.

Deuteronomy 31:1-8

"I KNOW FOR CERTAIN!"

Then they came to Elim, where there were twelve springs and seventy palm trees, and they camped there near the water.

~ Exodus 15:27 ~

In contrast to the oasis of Marah and its bitter water, the people arrive at Elim with its abundance of water and trees. Here the Lord demonstrates the extent of His care. This is how God's grace manifests itself in practice when we obey Him. It is an inspiring thought for our everyday lives. A fountain always speaks of abundance and contentment and life. Without water we cannot live, but where there is water, there is life.

Jesus Christ is the true fountain of life! He grants His children contentment and abundant life so that they may live in prosperity (cf. Jn. 10:10). In every sphere of life, perfect contentment is found with Him.

The palm trees provided a welcome shade against the scorching sun that blazed down on them, and they would also have been beautiful to behold. The date-palms provided the people with fruit to eat. Throughout our lives we can be assured of God's protection and provision. He not only gives us life's essentials, He also gives us that which is good and beautiful.

Without doubt we can picture God's unfathomable love and faithful care. Twelve fountains and seventy palm trees! I know for certain that when God gives, He gives abundantly and generously. We can trust in Him every day of every year to provide in every need. Joy and happiness are ours and we are shielded by His immeasurable love.

Heavenly God and Father, thank You for Your faithful care from day to day – also that, through Your Spirit, You take care of our spiritual needs. Amen.

Exodus 15:22-27

"I KNOW FOR CERTAIN!"

... I will counsel you and watch over you.

~ PSALM 32:8 ~

The psalmist is so joyful about being forgiven and God's encircling love, that he wants to teach people how to go get it. He pleads: Do not be as foolish as a stubborn mule that has to be controlled by bit and bridle! Trust in the Lord, confess your sins to Him, because everyone that does so, He enfolds with His love.

What a comforting and blessed promise to take with you on your pilgrimage through the world. This encourages and supports us, especially if we are confused and uncertain about the right road to follow. There are many people who wish to give us advice and who recommend some kind of action. Often it is useful and professional advice, but we still remain unsure whether it is really the advice that we need.

There is one Friend who not only promised to be our Counselor, but who will do it. He will always watch over us for our good. We only need to ask His advice: He knows the road from beginning to end and He knows what is best for us. Then we will never have to live with uncertainty.

Let us ask His guidance from day to day, and believe without a doubt that He *will* advise us and that He *will* watch over us.

Governor and Lord, thank You that You keep watch over me. In the darkest hour it is a comfort and encouragement to me. Amen.

Psalm 32:1-11

"I KNOW FOR CERTAIN!"

Then the disciple whom Jesus loved said to Peter, "It is the Lord!" ...
~ JOHN 21:7 ~

When the disciples beached at dawn, following a night of fishing, they recognised Jesus on the beach. He had prepared a meal for them. Jesus was the host for this meal. This tells us of the Lord's care who, even after His resurrection, stayed close to His followers and His church. He will care for His children and His congregation. Wonders will happen, but His children need not ask why they happen. They happen because the Lord is with His church and His children to provide for their needs.

We will get rid of a multitude of anxieties and confusion from our lives if only we would recognize the Lord's hand. Much of our anxiety and stress will be prevented if we know for certain that He is by our side under all circumstances.

If we persist on our own path without asking for His guidance and presence, we cannot say that the Lord caused some accidents and disasters to happen. The Lord could allow these things to happen so that we will once again turn to Him and ask Him to be our Guide on our pilgrimage.

When we walk in fellowship with Christ, looking to Him for guidance, we receive the strength to accept His holy will, regardless of our circumstances. Then our hearts are strengthened by the consoling knowledge, "It is the Lord!" Then we find peace and rest. We know that He guides us on our path with that which is best for us. If we meet Jesus with unfailing certainty every day on our path through life, we are amongst the most fortunate of all people on earth.

I praise and glorify You, Lord Jesus, because I see Your hand in every situation in my life and I know for certain that You will never forsake me. Amen.

John 21:1-11

"I KNOW FOR CERTAIN!"

My God will meet all your needs according to his glorious riches in
Christ Jesus.

~ PHILIPPIANS 4:19 ~

Paul assures the Philippians that God will meet all their needs.
However, that does not mean that He will grant everything that
the faithful think they need. The faithful suffer and even die violently.
According to tradition, Peter was crucified upside down. The Lord does
not always intervene in order to save. There is a subtle difference
between that which we would like to have and that which is necessary
for our own good. Our God does not promise to provide everything
that we want or that others think that we may need. No, He promises
that He will richly meet our "needs".

We think that we will be very happy if only we possessed certain
things and so we ask God to give them to us. We often forget to add: If
it is Your will! God does not deprive His children of certain things
merely to make them unhappy, or because He cannot give them to
them. Like every right-minded father, there are times when He says to
His children, "No!" or, "Wait a while."

The love of our God is boundless and unfathomable, His wisdom
endless. He knows exactly what is best for each of us. He rejoices in
giving us that which we really need, but He also loves us sufficiently to
refrain from giving us that which will not benefit us. Hence, we must
trust in His wisdom and love with the certain knowledge: God will
provide! This promise brings consolation. Ask Him every day to give
you what you really need according to His will, and know for certain:
"Jehovah Jireh!" – the Lord will provide!

> Our God and Provider, thank You that I have Your promise that You
> will meet every need according to Your will. Therefore, make me
> content with my circumstances. Amen.

Philippians 4:10-19

"I Know for certain!"

The LORD loves the just and will not forsake his faithful ones.

~ PSALM 37:28 ~

This is a psalm of wisdom in which the poet encourages the faithful to turn away from evil and do what is good. The reason is that the Lord loves the just and He rewards those who live righteously and punishes the wicked. He adds that the righteous will acquire wisdom if their tongues speak what is just according to God, and if the law of God is in their hearts.

This promise provides certainty in faith: the Lord does not forsake His faithful ones! This causes our hearts to rejoice, even in the midst of tribulation and disappointment. Therefore, whatever happens in our lives, wherever we have to go, we carry the definite and validated promise of the Lord in our hearts.

Most of us experience times when it seems as though everything is becoming too much for us. We might experience one disappointment after the other and are tempted to wonder whether God has forgotten about us. Possibly there is illness, or problems that have to be handled, and we cannot see the road ahead or believe that we will live through it all.

Sometimes we ask the Lord something specific and He withholds it. Let us then remember that if He has not approved our request, it would not have been for our ultimate good. We dare not become despondent or dejected; we dare not harbor doubt in our hearts. We must look up into the loving countenance of our Master and remember our text for today with trust and certainty, "He will not forsake His faithful ones!" Not by day and neither in the darkest night. When we arrive in His glorious presence one day and are with the Lord forever, we will understand everything and express our stammering thanks for every step of the way that He was by our side.

Eternal God, thank You for the certain knowledge that You will not forsake Your faithful servant – not even in my darkest hour. Amen.

Psalm 37:23-30

"**I** Know for certain!"

"Peace I leave with you; my peace I give you..."

~ John 14:27 ~

Jesus promises peace to His followers. He emphasizes that it is a peace that differs in nature and content from human peace: His is peace with the King of the universe. With this, Jesus gives us another perspective on life: He wants us to look at life through God's eyes. Then worldly things suddenly do not seem to be that important any longer. What God thinks of you and how you relate with God, now form the foundation for your peace.

Often God's blessing and peace are all that we desire here on earth. We need His peace in our everyday life, in our homes, in our world, but most of all, in our innermost being. There is often discord in the world around us. There are times when the situation in our homes is disturbing and the peace is disturbed. This adds to the discord in our lives. All of these contribute to the disturbance of the peace in our innermost being.

The Lord does not want us to suffer stress about everything that is happening around us. He did not promise a universal peace to all. He did, however, promise: *"The Lord blesses his people with peace"* (cf. Ps. 29:11). It is easy to allow external things to upset us. If only, in all the confusion, we would look away from the world and look up to God who is waiting to grant us His peace and love, it would make a radical difference to our lives.

The Lord does not force His gifts upon us, but He is always ready to grant them to us when we are spiritually ready to receive them. We must ask for it in prayer. Then the Lord will bless us with His peace in our innermost being, so that we may already know His peace here on earth.

Prince of Peace, Jesus my Savior, thank You that I know for certain that You have not only redeemed me, but that You also grant me Your heavenly peace. Amen.

John 14:25-31

"I Know for certain!"

And God is able to make all grace abound to you, so that in all things at all times, having all that you need, you will abound in every good work.

~ 2 Corinthians 9:8 ~

God loves the generous giver (cf. Prov. 22:9). God always blesses the giver. God Himself gives abundantly so that His children may have enough in all things. He gave His Son, the Holy Spirit, and all the excitement of a new, redeemed life. God also gives the means for daily life in abundance, therefore we must contribute generously towards good works.

Are you looking for something big in your life? Do you wish that you had more money, more time, more friends or more opportunities? That is not at all how God wishes us to live. Nowhere did He promise us more than what we need to make a living – nor excess – but all that we "need".

We can therefore be certain that in anything we encounter, whatever battle we are called to fight, we will always have enough strength for that. If we trust in the Lord completely, we can be certain, regardless of how dark the storm clouds are above us, regardless of how great the need, that in God, we will have enough to face every difficulty.

It is a privilege to know that we will always have sufficient strength and sufficient grace. We only need to ask our merciful God to provide, in our need and poverty, from His treasure-chamber. Then we will know for certain that God is all-sufficient. He will deal with us according to His Word. From His unfathomable grace, He will, every day, in every way, provide in all our needs through all our life. His love knows no bounds!

> Thank You for the quiet assurance, Lord Jesus, that I will always have sufficient strength and grace for every situation in life. Amen.

2 Corinthians 9:6-14

"I KNOW FOR CERTAIN!"

With joy you will draw water from the wells of salvation.

~ ISAIAH 12:3 ~

God saves! That is certain. Trust in Him and you will draw water from the wells of salvation. Water is a metaphor for the salvation that God grants. In an arid and barren land, a well is a source of joy and refreshment. For God's children, His presence is the source that gives them life. Everybody who experiences salvation is called upon to praise Him and to proclaim His deeds. A redeemed person cannot remain quiet, and has this blessed assurance: God is with us. Every child of God can draw joy from this knowledge.

Even though we know that we have been redeemed, and we draw comfort from the deep wells of salvation, we nevertheless lose some of the joy that the Savior wants us to experience. There is no doubt that the life of a Christian is fraught with problems; troubles and confusion are too often our lot. There are even times when we are called upon to go through periods of suffering and persecution.

The Master does not want us to be despondent or dejected. There are so many wonderful promises in His Word and so much that should fill us with heavenly joy and peace. Let us therefore remember that the Lord is always with us. He loves us with a constant love and it is His holy desire that, at all times, we will "with joy draw water from the wells of salvation".

Let us then also bring that joyous living water to all who need the Water of Salvation. Then our hearts will rejoice with theirs. All our doubts will disappear because we will see Christ in His wondrous grace and love!

Lord Jesus, You are the Source of all my joy and happiness. Let the world around me take note of this every day. Amen.

Isaiah 12:1-6

"I KNOW FOR CERTAIN!"

Jesus Christ is the same yesterday and today and for ever.

~ HEBREWS 13:8 ~

What a reassuring consolation to cherish in one's heart: our Lord and Savior constantly remains the same. Our circumstances constantly change. At times we even change friends. There is nothing in this world that we can really be certain about.

The author of Hebrews says the church leaders represent Jesus Christ and must therefore, in certain respects, be just like Him. They should be measured against the profile of Jesus as people who serve and do not want to be served, who are first because they are last. Possibly, the things that change most and which cause us the most trouble, are our feelings. Some of us are on the mountain peak of joy one day, and the next day we are in the valley of despair; all because our feelings have changed. Sometimes we are certain of our love for God and of His love for us, and at other times we are tragically aware of a coldness and lukewarmness in this relationship. We must strive to be constant as is our Master.

Let us stop depending on our feelings and look to the living Christ, remembering the strengthening assurance that His Word teaches us, "Jesus Christ is the same yesterday and today and forever". We can meet the future with this blessed assurance: Christ is our constant friend and example who always remains the same. Praise the Lord! His love is endless.

> You are our unchanging friend and Example. I will praise You because of Your unfailing love. Amen.

Hebrews 13:1-9

"I KNOW FOR CERTAIN!"

"The LORD is my strength and my song, he has become my salvation."

~ EXODUS 15:2 ~

oses' song of victory is one of the oldest examples of Hebrew poetry. Creation and salvation are often regarded as separate theological themes, with the one often played off against the other. According to this tradition, creation maintains the status quo, while salvation points to a radical new break through. Moses' poem tells us that this is a false distinction. The Creator is also Savior and Redeemer. The Redeemer of Israel is both Creator and the God of the forefathers.

We need strength to keep our footing in the battle of life. Day after day we are confronted with things that are wrong and which must be rectified, or evil that must be combated. Our enemy, the Evil One, is always ready to trip us and we require self-control and vigilance to remain standing. There is but one Source of true strength. There is but one true path of victory that we can walk. That is through Jesus Christ, the Victor over Satan, sin and death. He is our Savior and if we can trust in Him with certainty in our hearts, we will know what it means to live on victorious ground.

It is one thing to be the victor, and another to be happy about it. Hence, Moses says, "I will exalt Him!" It is a glorious truth to live in this experience and to realize that He is my Redeemer and I can thus praise and glorify Him with joy. If we carry this certainty in our hearts, every moment of our lives can be happy, because the Master to whom I belong works as Redeemer in and through me.

Triumphant Jesus, thank You for granting victory to me as well. I praise Your holy Name and kneel in wonder before You. Amen.

Exodus 15:1-11

"I KNOW FOR CERTAIN!"

For this God is our God for ever and ever; he will be our guide even
to the end.

~ PSALM 48:14 ~

This Psalm of the Sons of Korah is about the temple and the God of the temple. The God of the temple is more important than the temple itself. This must still be true of us as well: our religion points to God and not to the structures that we erect around our religion. We must worship the Lord in such a way that people notice *Him* rather than beautiful clothes, expensive church buildings or lofty prayers. Then our lives will also have the quality of Jerusalem, the city that points to God and displays the glory of God.

We all like to say, "That is mine!" or, "It is my own!" The joy of possession is strong in most of us. Here is something that each of God's true children can say with certainty, "For this God is our God for ever and ever." What an overwhelming thought. The Almighty God of the universe, the God of the fathers of old; He is also my God! Do we ever pause to reflect upon this truth?

"He will be our guide even to the end." We so often need a reliable guide who can show us the right path and warn us against the pot-holes and stumbling blocks in our path. Could there ever be a more reliable guide than God? Let us then exult and rejoice with trust and confidence, *"For this God is our God for ever and ever".* He will lead us through life, through dark depths, the valley of death and into the Father's house. What more could we ask of life, of God! With Him as our guide, we are sheltered against all dangers on our uncertain pilgrimage.

> Eternal and Unchanging God, thank You that You are also my God and that You will guide me safely into the House of the Father. Amen.

Psalm 48:1-14

"I KNOW FOR CERTAIN!"

The LORD Almighty is with us; the God of Jacob is our fortress.

~ PSALM 46:11 ~

In this Psalm, the psalmist tells us why the children of God do not have to fear anything: in their distress they thought about God's deeds of the past and knew that they could trust in Him and that there was no longer any need to fear. We may walk the same path. If we are afraid of anything – disasters or war, violence or pain, illness or death – we should think about what God did for us in the past. This confirms His loving care for us: He gave His Son to die and rise from the dead in our place. Hence, we need not fear anything any longer.

I know for certain that, in an ever-changing world, there is always stability and assurance with God. My cherished plans might have come to nothing. I possibly suffered deep disappointment; there might have been sorrow and loss; unsure and confused, I might have drifted away from God. Then it is comforting to know: *"The Lord Almighty is with us!"*

The Lord does not want us to minimize the reality of problems, pain and suffering. He allows them so that we will place our faith and trust increasingly in Him, forcefully holding on to Him and learning more about His untold love. He wants us to know that He has not forgotten us and that we are not alone. Let us find steadfast consolation in the words: "The Almighty is with us!" He is with us to support us every day in our weakness: in sorrow, pain or joy. He is our heavenly Consort for the whole journey. Praise the Lord, because He is good!

> I know for certain: the Lord, the Almighty, is with me! Therefore I can face tomorrow without fear; my God is already there! Amen.

Psalm 46:1-12

No, in all these things we are more than conquerors through him who loved us.

~ ROMANS 8:37 ~

Paul maintains that one of the ways to experience peace with God, is by realizing that, together with Christ, you are a conqueror. He declares God's pardon. His words forcefully declare: God is for you! This turns the faithful into more than conquerors. Paul turns this into a song of triumph and a creed. He reveals our debt before God, Christ's payment of that debt and our pardon through faith in Jesus Christ. This is a positive point of departure for your spiritual life: God is for me!

The children of the Lord desire to live a life of victory in which sin and weakness are conquered. But all too often we have to confess with Paul: *"When I want to do good evil is right there with me"* (cf. Rom. 7:21). Then we humbly confess to the Master that we are not conquerors, but that our circumstances have conquered us.

That is not what the Master wants for His followers. He desires that we live a life of victory and triumph in everything. Thank God that we do not have to triumph in our own strength. His Word declares that it is through Him who loves us that we not only become conquerors, but more than conquerors!

To experience this wondrous promise fully, we must meet with Him every day to receive new strength from Him. We will never be denied that. Whatever happens, whatever afflictions and problems may surface, you must remember that "in all things" He grants us victory. Then we will be overcomers through the strength of Somebody who loves us and who always fulfils His promises.

I praise and thank You, Lord my Savior, that in Your strength I may be the conqueror. Let me never again live as though I was the conquered. Amen.

Romans 8:31-39

"I KNOW FOR CERTAIN!"

He led them by a straight way ...

~ PSALM 107:7 ~

This Psalm describes the various phases in God's guidance of His people to the Promised Land. Today's section refers to those who came through the desert. Those were people who suffered, got lost, and were hungry, thirsty and exhausted. They represent people who get lost in a spiritual desert. Whether literal or figurative, these lost people could pray, and that made all the difference. The Lord saved them and gave them abundance and put them back on track.

To lead someone else onto the right road, means we need to know the road ourselves. If those who are being led are to feel safe and free, they must have unshakeable faith and trust in the one who leads them. Does it seem that you are following a strange road? Are the problems that you encounter on the road causing a trace of doubt in your heart? Never doubt the Lord's guidance. If you are willing to allow Him, He will surely and safely lead you down the right road, just as He has done through the ages with all His children.

He knows every step of the way and we can follow His lead with absolute trust, while we remember the words of the psalmist, *"He led them by a straight way"*. He is, indeed, the way that we must follow, the truth that we know and the life that we must live (cf. Jn. 14:6). If He led His people safely in days gone by, we can trust in His guiding hand to lead us, even through dark depths. Eventually, we will reach our heavenly home and our problems will be something of the past. We simply have to trust in His wisdom and know for certain that His loving hand will always hold onto our unsteady hand.

God of the pilgrim, thank You that I have Your Spirit to accompany me on my journey to the House of the Father. Amen.

Psalm 107:1-9

"I KNOW FOR CERTAIN!"

He who dwells in the shelter of the Most High will rest in the shadow of the Almighty. I will say of the LORD, "He is my refuge and my fortress, my God, in whom I trust."

~ PSALM 91:1-2 ~

H ere we learn that our lives can only be safe if we trust in the Most High. His protection is not limited to certain times. Every moment, night or day, you are under God's protection. You need not fear anything: neither the dangers of night nor the attacks of day; neither illness nor plague; neither war nor the hate of the ungodly. His protection is also not limited to certain places. God is with you everywhere: your home, the roads, your workplace or your playground. You will be enabled to conquer threatening dangers.

To enjoy the protection and shelter of the Most High, speaks of peace, grace and security. It is, without doubt, something that man in his haste desperately needs. Our lives are usually filled with obligations and we live in a flurry of panic. But here we discover tranquility and stillness such as the person who does not know God cannot experience. How much do we need this assurance in our time! And how fervently does the Lord desire it for us!

The thoughts of "shelter" and "protection" imply permanence. Once we have come to know the joy of the protection of the Almighty, we will know what it means to trust in God. It is a secret that each of God's children gets to know firsthand. As we increasingly stay in fellowship with Him, we also increasingly realize the meaning of our text for the day and to Whom we may go with all our problems and burdens. Therefore, we always want to shelter under His wings and be assured that we have a safe refuge. Nowhere else are peace and safety to be found.

God of Ages, Your children have always found shelter and protection in You. Thank You that I know for certain that I will also find it. Amen.

Psalm 91:1-16

"I KNOW FOR CERTAIN!"

"Praise be to you, O LORD, God of our father Israel, from everlasting to everlasting. Yours, O LORD, is the greatness and the power and the glory and the majesty and the splendor, for everything in heaven and earth is yours ..."

~ 1 CHRONICLES 29:10-11 ~

The joy and gratitude of David became a song of praise. He was excited and joyful about the temple of God. This is a spontaneous, wondrously beautiful prayer of praise in which David celebrates the majesty of God. Everything in heaven and on earth belongs to Him. We cannot lay claim to anything. All are but gifts of grace. Even life fleeting as it is, is a gift. Everything is only borrowed.

It is a sad truth that, even if we belong to the Lord, and even if we have been reborn through His Holy Spirit, we so often fall short of the standards that the Lord sets for us. There are times when we specifically want to stand firm, and yet we have to admit failure and defeat. This could be caused by several things. We might have lost contact with the Master or our communication with Him might have been short-circuited.

One of the Evil One's easiest ways to trip us in our spiritual life, is to convince us that we can achieve things in our own strength. How often does this cause us discouragement and failure, and our Master grief? He is always ready to strengthen us, if only we will ask.

Remember that it is not in our might that our strength lies or that victory is ensured. Reaffirm that the power, the splendor, the fame and the majesty belong to God. Then we will be more than conquerors, through the strength that He gives us. It is only when we ask Him that we will know how much strength He can give to us.

Lord, all power, glory and majesty belong to You. You alone are Lord. You are above all others. Amen.

1 Chronicles 29:10-19

"I Know for certain!"

The hour has come for you to wake up from your slumber, because
our salvation is nearer now than when we first believed.

~ Romans 13:11 ~

In Revelation, John explains that the devil knows that his time is
short (cf. Rev. 12:12). Now Paul encourages you with the same
thought. You cannot afford to take note of God's expectations of you
and then carry on with a life that is geared to your own and other
people's expectations. *Let us behave decently, as in the daytime, not
in orgies and drunkenness, not in sexual immorality and debauchery,
not in dissension and jealousy* (Rom. 13:13). In order to do this, God
gives the armor of light (cf. Rom. 13:12). In Ephesians 6:10-17 Paul
tells us what this armor consists of.

It was a joyous and happy day when we first got to know Jesus as
our Savior and Friend. All our sins were washed away by the blood of
the Lamb and we started a new life. We were on our way to heaven
with a heart filled with joy and with a new song on our lips.

In spite of this exciting time in our lives, day after day, we experience
temptations, disappointments and failures. Sometimes we become
battle-weary and discouraged. We look around us instead of looking
up; we look backwards instead of forwards. That is why our text contains
such an inspirational thought. Every day brings us closer to heaven and
to the full knowledge and insight of Him that redeemed us and whose
love is perfect. Let us then look forward to that encounter and cherish
the rich word of comfort in our hearts, *"Our salvation is nearer now
than when we first believed."* Let us rejoice in this statement in the
sure knowledge – He will return – and live accordingly!

Living Lord Jesus, thank You that we may know for certain that You
will return – You have promised that. Let us be prepared for that.
Amen.

Romans 13:4-14

"I KNOW FOR CERTAIN!"

For the Lord himself will come down from heaven, with a loud command, with the voice of the archangel and with the trumpet call of God.

~ I THESSALONIANS 4:16 ~

The separation between spirit and body at our death, and the separation of the faithful, are only temporary. With Christ's return, the spirit and the transfigured body will reunite and then all the faithful, those who are already dead and those who are still alive when Jesus returns, will be together forever with the Lord. Paul assures the faithful that the dead in Christ will not be forgotten at the return of Christ.

There are many ways to receive guests. We may visit a friend or family member for the first time. Maybe we do not know the neighborhood all that well and we wonder whether we will lose our way. Then we suddenly receive a letter with full directions to find the place and we have peace of mind. We know for certain that, if we follow the instructions carefully, we will reach our destination safely.

It is even more pleasant if our friends can meet us at a specific place and accompany us to their home with love. Then we do not have to worry about finding the road. In this way, the last part of the journey becomes very pleasant, because we are in the company of our friends.

We are all *en route* to our heavenly home. The Bible provides us with full instructions regarding the route. The Holy Spirit is our guide, but for the final entrance into our Father's dwelling, none other than Jesus Himself will be our guide. It is wonderful to know for certain that He will not entrust us to angels or heavenly beings. We have the comforting thought of His holy Word that the Lord Himself will come down from heaven to take His loved ones to His heavenly dwelling.

Lord, who will return again, we thank You that we will go with You to the eternal Home of the Father and that we will be with You forever. Amen.

1 Thessalonians 4:13-18

"I KNOW FOR CERTAIN!"

Do not be afraid or discouraged, for the LORD God, my God, is with you.

~ I CHRONICLES 28:20 ~

M any tasks are started and then left hanging; sometimes because of a lack of time, money and interest, or because of laziness. We simply do not finish that which we have started. Therefore, David encouraged his son, Solomon, to persevere in the building of the temple. He could do it, David said to Solomon, *"For the Lord God, my God, is with you."* Over many years and in all his adventures, David had experienced the help, the nearness and the support of his God. Therefore, he could pray for his son to know the same. It is so important that we state it once again: if we pray the blessing of the Lord for our children, it must be because we have experienced it as a reality in our own lives.

No problem is too overwhelming if we have a friend to share it with. No road, regardless of how long or steep it may be, looks nearly as long or steep if we have a companion who knows the way. Our text for the day gives us a glorious idea of comradeship. It is the Lord Himself who accompanies us and we have the assurance that He will walk the whole way with us.

If life gives us pleasure, it is pleasant to share it with a friend. Just as shared problems are problems halved, so shared happiness becomes double happiness. Our problems and troubles become so much fewer and our happiness becomes so much greater if we cherish the assurance of our text for the day in our hearts. Then our path through life becomes a path of joy because Christ Himself walks with us, and like the men from Emmaus, our sunset road becomes a sunrise road. His living voice is always there to encourage us and to speak words of blessing to us.

Faithful Lord Jesus, thank You for changing our sunsets into sunrises. Let us take courage from that for the road ahead. Amen.

1 Chronicles 28:20-21

"I KNOW FOR CERTAIN!"

For the eyes of the LORD range throughout the earth to strengthen those whose hearts are fully committed to him ...

~ 2 CHRONICLES 16:9 ~

Asa's behavior towards the Arameans was incomprehensible. Hanani, the seer, could also not understand it, and therefore he told Asa pointedly: You have not relied on the Lord your God. He trusted in God against a *strong army*, but in his battle against the weak Baasha, he expected help from Ben-Hadad. Hanani put it excellently: God looks around and helps the helpless who trust in Him.

Let us never think that we are drifting out of the sphere of God's love and omnipotence, or that He will forsake us. We read in His Word that His eyes range throughout the earth in order to help those who put their trust in Him. The Lord always knows those who place their expectations in Him: He shelters them in times of danger, helps them handle temptations and problems, and comforts them in sorrow. He is always *there* to guide us, if we would only allow Him to do so.

What a blessed privilege it is to have such a God as our protector. Wherever we find ourselves while living within His will, we can rest assured that His eyes keep a loving watch over us and that He is ready to hear when we call and to help when we need Him. We must keep this comforting and strengthening truth in mind, not only in times of problems, trouble or sorrow, but also in times of happiness and joy. It is a privilege to know that, wherever you may go, His eye watches steadily over you. If we walk in His path and do His will every moment of the day, we will have the assurance in our hearts that our Master and Savior is always near us. The alternative is the disastrous road that Asa chose.

We praise Your great Name, oh God, because You never forsake those who trust in You. Let me also not forsake You. Amen.

2 Chronicles 16:7-14

"I Know for certain!"

"... The joy of the LORD is your strength."

~ NEHEMIAH 8:10 ~

Our Christianity, and especially the reading of the Word, is clearly a serious issue. Through it, we experience something of God's grandeur and so call upon Him with awe. We become aware of our sins and are disturbed about them. But we also rejoice in the God who forgives us our transgressions, who listens to us, who hears our prayers, who cries with us and rejoices with us, who wishes to grant us joy. There is a place for the expression of all the human emotions: sorrow, jubilation, grief and joy. With the reformation in Israel through the reading of the Word, the people were initially sad and disturbed, and Ezra and Nehemiah had calmed them with the words of our text today.

There are times when we feel powerless and weak, and grief and dejection seem to take hold of our hearts. Maybe you have had a very difficult or demanding day. Maybe disappointment stood squarely in your way today. Your problems made it difficult – if not impossible – to keep a smile on your face.

Note that our text does not state that our joy lies in our own strength. If our joy resided in our own strength, it would have fallen lamentably short. But it says that, if we serve the Lord joyously, He will protect us. That is something entirely different. Our feelings are uncertain and unstable, but the Lord never changes. He is always there, but we must not allow clouds of uncertainty to hide His face.

If we live in loving fellowship with our Father, allowing nothing to come between us, we will be able to understand the meaning of this promise so much better. It is a precious assurance for the pilgrim: I serve the Lord joyously and I am sheltered by Him. Praise the Lord!

Please, Lord Jesus, let me serve You with happiness and joy and, in so doing, become a powerful testimony to You in this dismal world. Amen.

Nehemiah 8:6-13

"❡ KNOW FOR CERTAIN!"

"The LORD your God will be with you wherever you go."

~ JOSHUA 1:9 ~

God's guidance and presence take anxiety away. He gives courage to the weak. If you are dependent upon the Lord in everything, He will care for you. You will succeed and be prosperous. This means that He will support you in all circumstances. Wherever you go, He will be present to help you. The Lord supports His children practically. They receive guidance through His Word. It is therefore everyone's responsibility to hold on to Him by carefully studying the Bible and reflecting on His will. Moses' Book of the Law was the guide for everything that Joshua had to say or do. In the same way, the believer must always search for God's will.

To walk alone in life can be very lonely. To have a fellow-traveller can make a big difference to our lives. Under certain circumstances it is unavoidable to live without comradeship or to spend time in the company of unfriendly people. We all, at times, yearn for a companion who understands us and who can cheer up our lives.

The promise that we receive from the Word today is possibly one of *the* most reassuring and comforting that one can hope to find. Nobody can really be lonely if one is aware of the presence of the resurrected Savior. No road can be lonely if we are certain that Christ is walking next to us. We can always look away from the present scene with joy in the heart and a song on the lips, and experience the full impact of this blessed assurance: *"The Lord your God will be with you"*.

He is present every moment to help you and to cheer you up. You can talk to your Savior and walk with Him. He brightens every step of the way.

Omnipresent God, thank You that I am never alone in this world and that You are always there when I am in distress – but also when I am filled with joy! Amen.

Joshua 1:1-10

"I KNOW FOR CERTAIN!"

"... No one will take away your joy."

~ JOHN 16:22 ~

Jesus tells His disciples that He will be separated from them for a short while because of the crucifixion, but the separation will only be temporary. He will return once again to His church, but through the Holy Spirit. Then they will no longer be distressed, but will be filled with joy. The parting will be difficult for the disciples and the world will rejoice because it will now be rid of Jesus. But that will be short-lived, and then the sorrow of the disciples will change into joy: a joy that no one can deprive them of. Through His Holy Spirit, He will live permanently with His followers.

The world's joy is temporary and transitory. It disappears so quickly. Christ's joy is a deep well of quiet happiness and, because the source of it is in the Lord himself, it is stable and steadfast.

There may be no outward reason for joy. In the eyes of the world, it may even seem that conditions should render us disturbed and desolate. But with Christ's peace that fills and encircles our lives, and our hearts, we may rest assured that His eternal fountain of inner joy is guaranteed and that no one can take it away.

Therefore, I can rejoice: everlasting joy is mine. The promise comes from my Savior Himself. Therefore I rest cheerfully and peacefully in my Friend and Savior, Jesus my Lord. He will see to it that no evil power will rob me of my joy.

> Holy Spirit of God, thank You that one of Your gifts is joy. Let me never disappoint my Lord by being a despondent Christian. Amen.

John 16:16-24

"I KNOW FOR CERTAIN!"

"We believe and know that you are the Holy One of God."

~ JOHN 6:69 ~

Because the theme of Jesus' death is emphasised in this section, the implication is that the disciples, like Jesus, should be willing to sacrifice their lives. Peter's confession is poignant and informative. What is the difference between people who want to remain with Jesus and those who want to leave Him? The difference is Jesus! Who Jesus is to you and what He does for you, makes the difference. He is the unique Son of God with whom alone eternal life may be found.

So often we look for exact information but are told, "I think ..." or, "I imagine that ...". We know that in many matters of a temporary nature, we have to confess our lack of knowledge and certainty. However, when it comes to spiritual matters, there is a world of difference. There are many things in which we can believe and of which we can be sure. Together with Job we can say: *I know that my Redeemer lives, and that in the end he will stand upon the earth* (Job 19:25). Together with Paul we can say: *... I know whom I have believed, and am convinced that he is able to guard what I have entrusted to him for that day* (2 Tim. 1:12).

At all times and under all circumstances we may be sure of His help and support; of His power when we are weak (cf. 2 Cor. 12:9); of His solace in our sorrow. How wonderful to think that He will return to fetch us and that we will be with Him for eternity. This assurance enables us to profess that Jesus is the Holy One of God. Oh, the blessing and grace to be certain and convinced, to know that His promises are constant, that His love and care for us will never cease, that Jesus will always be *there* for us. The joy to be able to rejoice, "I know for certain that Jesus lives!"

I praise and thank You, Savior and Lord, that I could rejoice during this month: I know for certain that Jesus lives! Amen.

John 6:60-71

September

See! The winter is past;
   the rains are over and gone.
Flowers appear on the earth;
   the season of singing has come,
the cooing of doves
   is heard in our land.

~ Song of Songs 2:11-12 ~

Prayer

Oh Lord, our Lord, how majestic is Your name in all the earth! We worship You this month as the God and Creator who also maintains Your creation.

We praise and thank You for the world – our home; for spring that is once again bursting out around us; for new, tingling, tender life that awakens; for our senses, to hear the voice of the turtle-dove; see the splendor of flowers, taste the fruit, smell the spring; and sense the spring-feeling in our hearts.

Preserve us from walking past without noticing it and praising and glorifying You for it while every tree, shrub and bird is singing Your praises.

Loving Savior, also touch my heart and life with new life and vitality in Jesus Christ, my resurrected Redeemer.

Let my gratitude and joy inspire a dynamic ode to spring in my heart.

"Praise the Lord, O my soul!"

Amen

BORN AGAIN TO GROW IN GRACE

"... You must be born again."

~ JOHN 3:7 ~

But grow in the grace and knowledge of our Lord and Savior Jesus Christ.

~ 2 PETER 3:18 ~

Spiritual rebirth is a Scriptural truth and a vital experience for those who embrace Christ as their Savior and allow their lives to be controlled by His Holy Spirit. However, many born-again Christians do not understand that this wonderful relationship with the Savior could be experienced in various ways: through gospel revival services, or in private quiet time with God. The living Christ is not bound by stereotyped methods. If a hungry, searching soul searches for God, He will meet that person wherever he may be. The important fact is not the method used, but whether you are truly born again and know Jesus as your Lord and Savior.

In your spiritual life, you *must* grow "in the grace and knowledge". As you grow in the Spirit of Christ, you may sometimes look back to a point where everything began, but do not try to cling to that moment. If you do not grow, you will decline spiritually. To grow spiritually, to cultivate an increasingly profound love for God and your fellow man, is as important as the experience of a new birth. May both be blessed experiences for you.

Lord Jesus, through the guidance and edification of the Holy Spirit, help me to grow in grace and knowledge so that I may experience spring in my life. Amen.

John 3:1-13

BE TRUE TO YOURSELF

"I no longer live, but Christ lives in me ... "

~ GALATIANS 2:20 ~

Through the ages, Christians have been called upon to choose between church and state; between God and the emperor. In these uncertain times, it seems as though the pressure is even greater and the Christian's choice is made even more difficult by the standpoints of various church leaders. Some of them openly support violence and revolution, or question Biblical truths. In the midst of conflicting and confusing opinions, the man in the street asks, "What must I do?"

The enemies of Jesus attempted to trap Him by asking Him well-planned and cunning questions. They hoped that confusion would develop, should He hesitate to answer. They knew that His answers would disturb either the Romans or the Jews. Thus, He would have destroyed His integrity, and possibly Himself as well. But the Holy Spirit was in Jesus and enabled Him to speak with the authority that could only come from God.

If you sincerely believe in the Lord Jesus and His Holy Spirit resides in you, because you are a new creature in Christ and because the perfect love of God in Christ drives out all fear, decide then for yourself about every question that comes your way by taking it to God in prayer. Then allow His Holy Spirit to speak through your conscience. Only then can you be sure of the fact that, regardless of what you do, it will be in harmony with the will of God.

> Lord, my God and Father, help me to be unmoved or unconvinced by others, but let every decision that I take be in harmony with Your Holy will. Amen.

Galatians 2:15-21

Have you had an experience with Christ?

Afterwards Jesus appeared in a different form to two of them while they were walking in the country.

~ Mark 16:12 ~

It is possible that you are one of those people who is jealous of others who have had a dramatic and personal encounter with Jesus Christ. They could have been converted or received the baptism of the Holy Spirit during a prayer meeting or a gospel campaign. Regardless of how it took place, it was without a doubt with great joy. Now you are wondering why it did not happen to you!

Never allow this to dampen your spirit or affect your relationship with Christ. Always bear in mind that Christ has made us unique creations, and that not all Christians have an encounter with Jesus that is as dramatic as Paul's.

Jesus knows every one of His disciples personally – including you – better than we know ourselves. He is fully aware of our nature, how we react, our ability to handle an emotional high. As the psalmist writes: *O Lord, you have searched me and you know me. Search me, O God, and know my heart; test me and know my anxious thoughts* (Ps. 139:1, 23).

Do not brood on this issue, but persevere in prayer and meditation and wait on the Lord. The living Christ will appear to you in a manner which *He* will choose, as He has always done in the lives of those who love Him dearly.

Come, oh Holy Spirit, and visit my soul and innermost being and fill it with Your precious fire. Amen.

Mark 16:9-20

STAND BY YOUR CONVICTIONS

Simon Peter answered, "You are the Christ, the Son of the living God."

~ MATTHEW 16:16 ~

$\mathcal{T}$ here are many people who wish for stronger faith. Many of them attend services and are active in church affairs; some have been involved with the Christian faith for many years. Notwithstanding, their spiritual life has become lukewarm and their relationship with Christ humdrum.

There comes a time when all of us are confronted with the question that Jesus put to Simon Peter: *"What about you? Who do you say I am?"* This question may be put to us at a time of our lives when we do not know who to turn to for help or what we must do; it might loom before us when we are frustrated and dissatisfied with our own seemingly empty and aimless spiritual life. This is a question that you cannot avoid; you have to answer it.

In order to get the maximum benefit from Christian experience, and to know the fullness and abundance of true life that Jesus offers us, it is essential for you to have a personal knowledge of the living Christ. This does not only mean to learn everything about Him that there is to learn; it means to know Him personally and to surrender to Him; to open your life and allow His Holy Spirit to take control. Acknowledge Christ's sovereignty and then abundant life will be yours. That is why Jesus came to this world.

Make me Your prisoner, oh Lord, because only then will I be truly free. Amen.

Matthew 16:13-20

CHRISTLIKENESS REQUIRES GROWTH

Instead, speaking the truth in love, we will in all things grow up into Christ.

~ EPHESIANS 4:15 ~

The moment you embraced Christ as your Savior and Redeemer, you accepted certain responsibilities. Refusal to accept them reveals a weakness in your devotion that could cause a slackening in your spiritual life, including a weakening in the relationship between you and the Lord.

When you become a Christian, you start a new life with new values and fresh objectives. You no longer live to please yourself, but to please God. The biggest purpose in your life will be to serve others. The good deeds that you do for others are a practical expression of your faith. It is not faith in itself, because a person who is not bound to Christ can also do good deeds.

The "new life" in Christ has requirements that you must honor if your inner spiritual strength is to be maintained and developed. As a Christian disciple, you have a solemn obligation to revere your Master and the main motive for your existence must be to satisfy Him. You can no longer live for your own pleasure. You must be totally obedient to the will of God, as it has been revealed to you in His Word. You must confess your sins to God and to those against whom you have transgressed.

Paul insists that Christians must be filled with the fullness of God. "God in me" is one of the themes that he constantly emphasized. Every Christian, who loves his Lord, is compelled to grow into Christ.

I plead for strength, oh Lord, to strengthen the ties between us, so that I will never lose the awareness of Your presence. Amen.

Ephesians 4:1-16

ℒET GOD BE YOUR COUNSELOR

"I am the vine; you are the branches. If a man remains in me and I in him, he will bear much fruit; apart from me you can do nothing."

~ JOHN 15:5 ~

Ｐeople often express disappointment when well-laid plans come to nothing. Much time and energy are invested in planning, only to see dreams and hopes turn into failure. What makes it even more difficult, is that, in the minds of the people who did the planning, their objectives were noble. Some people become disillusioned and withdraw from further action.

Regardless of how commendable the cause to which you aspire, or how much effort you put into something, it is essential – should you strive towards the very best – that you take your aspirations and hopes in prayer to the Lord and seek His guidance. Remember, Jesus said that He was the vine – the life-giving support – and that you, as a branch, are totally dependent upon Him for everything. This is especially true of your spiritual growth.

Whatever you may undertake in life is important to your Master. He cares for and takes care of you. For this reason it is essential to turn to Him for guidance before deciding on a specific plan of action. God knows what is best for you and He knows the future. Put your trust in Him for guidance and surrender your hope and expectations to Him. Wait for His guidance and then act according to His will, and you will not be disappointed.

Not my will or my choice, loving Counselor, in matters great or small.
Be my guide, my strength, my wisdom, and my all. Amen.

John 15:1-8

LIFE'S MOST ENRICHING EXPERIENCE

"Remain in me, and I will remain in you ..."

~ JOHN 15:4 ~

It is worth remembering that the stars are still shining, even when they are hidden by clouds. On your spiritual pilgrimage, remember that behind the dark patches of life, the eternal love of your heavenly Father is still shining brightly. If you have cultivated trust in Him, your faith will carry you in the darkest moments of life. You will possess an inner peace and serenity that only He can give you.

While your Christian faith is a daily experience, it is necessary to have a vision that rises above all time into eternity. When Jesus lived amongst ordinary people, His oneness with His Father enabled Him to act with the authority of God. Through the Divine love that radiated from Him, He invited people to share that Divinity with Him. When Jesus said, *"Remain in me, and I will remain in you"*, He invited us to a most noble lifestyle of which we could only dream before.

The life that He promises if we "remain in Him", is such a challenge that people hesitate to accept it and choose to stay in a religious rut that promotes neither joy nor spiritual growth. The life that Christ promises is much more than an emotional experience. It creates inner peace, a constructive purpose in life, and also provides the strength to achieve and maintain such a life through the power of the Holy Spirit.

Holy Father, I praise and glorify You for the life-changing strength that flows from the living Christ. Amen.

John 15:4

You are a child of God

The Spirit himself testifies with our spirit that we are God's children.

~ ROMANS 8:16 ~

Books, enough to fill libraries, have been written about the fatherhood of God. Theories have been formulated and propagated, but when all that can be written has been written, the fatherhood of God is an experience of the soul that rises above all the theories, and which enables the most ignorant person to affirm: God is my Father.

Such intimacy, regardless of how simple it is, is not easily achieved. You must acknowledge and profess Christ's sovereignty in your life, and know the reality and joy of His residing presence within your spirit. Then you will not be controlled by your old sinful nature, but by the Spirit, because the Spirit of God resides in you.

To prevent this enriching experience from becoming pure emotion, it must be put into practice. This means the acceptance of God's discipline, as well as obedience to His holy will. The discipline of God requires you to live according to His standards and to be profoundly aware of your unique relationship with your heavenly Father. You dare not say, "I am a child of God!" and then live as though He does not exist. Obedience to the will of your Father can only be achieved if you know His will. This knowledge can only be obtained by a thorough study of His Word, in which His will for us is revealed through the Holy Spirit, and by waiting upon Him in prayer and meditation.

I thank You, my God and Father, that I may be Your child and that I inextricably belong to You. Amen.

Romans 8:9-17

THE POWER OF THE HOLY SPIRIT

Live by the Spirit, and you will not gratify the desires of the sinful nature.

~ GALATIANS 5:16 ~

*M*uch has been written and spoken about the importance of placing Christ first in your life. The call for subjecting yourself to His will and obeying His commands is often emphasized and Christians are encouraged to turn away from the world in order to follow Christ. Countless numbers of sincere believers attempt to meet these demands, in their efforts to lead a life that conforms to Christ's. If they are sincere and honest, they will confess that it is extremely difficult and much easier said than done.

Taking into account all the temptations and diversions that one has to contend with in daily life, it is understandable that it is very difficult to live a life that meets all Jesus' standards and demands. It requires an extremely strong will and character, which is far beyond the ability of an ordinary human being. The pace and pressure of modern life puts us under enormous stress. It becomes more intense when we are called time and again to observe circumstances and situations that do not contribute to a Christian lifestyle.

It is under these circumstances that you must open your life to the influence of the Holy Spirit. Invite Him to take control of your entire being, and then you will experience the power of Jesus Christ, which enables you to overcome every stumbling block while you live in and for Him.

Come, oh Holy Spirit, and fill my entire life. Then I will live courageously and be strong in my convictions and life. Amen.

Galatians 5:13-26

ᗷHE INFLUENCE OF THE RESIDING CHRIST

I pray ... that you, being rooted and established in love, may have power.

~ EPHESIANS 3:16-18 ~

ᗣ he average person is unaware that he is a slave to many hidden influences. His emotions, that change virtually from hour to hour, cause great joy or deep depression that sometimes cannot be brought under control. The stress of relationships often reaches breaking point, and the routine of everyday living sometimes becomes a soul-destroying monotony.

Because you are subject to all these forces, it is necessary to have the strength to choose the influences that control you. To insist that you cannot do anything about the forces that control you, means that you are unaware of the influence that the living Christ can have in your life. The only way in which you will gain the freedom to choose the influences that control your life, is to surrender yourself to the power of Jesus.

This act of surrender does not mean that you will never again be attacked by conflicting moods or moments of discouragement – they will certainly still be there – but you will be able to identify them that much easier and, in partnership with the Master, you will rise above their disturbing control. By being aware of the power and influence of the Residing Christ, you will be able to regulate and control your moods.

The acknowledgement of Christ as your Partner edifies you and delivers you from the bondage of the habits that tied you to slavery for so long. If Christ has set you free, you will be truly free.

I thank You, holy Master, that through Your residing presence, I am the ultimate victor. Amen.

Ephesians 3:14-21

DIRECTIVE FOR THE TRUE CHRISTIAN

In everything set them an example by doing what is good. In your teaching show integrity, seriousness and soundness of speech that cannot be condemned.

~ TITUS 2:7-8 ~

The Christian faith is something that many people take for granted. Their membership of the church of Christ grew from a habit of church attendance that was naturally expected of them. This is indeed a sad state of affairs derived from a complete misunderstanding by those concerned regarding the true meaning of discipleship.

When Jesus calls upon you to follow Him, He wants you, like His disciples of old, to testify of Him in your everyday life. As Paul said to the church of Corinth: we are ambassadors of Christ. As a Christian, you are privileged, through the grace of God, to represent the resurrected Savior in this world. He wants devoted and committed people to do His work. Therefore, you act, for and on behalf of Him, to spread the love of God through the world. In so doing, you will make a contribution to bringing people increasingly closer to Him.

There is no method more effective than instruction through own example. For this reason, it is of primary importance that you live a life that will conform to that of Christ. In your dealings with other people, you must manifest the mercy, grace and love that Jesus showed to you. If you devote your life to bear testimony to Christ, then open your life widely to the influence of the Holy Spirit. He will not only lead you on paths of service, but He will enable you to reflect the glory of God, without your being aware of it.

"Recreate, oh Spirit, let live, oh Spirit, let Your kingdom come in force. Let people come to worship, persuaded by Your power of conviction" (Hymn 216:1).

Titus 2:1-15

WHO AM I?

Yet to all who received him, to those who believed in his name, he gave the right to become children of God.

~ JOHN 1:12 ~

In the lives of all of us, there are days when everything looks bare, barren and dismal. You then question the purpose of life by asking yourself, "Who am I really?" In times of dejection and depression, which can be caused by a number of factors, and which lead to emotional disruption, it is not uncommon for people to question their identity, as well as the purpose of life. This confusion could be caused by a change in lifestyle or workplace, deep disappointment, illness, death, and any of a number of factors that rattle your stability and tranquillity and cause you to sink into a well of despair, helpless and hopeless.

If you find yourself questioning your identity and the purpose or meaning of your existence, remember then the glorious heritage that you have received through the grace of God. Through your faith in Jesus Christ, and by embracing Him as your Savior and Redeemer, your life will find new meaning and purpose, because you no longer search for your lost identity or the purpose of life. He offers you the greatest of all privileges and the only true life when you, by identifying with the living Christ, become a child of God. Life can have no greater meaning than that.

God of grace and love, help me when life is at its lowest ebb, to put my hope and faith in You and to cherish the truth in my heart that I am a *child of God!* Amen.

John 1:1-13

BE AN ENTHUSIASTIC CHRISTIAN

And if the Spirit of him who raised Jesus from the dead is living in you, he who raised Christ from the dead will also give life to your mortal bodies through his Spirit, who lives in you.

~ ROMANS 8:11 ~

Uninvolvement and nonchalance concerning spiritual things are weaknesses in the lives of many Christians. It is not that they differ from Jesus Christ and His doctrines, but they have become so familiar with Biblical truths that they no longer experience the impact of their life-changing power. It is possible that they have become so accustomed to sacred and holy things, that they are no longer affected by them.

To give expression to sincere enthusiasm may, for some people, mean physical and emotional demonstrations. If that is the way in which you express your spiritual enthusiasm, do not restrict yourself. However, there is a more profound and more meaningful, constructive way to be an enthusiastic Christian. That is to lead a life that is filled with the Spirit of Christ.

If the Spirit of the living Christ fills you, He encircles every facet of your life and existence. Your thoughts, your spirit, your emotions, your likes and dislikes, your fears and convictions, everything is surrendered to His control. When this happens, the holy flame of enthusiasm is lit in your life through the ministry of the Holy Spirit, and your whole life is inspired by a Power that is not of your making. Every part of you reflects the love of Jesus, even if it is sometimes imperfectly. You become truly enthusiastic about Him in the life that you live for Him.

Holy Spirit of God, revive my weak and imperfect faith with Your Divine power. Amen.

Romans 8:1-17

$\mathcal{O}$HE FUTURE IN CHRIST

When the foundations are being destroyed, what can the righteous do?

$\sim$ Psalm 11:3 $\sim$

$\mathcal{F}$rom the moment Jesus delivered His first prophetic message in the synagogue of Nazareth, there were forces at work in the world to undermine and destroy His doctrines. Some of these took the form of blatant persecution and vilification of the faithful, while others made use of more subtle and cunning methods.

As a Christian, you are required to guard, protect and maintain all that is good in life. It is your duty to reveal the beauty and love of God through your life, in contrast to external influences that attempt to malign and destroy the virtue of a life in Christ. In a world in which standards are increasingly declining, and honesty and integrity are often regarded as old-fashioned, the onus rests squarely upon you, the Christian, to set the high standards that are naturally expected of you and to lead an honest life of integrity, regardless of what others may do or say.

It seems unnecessary to emphasise the fact that you cannot do it in your own strength.

Nevertheless, Jesus does not expect you to start an undertaking or work in His Name without giving you the strength to do so. Your first obligation is therefore to move closer to the Master through prayer and Bible study. With the Rock of Ages as your foundation, you can go out into the world in the Spirit of the living Christ and live as a conqueror for Him.

It is a glorious privilege, my Counselor and Lord, to face the future in Your strength and with the guidance of the Holy Spirit. Amen.

Psalm 11:1-7

And in that place many believed in Jesus.

~ JOHN 10:42 ~

The instruction of the Master to go and make disciples of all people, is just as relevant to you as it was to the eleven disciples to whom He spoke following His resurrection and just before His triumphant Ascension. This obligation rests squarely on the shoulders of every Christian. It requires of us to bring other people to an intimate and personal relationship with the Lord. They have to get to know Him as the Lord of their lives, and in this way share in the saving grace of God.

Various people have different theories about how this command should be implemented. Some prefer a bold approach and are dogmatic regarding their beliefs, others trust in emotion, and others again trust in instruction and edification as a method to lead people to God. There is a wide variety of methods which unfortunately causes division in the church, because people differ from one another and refuse to work together.

However, there is one tried and tested method to lead somebody to Jesus, and that should be generally accepted by all who bear the Name of Christ. If you are true to your faith, people who come into contact with you will observe something of Christ in you. Everything that you say or do, should bear the stamp of the love and mercy of Christ. Your life must be a living example of the life of the Master. Then, without your being aware of it, other people see Christ in your life, and you will lead people to God through Christ.

Holy Lord Jesus, while I tell other people of Your saving grace, may they see Your image in all that I do and say. Amen.

John 10:22-42

He is the image of the invisible God.

~ COLOSSIANS 1:15 ~

Here we have to do with the boldest pronouncement that Paul ever made. He classifies Jesus Christ as equal to the eternal God and declares, with outspoken courage, that the One is like the Other. There are two ways of looking at this breathtaking truth. You may be overwhelmed by the fact that you can see the person of God in the living Christ. This is soul-stirring and you may feel that such spiritual heights do not apply to you. Jesus lived on such a high level, setting examples of how to respond in certain matters and situations. You cannot achieve this without His help.

On the other hand, it is also true that this great truth inspires and elevates us. The living Christ does not condemn people for their sins, but inspires them to reach unprecedented heights. The eternal God held Jesus Christ as an example to us. That is what we must aspire to. Depending on the strength and intensity of our devotion, we can, in a small way, become like Jesus.

That is God's purpose for your life. As you attempt to reach this objective, you will find that you are walking the path of fulfilment, peace and happiness.

Stand by me, gracious Lord Jesus, helping me to grow in likeness into Your image through the power and guidance of the Holy Spirit. Amen.

Colossians 1:15-20

Instead, speaking the truth in love, we will in all things grow up into him who is the Head, that is, Christ. From him the whole body ... grows.

~ EPHESIANS 4:15-16 ~

It is a glorious truth to know that faith in Jesus Christ redeems us of sin. This is the foundation of the Christian gospel. However, you must not forget that, after you have accepted Christ as your Savior, the process of spiritual growth only begins. If you ignore the necessity of growth, it will not be long before your spiritual life will run aground on the rocks of disappointment and despair. There must be growth and progress, otherwise your spiritual life will waste away and die. That is the law of atrophy.

The Master promised us many means for spiritual growth. But we must guard against these means becoming objectives in themselves. Fellowship is essential, but brotherhood that is not centered in Christ serves no constructive purpose. Study of the Scriptures will be a continuous source of infallible inspiration and guidance, but remember that the purpose is to point the disciple towards Christ as our Example and Guide. Good works and caring about the less privileged are without a doubt acceptable to God, but these must be the fruits of a knowledge of Jesus Christ. In themselves they do not necessarily lead you to Christ.

There can only be spiritual growth if your objective is to become more and more like Jesus. This should be the heartfelt desire of every follower of Jesus. This lifestyle rises above emotion and requires your all.

Let Your Spirit possess me, Lord Jesus, so that I may increasingly reflect Your image. Amen.

Ephesians 4:1-16

GROWTH IN FAITH

He who has the Son has life; he who does not have the Son of God does not have life.

~ 1 JOHN 5:12 ~

There are people – often good, kind, church-going people – who sadly maintain that their spiritual life has lost momentum, that the spark of their faith has been extinguished and they feel empty and lack faith. The great danger is that, unless something drastic is done about it, these people will be lost forever to the cause of Christ. They will look for other ways to find spiritual fulfilment; ways that, without a doubt, lead to disaster.

Jesus Christ came to this world so that we may have life, and have it to the full (cf. Jn. 10:10). This was an important component of His Divine mission. He died and rose from the dead to destroy the fear of sin and death, and to give us everlasting life. Then, to make His promise an effective reality, He gave the Holy Spirit to all who believe in Him and, through His blood, make redemption their own.

If your faith has reached a low, or if you are experiencing a barren and arid patch in your spiritual life, it is time to open your life to Christ and His redeeming grace. Ask Him to come in and take control of your life. This will require you to subject your will to the will of the Lord. In exchange, He will transform you into a new creature and, while He lives in You, He will grant you faith, joy and peace. This is only possible if you have an intimate relationship of faith with Christ.

Powerful Savior, let the wind of Your Holy Spirit blow through my spiritual life and bring with it new life and vitality in faith. Amen.

1 John 5:1-13

BREAK THE TIES OF BONDAGE

It is for freedom that Christ has set us free. Stand firm, then, and do not let yourselves be burdened again by a yoke of slavery.

~ GALATIANS 5:1 ~

The greatest gift that an owner could give a slave, was unconditional freedom. To be freed of the ties of bondage brought immense joy and happiness to the one whose life was returned to normality and independence. You can be certain that, after all the suffering and humiliation, the slave would have done everything in his power not to become a slave again. He would then have forfeited the life that he had received for nothing but an existence. He would, once again, become merely a part of the landscape of his master's property.

There are very few people – if any – who have not fallen prey, at one time or another, to the bondage of some form of slavery. People become slaves to habits that are not beneficial to their prosperity. There are those to whom wealth and status are of the utmost importance. Many get addicted to drugs or alcohol, with disastrous consequences. It is a fact that anything that becomes an obsession and has a hold on you, reduces you to the status of a slave.

The living Christ, through His great sacrifice of love, offers you true freedom, together with abundant life. You must simply be willing to embrace Him as the Savior in your life and make Him an integral part of your life. Can you afford to refuse His offer?

Living Master and Lord, in You my soul found true freedom. And with that, I have found the joy for which I have been yearning for so long. Amen.

Galatians 5:1-12

INEXTRICABLY BOUND TO CHRIST

Who shall separate us from the love of Christ?

~ ROMANS 8:35 ~

Paul asks a penetrating question here. He implies that nothing can separate us from the love of Christ. He mentions the things that could attempt to do so: trouble or hardship, persecution, famine or nakedness, danger or sword. He comes to the conclusion: nothing will be able to separate us *"from the love of God that is in Christ Jesus our Lord"*.

God loves you: this truth is comfort, strength and encouragement. Although it is a fact that God's love encircles you, many people do not experience it because they erect barriers against it. It is wondrously true that nothing can separate you from that love, unless you isolate yourself from the awareness of His presence. Then you will fail to experience His love in your daily life.

If God is to be effective in your life, He must receive your full surrender and devotion. This means cooperation. Unfortunately, there are elements in our personality that do not contribute to spiritual growth. These are often revealed in indifference to spiritual matters, disinterest in the despair of others, spiritual arrogance, and many other soul-destroying forces that succeed in damaging your relationship with Christ.

If you acknowledge and accept Christ's sovereignty in your life, you open the door to a totally new life. He has promised that His Spirit will reside in you and manifest Himself through you. Growing in the image of Christ is the start of an exciting pilgrimage. When this happens, nothing can separate you from the love of Christ.

Holy Master, make me aware of Your Holy Spirit residing in me, so that my life will reflect Your glory and love. Amen.

Romans 8:31-39

DO YOU TRULY WISH TO CHANGE?

Therefore, if anyone is in Christ, he is a new creation; the old has gone, the new has come!

~ 2 CORINTHIANS 5:17 ~

It seems as though everyone is focused on doing something "one day" in the future: the schoolboy thinks of playing for a national team, the young clerk dreams of the day when he will become company manager, the shop assistant lives for the day when he will have his own business. We all have the right to dream, but the tragedy is that so many dreams remain only dreams and never become reality.

As it is in daily life, so is it in spiritual life as well. Christianity is filled with people who will live a more devoted life "one day", who will practice a more meaningful and more profound prayer life, who will make a thorough study of the Word of God, who will strive to be a better Christian "one day". Unfortunately, that "one day" seldom arrives.

One of the challenges that you will have to face, is whether you truly wish to change or not! There is a world of difference between a desire to change "one day" and to really do so. The Lord never changes a person against his will. Before change can take place, there must be cooperation with the living Christ. He asks you to submit to His will before He can put new life into your old, rigid life. The moment when you sincerely desire to change, the transformation begins – and that, which you once regarded as impossible, becomes a glorious reality in the strength that Christ grants you.

I praise and thank You, Heavenly Father, for the new life that You granted me through Jesus Christ, my Savior. Amen.

2 Corinthians 5:11-21

LIVE A LIFE OF ABUNDANCE

Give ear and come to me; hear me, that your soul may live.

~ ISAIAH 55:3 ~

Any living being that is deprived of food for an unlimited period of time, will waste away and die. The human body cannot, in the long run, withstand the torment of hunger and thirst. The body becomes increasingly weaker until death comes. In a similar fashion, a plant or a tree will die if it is not watered or does not have good earth to grow in.

Your spiritual life is also subject to the results of hunger and thirst and, if it not properly nourished, it can also wither and die. Just as your physical body is dependent on good food and water for life and growth, so your spiritual life must be nourished in order to exist and flourish.

Jesus Christ, the Bread of Life, invites us to come to Him and He assures us that we will never go hungry or thirsty again. This does not imply a short-lived and shallow relationship with the Lord, like attempting to study His Word superficially. It means surrendering your entire life unconditionally to Him, so that the Holy Spirit can take control and give purpose and meaning to your life, thoughts and deeds. Then you start living *in* and *through* Christ.

This challenge is as valid today as it was when Jesus said to His followers, *"You diligently study the Scriptures because you think that by them you possess eternal life. These are the Scriptures that testify about me, yet you refuse to come to me to have life"* (Jn. 5:39-40). Take up this challenge by turning to Christ for your salvation and you will experience life in abundance.

Lord Jesus, You are eternal life and I come to You so that I may experience life in all its abundance. Amen.

Isaiah 55:1-13

It is because of him that you are in Christ Jesus, who has become for us wisdom from God – that is, our righteousness, holiness and redemption.

~ 1 CORINTHIANS 1:30 ~

There are various degrees of life. There is life that sinks to the lowest depths. At that level, there is no desire for improvement, because it is suffocated by laziness, lack of ambition and the fear of parting with familiar friends and surroundings. The large majority of people belong to this group of mankind – those who always battle to maintain the status quo. They refuse to part with the old, even though something much better is offered to them. There are also people who are sharp and awake – in mind and in spirit. They believe that their best days are still ahead. Each person belongs to one of these categories.

You decide for yourself how to live your life depending upon the source from which you draw your inspiration. If you are a self-centered individual, you will be driven by arrogance, desire and self-glorification. If you live to satisfy the masses, your inspiration will be born from popular opinion and the emotional pace of the moment. If you are pursuing a better future, you will have an affinity in your soul for the Eternal: *there* God is in control and He directs your spirit and your mind.

It is only when the living Christ is the inspirational power in your life that His Holy Spirit can work in and through you, making it visible in your everyday life.

> You are the source of inspiration and strength in my life, my Lord and my God! Amen.

1 Corinthians 1:20-31

... (May you) know this love that surpasses knowledge – that you may be filled to the measure of all the fullness of God.

~ EPHESIANS 3:19 ~

It is true that one of the Master's most difficult commands is to love one another as He loves us. The question that immediately arises is: How can I love a cold-blooded murderer? How can I show love to someone who has harmed me? How can I love a child-molester? These are but a few of the questions that come to mind when you think about this irreversible command that the Master gives to us.

In our own strength it is impossible, because human nature still clings to the principle of an eye for an eye and a tooth for a tooth. However, history has proven that these are not the solutions. The only way to restore reason and stability to our world, is through the all-embracing, all-powerful love of God that can soften the hearts of the most hardened of men.

Jesus needs people who will display His love by praying for all people, regardless of how appalling their deeds may be. The Evil One has never had the power to conquer the power of prayer and love that comes in the Name of Christ. It is your privilege to be part of this miracle.

Loving and merciful God, help me set aside all personal feelings and to offer myself to be an instrument of Your love in this afflicted world. Amen.

Ephesians 3:14-21

Do not conform any longer to the pattern of this world, but be transformed by the renewing of your mind.

~ ROMANS 12:2 ~

Long before the term psychology became popular in modern-day society, the Bible taught us the necessity to be renewed by an inner strength. Man was created in the image of God. Since his fall from former glory, he has been trying to restore his unity with God.

For the renewed soul, there is an ongoing battle to become that which he instinctively feels that he should be: a child of God who is worthy of this high honor. Man has tried hard to achieve this goal, using all the means at his disposal to rediscover a meaningful relationship with his God. This battle often results in frustration and disappointment. He, who does not find and embrace God outwardly, will also not discover God inwardly.

Once we have developed a positive relationship with the living Christ, our mental outlook will also be renewed. Instead of living a life filled with fear, you will face life with confidence. Instead of frustration, a sense of purpose will enter your life; your spirit is filled with joy, happiness and contentment, inspired by the Holy Spirit of God. Such a transformation takes place because your mind has been possessed by the Spirit of God. This is what Paul is talking about when he says in Philippians 2:5: *Your attitude should be the same as that of Christ Jesus ...*

Living God, I humbly ask that You will renew my spiritual life through the Holy Spirit residing in me.

Romans 12:1-8

... (He abolished) in his flesh the law (of Moses) with its commandments and regulations. His purpose was to create in himself one new man out of the two (Jews and Gentiles), thus making peace, and in this one body to reconcile both of them to God through the cross, by which he put to death their hostility.

~ EPHESIANS 2:15-17 ~

It is a sad but indisputable fact that the fallibility of man in the church is as evident as in any other place. Since the founding of the early church until today, there have been division, fragmentation and dispute about dogmatic and theological issues. This has resulted in the founding of a large number of denominations and sects – and each believes that its interpretation of the Scriptures is the only one that is correct. In many cases this leads to hostility, conduct that is directly in conflict with the doctrines of Christ.

The foundation for our Christian faith is love. Jesus was born in this world as a result of God's love. He came to live a life of love in this world. He died on the cross, because of His love for the world. He rose from the dead, ascended to heaven and the Holy Spirit was poured out onto the world so that His love could be preserved throughout the world.

In these uncertain times, there is much testimony to Satan's work. It is very important for everybody who adheres to the Christian faith to set their differences aside right now and to respect each other's faith and feelings. We must be united in the love of the living Christ in our efforts to emphasize the glory of God.

In Your love, blessed Lord Jesus, I am reconciled with my fellow Christians so that I may serve You better in this world.

Ephesians 2:11-22

From the Lord comes deliverance.

~ PSALM 3:8 ~

Ꮗnfortunately, many people live in the conviction that they are "born losers". They complain that nothing ever goes right for them, that their plans are always thwarted, that their life is a succession of lost opportunities, that – regardless of what they undertake – they will never achieve success. It does not take long for such a person's outlook on life to become totally negative as a result of a pessimistic disposition.

If you resolve to live your life in your own strength and to trust in your own abilities to see you through, you may indeed, sometimes, achieve a measure of success. However, your existence will lack the self-confidence that only God can give you. If you then have to face problems and setbacks, you will discover, to your disillusionment, that there is no depth in the abilities of man. It will therefore become all the more difficult for you to handle the situation.

The manner in which you handle your life in all its facets, will depend on your faith in Jesus Christ. Surrender your life, your business, your decisions, in fact everything, to Him, and wait on Him to guide you through the labyrinth of life. If you live in obedience and loyalty to Him, you will live confidently and triumphantly in the knowledge: *No, in all these things we are more than conquerors through him who loved us* (Rom. 8:37).

I live my life in the quiet faith of knowing You, Lord Jesus, and I thank You that I am growing in self-confidence and faith in You. Amen.

Psalm 3:1-8

ᴛHE POWER OF INSPIRED THOUGHTS

Above all else, guard your heart, for it is the wellspring of life.

~ Proverbs 4:23 ~

Our thoughts motivate our lives. The person who thinks positively, acts constructively. Without creativity, our thoughts wander aimlessly, often with disastrous consequences. To have an active mind, does not necessarily mean that you will be a brilliant student. Many intelligent people miss the true purpose of life and do not succeed in identifying the spirit that stimulates thoughts, and which is as important as the thoughts themselves.

If your spirit cherishes thoughts of bitterness, hate, lechery and envy, your mind is drenched with negative and destructive thoughts, and you will never experience the fullness of a pulsating Christian faith. By living in harmony with the living Christ, and allowing His Spirit to become an inspiration to your spirit, you can achieve the impossible.

The Master puts to us the challenging, though merciful invitation, *"Remain in me, and I will remain in you ... "* (Jn. 15:4). To "remain in Christ" means a joyous embracing of the way of Christ. It implies a healthy and increasingly profound prayer life, supported by faithful Bible study. It gives your mind the inspiration and strength that are only experienced by those who have put Jesus Christ foremost in their lives.

Through Your enabling grace, Lord Jesus, my mind is opened to the inspiration of the Holy Spirit. Amen.

Proverbs 4:18-27

I want to know Christ and the power of his resurrection and the fellowship of sharing in his sufferings.

~ PHILIPPIANS 3:10 ~

𝓜any of God's servants are so busy working for Him, that they do not have the time to spend regular quiet moments with Him. Christian service without prayer is never filled with purpose. Few people will say, "I work for the Lord, therefore I do not have to pray." The truth is rather that they are so actively at work for the kingdom that, gradually and without noticing, their activities become more important than their quiet time with the Father. They are active for God without experiencing the presence and power of the living Christ.

Attempting to serve the Lord without the motivating strength of the Holy Spirit results in frustration and ultimate disaster. If the vision of what you are trying to do for Him fades, your service will become powerless and ineffective. And it will happen if your spiritual reserves are not regularly replenished through prayer and meditation. Furthermore, you cannot attempt to maintain Christian testimony without the experience of prayer.

Regardless of the sphere of life in which you are trying to serve the Master, you must put Him foremost in all your activities. The service that you render to Him must be the result of your intimate knowledge of Him. Only when He enjoys priority in all things, can you understand life the way He sees it. Putting Christ foremost in your life and work, makes you a more efficient and acceptable servant of God.

Savior and Lord, help me to put You foremost in my life. You are the inspiration and power of my service to You. Amen.

Philippians 3:1-14

CREATE AN ATMOSPHERE

Finally, be strong in the Lord and in his mighty power.

~ EPHESIANS 6:10 ~

There are certain things in life that can be experienced, but that are very difficult to explain. Atmosphere is one of them. You can enter a room feeling completely normal, and suddenly you are over-whelmed by a feeling of dejection. In many ways we are subject to atmosphere, but we must never forget that we can create our own atmosphere.

Acknowledging this could play an important role in your life. If you realize that you can create your own atmosphere, you will be able to face life with self-confidence. If you ignore this fact, you will be the target of negative influences that surround you every day. If you welcome this ability, you will become a blessing to everybody that you come into contact with. In this way, your life becomes meaningful and blessed.

It is by creating an atmosphere of blessing that the doctrines and presence of Jesus Christ can play such an important role in your life. The living Christ promised us that His Holy Spirit would reside in the hearts and minds of those who love and serve Him. If Jesus is in control and His Spirit controls your life, He is also in control of the atmosphere that fills your days.

A personality that is centered on Christ, reflects an atmosphere that can be sensed, even by people who do not know Him. The words of the old Hallelujah song should be a challenge to all Christians: *I so much want to be like Jesus, so humble and so good; His words were so friendly, His voice always sweet* (Hall. 439:1). Then a spirit of confidence and love will flow through your life and create an atmosphere that makes life meaningful and worthwhile.

Counselor and Master, may my Christian experience be great enough to influence the atmosphere of my daily life. Amen.

Ephesians 6:10-20

October

Carry each other's burdens, and in this way you will fulfill the law of Christ.

~ Galatians 6:2 ~

Prayer

We need each other. Caring month.

Holy Jesus of love and grace, there are many people who urgently need Christian love: The aged, the sick, the poor, the mournful, the lost, children and young people; this world is indeed a vale of tears.

You challenged us to love one another as You love us: We so easily profess our love for You, but when it comes to our neighbor, we fail dismally.

Give us eyes to see the distress around us;

Give us ears to hear the plea for help;

Give us a mouth to preach Your message of love;

Give us hands that will do something to alleviate sorrow;

Give us a heart that will have compassion for the pain and suffering of our day.

We worship You as the Lord who can make all of life beautiful: youth with its strength and invincibility, its life-expectancy, idealism and dauntlessness; the full power and ripeness of maturity; the serenity, peace and wisdom of age.

Teach us all to care for one another with Your love in our hearts.

You are indeed our Perfect Example in everything, be so in this as well, Lord Jesus.

Amen

"By this all men will know that you are my disciples, if you love one another."

~ JOHN 13:35 ~

C hrist makes many demands on His disciples. It is how we respond to these demands that distinguishes us from those who do not acknowledge the sovereignty of Christ in their lives. The Christian's standards are the standards of Christ and, in his entire conduct and disposition, he strives to reflect the image of Christ.

Christian discipleship implies an honorable way of life and good deeds. It is impossible to live in intimate harmony with Christ without something of His loveliness being reflected in our lives. Because you are a Christian, your life should differ in many ways from that of the non-Christian. The Master not only expects this difference, but the ungodly world expects it of you as well; those who have not sworn allegiance to Him or give Him any love. What is the decisive difference?

The litmus test of true Christlikeness is the love Christians have for one another. There can be no good deeds without love. These would lack the penetrating power of inspired discipleship, and faith would become a series of good deeds that lack inspiration and purpose.

Christ knows all our human weaknesses and offers us the love that we lack in order for us to achieve His objective with our lives. If we find it difficult to love, we need only open our lives to His Spirit, and allow Him to love others through us. It is this true love of Christ that flows through us that will demonstrate to all that we are His disciples.

I plead that Your love will take possession of my life, oh Master, so that I will reflect the quality of Your love. Amen.

John 13:32-38

ℬE A COMFORTER

They approach and come forward; each helps the other and says to
his brother, "Be strong!"

~ Isaiah 41:5-6 ~

ℒ ife is not easy for the average person. The ever-increasing cost
of living, tense human relationships, the fear of unemployment,
the spectre of ill-health, all contribute to make life difficult. Unfortunately,
many people accept these unfortunate circumstances as the norm. They
believe that the disappointments and the misery that emerges from it,
are things that cannot be avoided.

As a Christian, you are not guaranteed freedom from temptations
and problems. The difference lies in your approach to these things. If
you bemoan your fate and feel that God has disappointed you when
these things happen to you, you become part of the big choir that sings
a song of woe about the afflictions and the unfairness of life. Then you
only succeed in creating more misery and despair.

If you have the Eternal Spirit of the living Christ in your spirit, He
will prevent you from sinking into the quicksand of a depressed and
negative disposition. You will look for solutions for life's problems, and
if the answers escape you, you will be content, in childlike faith, to cast
your cares upon Christ. After all, He knows about everything. Then
you will be able to live, creatively and unafraid.

Because you know that, through the power of Christ's residing Spirit
you can triumph over negative circumstances, you are able to comfort
others. Then they, in turn, will be able to look past the temporary and
the negative, and see Eternity; a glorious future that God has planned
for them.

Powerful Savior, let my faith be so positive that I will be able to assist
others to overcome their despair. Amen.

Isaiah 41:1-7

KEEP YOUR SYMPATHY SENSITIVE

"Today, if you hear his voice, do not harden your hearts."
~ HEBREWS 3:7-8 ~

With so many organisations and welfare groups calling for assistance and attention, it is extremely difficult to know whom to support. Apart from these large organisations, there are also calls for our compassion from countless other sources. The beggar, the family in need, or any other urgent need that comes to our attention, makes it impossible for us to support them all. Your resources simply are not as big as your heart.

If it becomes impossible to meet the demands made on us, we must guard against developing detachment that gradually hardens our hearts towards the needs of the less privileged. Because you cannot help with material things, you can easily create the impression that you do not care.

Helping somebody in need keeps you spiritually sensitive towards the world you live in. There are other ways to help people than just with material things, and this enriches both the donor and the receiver. You may walk past a beggar without a cent in your pocket, but rather than look the other way and feel embarrassed, you can send up a quiet prayer on his behalf and follow it up with a smile. He will realize that the whole world is not against him, it will strengthen your spiritual sensitivity and you will be aware of the need of others.

Grant me, oh holy Master, the wisdom to keep my spirit sensitive to the needs of my fellow man. Amen.

Hebrews 3:7-19

CONFORMITY TO CHRIST

Jesus told him, "Go and do likewise."

~ JOHN 10:37 ~

Bookshops carry a prolific amount of literature on the various aspects of Christianity. Hundreds of authors produce thousands of books that are read by millions of people who want to know more about Jesus. They try and expand their knowledge of the great Scriptural truths.

Regardless of how laudable this may be, the danger exists that you could become so inspired by your studies, that you lose contact with the Christ about whom you are reading. You can know everything about Jesus, without knowing Him personally.

Jesus taught the early disciples by His example and on that He founded His church. The situation has not changed over the years. People still feel an affinity for the Christian faith through the example of compassion and love that is set by His modern-day disciples. A thorough knowledge of the Scriptures is essential as a solid foundation for any believer, but one should never allow study to replace one's personal knowledge or experience of Jesus. Neither should it hinder you from serving your fellow man in the same way as He served people when He walked this earth in His Name and to His glory.

Perfect Master, let my life reflect Your love and mercy in all that I do and say. Amen.

Luke 10:25-37

ARE YOU UNINVOLVED?

Then the LORD said to Cain, "Where is your brother Abel?" "I don't know," he replied. "Am I my brother's keeper?"

~ GENESIS 4:9 ~

Much of the evil in the world can be ascribed to uninvolvement in the face of the distress of our suffering fellow man. For a variety of reasons, there are so many people who are inclined to follow the example of the priest and the Levite in the parable of the Good Samaritan. They prefer "passing on the other side", instead of feeling deeply sorry for the victim of the crime.

Their reasons may differ and their attitude may be ascribed to embarrassment, inability or a fear of rejection. More often than not, they are so involved with their own affairs, or their own problems, that they do not have time to get involved with other people's problems. Even worse: they do not even notice the other persons' distress.

Jesus gave us two commandments that He emphasized as the most important. The one is to love God with your entire being, and the other is to love your neighbor as yourself. The Christian cannot ignore his fellow man. Uninvolvement has no place in the Christian faith and your concern for the welfare of your fellow man is a barometer of your love for God.

It does not require much effort to notice the distress in today's world. Reach out a helping hand to others and experience the presence of God in your service in His Name.

Use me, Lord, to serve amongst my fellow men. Amen.

Genesis 4:1-16

WE NEED EACH OTHER — AND CHRIST NEEDS YOU

Let us not become weary in doing good, for at the proper time we will reap a harvest if we do not give up.

~ GALATIANS 6:9 ~

Scientific, academic and technological progress has provided a sophisticated world to live in that can hold many advantages. However, there are also disadvantages that follow progress. It is difficult to live a simple and uncomplicated life in these modern times. Heavy demands are made on people of all genders and ages. Signs of stress and tension are noticeable as the qualifying requirements increase, greater productivity is required, and many people are regarded as redundant in the prime of their lives. We pay a high price for progress and people are suffering psychologically, mentally, physically and emotionally.

Now is the time for Christianity to be active for the sake of people in distress. We must draw from the wells of wisdom and discernment that are granted to us by the Holy Spirit, and utilize our talents to the full. We must always be aware of the needs of others. Lend a helping hand where required; be ready to listen and, if you are so guided, give advice; comfort those in despair and help to build their self-confidence. Christ expects His disciples to listen to the cries of distress around them and *to do something!*

Merciful Lord, stand by me while I try to serve You amongst those who are in need. Amen.

Galatians 6:1-10

REACH OUT TO OTHERS

"'Whatever you did for one of the least of these brothers of mine, you did for me.'"

~ MATTHEW 25:40 ~

Let us thank God for those people who take pleasure in helping others. No task is too small for them, and they rejoice in doing good unobtrusively. They do not seek any reward, except for making life richer and easier for their fellow men. People like that are usually happy. It is seldom that you will come across somebody who makes life more pleasant for others, who is dejected himself. To forget about yourself in the service of others, is not only the religious path of life, but also the path to a full and satisfying life. The only way in which you can be convinced of this, is by giving of yourself in the service of others.

Now is the best time to start. Find somebody who is in need. You will not have to look far, because the world is full of people who are destitute. A lonely person might welcome friendship; someone who is confused will appreciate a good and understanding listener; a lonely person might welcome visitors with all his heart; a single parent might welcome a responsible child-minder so that she could go out for an evening. There are so many different ways in which to help. While you are helping others, you will receive a rich blessing as your reward. Every good deed that is performed in the Name of Christ bestows a blessing on both the donor and the receiver. Most of all, it brings glory to His Name.

Lord and Master, make me sensitive to the needs of others. Amen.

Matthew 25:31-46

$\mathcal{T}$HE MINISTRY OF ANGELS

Do not forget to entertain strangers, for by so doing some people have entertained angels without knowing it.

~ HEBREWS 13:2 ~

$\mathcal{T}$he concept of angels does not meet with everybody's approval, but this does not mean that there aren't spiritual beings who serve God and assist people. There are many cases in the Bible where angels were sent as God's messengers to people. Obviously, the thought of a winged being is unrealistic and, even though they look beautiful in works of art, they cannot be accepted by the modern mind. If angels walked amongst us in our times, we would not be able to distinguish them from ordinary people. They would be known by their conduct and not by what they wear or how they look.

The thought that there could be angels in this world, presents us with a fresh approach and a new appreciation for our fellow men. Instead of looking for their faults, you will discover something of their God-given talents. Where the best in people is often concealed by layers of pride and self-glorification, you must look for something of the true glory that God has planted in the souls of all people.

God's serving angels often work unobtrusively as they attempt to make life easier and more pleasant for those they come into contact with: to look after little children while the mother is taking a well-earned rest; a visit to a lonely or depressed person; or to care for somebody who has nobody to care for him. These, and far more, are all tasks that are being performed by serving angels. Has it ever occurred to you that you could be a serving angel of God?

Lord Jesus, help me to practise my ministry of care towards all those that I come into contact with. Amen.

Hebrews 13:1-6

And do not forget to do good and to share with others, for with such sacrifices God is pleased.

~ Hebrews 13:16 ~

To do good can be the most exciting of all adventures. It might not sound enticing to those whose understanding of goodness is that it is nothing more than kind-heartedness in moderation. But for those who have experienced the dynamic impact of sacrificial "good deeds", it could be the most exciting and satisfying experience of their lives.

Those who need your help are often not aware of their needs. Their spirit may be closed to all sanctifying influences and be overshadowed by a cloth of bitterness. They may be cynical about everything that you regard as holy, and treat every offer of assistance with contempt. If you are determined to overcome their negative and destructive disposition through positive goodness, you will not be discouraged by the front that they put up. You will realize that, under that callous appearance, there is a spirit that is waiting to be liberated.

The liberation of spirit and mind is not always achieved by preaching or by arguing endlessly with the person that you are trying to help; to do any of these things will be harmful. Live in such a way that the desire is created within that person to have what you have. The best way of "doing good" to someone is not by an outward deed, but through the quality of your life which will serve as an inspiration towards a better life.

Loving Master, let the quality of my life improve the lives of other people. Amen.

Hebrews 13:7-19

ℒET YOUR LOVE BE PRACTICAL

Let us not love with words or tongue but with actions and in truth.

~ 1 JOHN 3:18 ~

True love is not something that can be fathomed by the human mind or by experience. It cannot be fully defined. Yet, of all the human emotions it is the most profound and dynamic. It is difficult to put the unique qualities of love into words. Unsuccessfully we try to express it in intelligible language. Compassion, friendliness, tenderness, and many other beautiful and soulful words do not succeed in describing the power and strength of love. There is an inclination to equate love with sentimentality, but that causes this dynamic force to become powerless and ineffective.

The basis for true love is identification with the loved one. The same joy, sorrow, temptations and disappointments are experienced. True love always comprises sacrifice, and often sorrow. The true quality of love surpasses sympathy and sentimentality, and manifests itself in loyalty and faithfulness when things go wrong for the loved one.

Love in action is more than doing good deeds, although such deeds can be an expression of love. Pure love is profound and unselfish and embraces the characteristics of faithfulness and high principles that enrich the mind and spirit of a person. It cannot be bought, borrowed, begged or stolen. That is why practical love is so precious.

Oh, Holy Father, enable me to love without counting the cost. Amen.

1 John 3:18-24

Each of you should look not only to your own interests, but also to the interests of others.

~ PHILIPPIANS 2:4 ~

Selfishness or self-centeredness undoubtedly stands out as one of the major causes of disturbed human relationships. Regardless of the level of the community where it may manifest itself – either on the national or international stage, or in our relationship with one another – a lack of "caring" and consideration for each other places a blot on society.

Jesus' whole life was devoted to caring for others. His love for people was all-embracing. This was obvious in His relationship with all that He came into contact with. Despite the circumstances, or regardless of the consequences, His first thought was always for others; even when He was nailed to the cross.

Jesus commanded His followers to love one another as He loves us. It is unavoidable that this will include self-sacrifice. In our ministry of love to one another, we must show others the same compassion and forgiving love that the Master has for us. Only in so doing, can the wounds of this world be healed. Harmony between people can only be achieved through obedience to Christ's commands. In this way you can personally play an important role – through His grace.

Holy Spirit of God, fill me with the desire and the ability to love my neighbor as You love me. Amen.

Philippians 2:1-11

ⅅO NOT DESPAIR

Let us not become weary in doing good, for at the proper time we will reap a harvest if we do not give up.

~ GALATIANS 6:9 ~

𝒯here are few things as sad as the failure to see results from your efforts. If after much effort and perseverance, you still see no signs of success, the result is discouragement that could easily lead to despair. We will never know how many worthwhile tasks were never completed because the people involved in them became discouraged. As a result, they were deprived of the wonderful opportunity to taste ultimate victory.

A study of the religious giants in the Bible will reveal the way in which they persevered against enormous odds in their efforts to do the work that God instructed them to do. Regardless of setback, ridicule, resistance from governments and churches, in the face of unbelievable suffering, they persevered with determination, until the glory of God's purpose was revealed, sometimes even long after their death.

There will come times during your life when things will become very difficult and you will be tempted to believe that your efforts are useless. That is the time to trust in God and devote yourself completely to Him. Set aside quiet time with Him and He will carry you through the days when despair gnaws at your soul. Let faith triumph over your feelings and rest assured that, in God's perfect timing, your efforts will bear fruit to the glory of His Name.

Enabling Lord Jesus, I thank You that you stand by me in days when despair threatens and that You comfort me in my task. Amen.

Galatians 6:1-9

"As the Father has sent me, I am sending you."

~ JOHN 20:21 ~

It is an overwhelming thought: Christians are called to a purposeful life. The delusion of wishful thinking that leads to the byways of life, is not our fate. You are in the service of His Majesty, the living Christ, and you have voluntarily accepted the responsibility of serving Him. This means that you accept all the disciplines of a spiritual life, so that your love for Him can increase and so that you can be His efficient messenger.

Where will you serve Him? For a privileged small number, their service will lead them to foreign countries and exciting circumstances, but for the majority of Christian believers it will mean service in an ordinary world. He sends you into the world that you know only too well. You may be in commerce or in a profession, hold a position of authority, or fill a humble post, you may be a homemaker; wherever you may be, you are His representative. People who know about your loyalty to Him, will expect you to maintain certain standards in your speech and in your conduct, that they will not expect from the world.

If your life is filled with the love of Jesus Christ, your infectious faith will bring a message of hope and love, wherever He wishes to use you.

Here am I, Master, send me to serve You wherever You may need me. Amen.

John 20:19-25

YOUR INFLUENCE DOES MATTER

> When we got to Rome, Paul was allowed to live by himself, with a soldier to guard him.
>
> ~ ACTS 28:16 ~

When this Roman soldier was instructed to guard Paul he was unaware of the influence that he would be subject to. It is improbable that he would have listened to Paul's daily testimony without being touched by it. The Gospel entered Emperor Caesar's palace, possibly through the influence and testimony of Paul's guards.

You may regard yourself as too unimportant to influence other people, but you do exercise an influence, often without being aware of it. This influence could inspire those who are dejected and feel that life holds nothing for them. If your influence is negative, it could darken the brightest of days for people. The influence that you exercise depends entirely on you. It is impossible to spread joy unless you are filled with the spirit of joy, or to spread peace, unless you live in peace with yourself and with God. The influence that you exercise originates from your innermost being and not from your appearance.

If you are a practicing Christian, who allows the Holy Spirit to work through you in order to enrich the lives of people around you, you must first have a personal experience with Christ, so that His influence can reach people through you.

Fill me with Your Holy Spirit, beloved Master, so that Your influence can reach other people through me. Amen.

Acts 28:16-25

Demas, because he loved this world, has deserted me and has gone to Thessalonica. Crescens has gone to Galatia, and Titus to Dalmatia.
~ 2 TIMOTHY 4:10 ~

N obody knows exactly why Demas, Crescens and Titus parted company with Paul, and whether the parting was temporary or permanent. It is possible that even amongst Christians there could be tense relationships, but it is what you do under these circumstances that is important. To ignore them only increases the tension, and to allow them to continue within a relationship, can destroy the spirit of unity in the group.

Even in the most intimate of relationships it is necessary to have areas where personal privacy is respected. Moments when a person wants to be alone with God, must never be invaded by another, regardless of the intimacy of the relationship. It is only by respecting the individuality of a person that a friendship can grow in strength and beauty.

Prayer, love and candor are agents which relieve the tension in relationships. Pray for God's blessing upon the person who has become estranged from you. While praying, you might discover something in your own life that contributes to the tension. Through the wisdom that the Holy Spirit grants us, we will be able to handle the situation correctly and possibly be able to rectify a misunderstanding.

Through prayer, love flourishes, and if a conversation is necessary, let it be tempered by love. Speak only the truth in love.

Wondrous Lord, teach me to appreciate friendship and to cherish it with care. Amen.

2 Timothy 4:9-18

In all your ways acknowledge him, and he will make your paths straight.

~ PROVERBS 3:6 ~

You meet people in your daily, or social life, and yet you never really get to know them. You greet them and are often impressed by their cheerfulness, without realising that behind the smile, a deep sorrow or a frustrated spirit is concealed.

Depression is an alarming experience and is the result of many possible causes. People who are lonely, often feel dejected. To feel that nobody loves you or needs you, can fill your spirit with pessimism. To have fought to conquer but to have known only defeat, could make one melancholic. These and similar factors all contribute to the feeling of depression that can overwhelm your spirit.

It is true that many people do not hesitate to tell the world of their depression, but others hide their feelings behind a smile. It calls for a sensitive and perceptive person to grasp the true situation. It is not always possible to evaluate people at face value. How different life would be if we made the time to understand people before we comment on their conduct. There would be less criticism and condemnation and much more love.

One of the Christian disciple's characteristics is an understanding heart. To be able to penetrate the mask of pretense and offer people understanding and comradeship, is one of the glorious results of the Holy Spirit in your life.

Grant me an understanding heart, oh Father, so that I may love people with more sincerity. Amen.

Proverbs 3:1-18

LIVE TO BLESS YOUR FELLOW MAN

"'Love your neighbor as yourself.'"

~ MATTHEW 22:39 ~

It is so easy to become self-centered. You talk about what you want and what you own, until you start to feel that this world has been created especially for you. If this happens, something of inestimable value dies within you and people will no longer seek your company. Self-centeredness can destroy the beauty of your character.

If you want to live a full, satisfying and free life, you need other people around you whom you can love and serve. It is only through loving service to your neighbor that you can grow to spiritual and intellectual maturity. Jesus emphasized this fact when He said, *"For whoever wants to save his life will lose it, but whoever loses his life for me will find it"* (Mt. 16:25). Live to bless other people, and you will be rendered speechless by how the quality of your own life improves.

If you want your life to have meaning and purpose, it is important to lose yourself in someone or a cause that is greater than yourself. It is at this level that Jesus Christ reveals Himself as the Great Inspirer of people like you and me, and who said, *"Remain in me, and I will remain in you..."* (Jn. 15:4). He also said, *"... Love your enemies and pray for those who persecute you..."* (Mt. 5:44). To bless in this way in the power of Christ, is to discover a full and satisfying life.

In Your power and through Your grace, Powerful Savior, I bless my fellow man and, in doing so, experience a full and rich life of service. Amen.

Matthew 22:34-46

ℱAITH AND PRACTICE

You foolish man, do you want evidence that faith without deeds is useless?

~ JAMES 2:20 ~

𝒯rue faith in the living Christ is an inspiration and a source of immense spiritual power. A positive faith makes Christ a living reality in your daily life, but it does not free you of the responsibility to practice your faith. We cannot merely believe and then neglect the practical application of Christian principles. Faith and practice go hand in hand and to neglect the one at the expense of the other, leads to an unbalanced spiritual experience.

In order to maintain a balanced Christian faith, through which the love and purpose of Christ can flow, we must draw inspiration from a positive and creative prayer life and the studying of God's Word. From these two sources, a spiritual life will emerge that is both inspirational and practical. To state that you believe in Christ, and yet refuse to allow Him to operate through your life, is a denial of that faith.

It may seem that who you are is irreconcilable with who Christ is, but when the Lord calls you, He also calls you to a life of growth. All growth is slow. Do not feel discouraged if your life in Christ seems to be frustrating and insufficient, but remain in close fellowship with Christ. By living in harmony with Him, you will grow in His image and demonstrate His ways in a practical manner. Then you will know how to reconcile faith and practice.

Savior and Redeemer, help me to live in You so that I may reflect Your life and act according to Your principles. Amen.

James 2:14-26

LOVE IS PRACTICAL AND SINCERE

This is how God showed his love among us: He sent his one and only Son into the world that we might live through him.

~ 1 JOHN 4:9 ~

If you make a study of the life of Christ, there is one outstanding characteristic that regularly comes to the fore: the fact that the Lord was practical. Read about the miracles and healings that He performed and the love that He showed. Regardless of the profound spiritual aspect of His ministry, we regularly notice Christ's practical nature. When He raised the little girl from the dead, He told the family to give her something to eat.

True love and caring requires more than mere words: it calls for action. It requires of you to support someone in prayer, but also to take some form of action to prove the extent of your love and caring, even if it causes you inconvenience. A visit to a patient in hospital or to an elderly person in a home for the aged, a card or a letter of consolation to someone who is experiencing difficult times, a call to someone who is lonely; all these things are practical expressions of love and they cannot but bring joy and happiness to the lives of others – as well as to your own.

By demonstrating your love for others in a practical manner, you follow the example that Jesus set for us. In this He is our example, because His love exceeds all other love.

Holy Jesus, help me to love others with a love that is sincere and practical. Amen.

1 John 4:7-21

DISCOURAGED?

Say to those with fearful hearts, "Be strong, do not fear; your God will come."

~ ISAIAH 35:4 ~

We all experience discouragement. It manifests itself in different ways, but always leaves you disillusioned, wondering whether all your efforts are worth the trouble. Only those who have aspired towards a goal can experience discouragement. If you feel that your dreams have been destroyed and your efforts have come to nothing, do not allow self-pity to sow the seed of discouragement in your spirit. There are spiritual reserves from which you can draw, that will give you hope and a sense of purpose. In the past, you might have trusted in sources of inspiration and strength that were of your own making. When these sources failed you, you lost your vision and life became empty and lacking in purpose. Without a constant source of inspiration, you will soon be discouraged.

God is your constant source of inspiration. He only asks that you come and draw freely from Him. Then you will be able to overcome discouragement. Remember: God is waiting to work in harmony with you. He does not work against you, but seeks your cooperation at all times in order to neutralize the influences that depress and overcome you.

You do not fight alone against discouragement and depression. God is on your side and He is waiting to pick you up so that you may proceed with joy and be ultimately triumphant.

I thank You, heavenly Father, that through the power of Your residing Spirit, I can triumph over discouragement. Amen.

Isaiah 35:1-10

DO YOU HAVE A HUMAN RELATIONS PROGRAM?

How good and pleasant it is when brothers live together in unity!
~ PSALM 133:1 ~

If you have to live with people, it is rewarding to understand them and to maintain a healthy relationship with them. In some cases this is relatively easy, but in others it could be exceptionally difficult. So much depends on the disposition of other people: with some it is easy to start a conversation and their pleasant personalities place no stress on human relationships. But not all people are like that.

There are many people who are abrupt and difficult and it seems as though they derive pleasure from making things unpleasant for those around them. At one time or another, such people enter the sphere of your life. If you try and solve the problem by ignoring them, you avoid the problem, but you do not solve it. At the same time you might miss the opportunity to get to know a unique, although difficult personality.

Handling the problem of human relations constructively, requires patience and sympathetic understanding on your part. You will keep quiet and give others the opportunity to talk and even if what they say hurts, you will maintain control over the situation by remaining calm. Under such circumstances, you will learn and discover that behind the rough exterior and apparent rudeness, there is a life that yearns for love and friendship.

Once you have discovered this distress, you can help meet the need. Then you have discovered the special art of freeing restrained personalities and making friends out of potential enemies.

God of grace and love, in Your strength I strive to obtain an understanding of all people so that I can live in peace with them. Amen.

Psalm 133:1-3

BY FORGETTING ABOUT
MYSELF I DISCOVER MYSELF

For none of us lives to himself alone.

~ ROMANS 14:7 ~

P eople always find the time to do those things that they would like to do, but are quick to find excuses for not doing the things which they don't like doing. This human characteristic runs right through life and our spiritual life is no exception.

In all probability you have occasionally stated that you do not have the time to pray and pointed to your hectic program. It would be beneficial to answer the question honestly, "How keen am I to make my prayer life more profound?" There is usually time for the newspaper, for your favorite author and time just to relax. If your spiritual life is at a low, you will continually multiply your excuses for a defective prayer life.

If this is your experience, it would be sensible to ask yourself why you are making excuses. Why have the splendor and power disappeared from your prayer life? Why has your religion become a burden instead of an inspiration of hope and faith? You will undoubtedly find the answer in the fact that your faith has become self-centered. This happens when you no longer reach out to God in prayer, or if all your prayers have become expressions of your personal desires. True prayer broadens your spiritual and intellectual horizons and, at the same time, makes your relationship with your Savior and Redeemer more profound.

Oh Lord, my God, help me to develop a meaningful and powerful prayer life under the guidance of the Holy Spirit. Amen.

Romans 14:1-12

"Do not judge, or you too will be judged."

~ MATTHEW 7:1 ~

ave you ever noticed the attitude towards life of a person who continually criticizes others? His disdain of his fellow man is reflected in his refusal to see any good in his neighbor. It does not matter what noble deed is performed, the critic will always come up with some disparaging remark. If a person's business is successful, there will always be some innuendoes of dishonesty. The critic finds it extremely difficult to give sincere praise and encouragement and, as a result, he is usually an embittered person.

Destructive criticism from a person who is not a Christian is bad enough. However, when a person maintains that he is a Christian, but refuses to encourage, inspire or elevate others, commits character assassination and discourages others at every possible opportunity, you will see the tragedy of failure in the Christian faith.

As a disciple of Christ you are called upon to live positively and constructively. If you are in company where disparaging remarks are being made about someone who is not present, it is your Christian duty to defend the absent person.

There are, however, times when constructive criticism is necessary. This must be handled directly with the person concerned and in a spirit and attitude of love and understanding. If your criticism is to be beneficial, you must take time to pray before you criticize. Only deliver criticism after you have shared it with the Master.

Loving Lord Jesus, if I have to criticize, make me constructive and loving at all times. Amen.

Matthew 7:1-12

DISCOVER THE GOOD IN OTHER PEOPLE

Finally, brothers, whatever is true, whatever is noble, whatever is right, whatever is pure, whatever is lovely, whatever is admirable ... think about such things.

~ PHILIPPIANS 4:8 ~

There are Christians who inadvertently attempt to do the work of the Holy Spirit. They are continually trying to convince people of their sins and constantly point out their mistakes. It is the sole right of the Holy Spirit to convince people of their sins and to bring them to a personal experience with the redeeming Christ. When a Christian spends all his precious time condemning sin, he is missing an important element of the Christian Gospel: that all people can become new creatures in Jesus Christ.

A new creature in Christ has received redemption and, although he is still tempted, he is able to handle it in the strength of his Savior. A true Christian will see the "new person" in a completely different light. He no longer sees the fallible side of the human personality; the side with all the weakness, unpleasantness and sin, but he starts to understand the good that there is in people he meets. He accepts the good points, even in those who have not sworn allegiance to Christ, and develops an appreciation for everything that is "right" and "noble".

When a Christian is looking for the good in his fellow man, he will discover that people gradually react to that which is being expected of them. When you intuitively expect the best in a person, you will often find that that person accepts the challenges of Jesus, the living Christ.

Lord and Savior, through enlightenment by the Holy Spirit, I increasingly see the good in my fellow men. Amen.

Philippians 4:2-9

ℬE SENSIBLE

Anyone who claims to be in the light but hates his brother is still in the darkness.

~ 1 JOHN 2:9 ~

There are many sincere people who find it difficult to be tolerant towards people who differ from them. Their love is limited by their small-mindedness and often their ill feelings cause relationships with their fellow men to be damaged.

Such a disposition limits your spiritual growth and prevents the Lord from finding expression in you. It is impossible to know Jesus Christ if small-mindedness and hate blunt your spirit and prevent you from loving others. There is no satisfaction in hatred. If you are one of those unfortunate people who stubbornly maintain that you cannot forgive, because of an injustice done to you, the time has come for you to take stock of your disposition. Who are you really hurting? It is possible that the person whom you hate has long since forgotten or does not mind in the least that you hate him? If you ruin relationships by keeping old wounds fresh, you will find that your own spirit becomes so bitter and perverse that even kindly disposed people will avoid you.

Regardless of how deep your hurt is, and even if you feel that it is too severe to forgive, you cannot afford not to do so. The cost of unforgiveness is too high. The price you pay is that you are separated from God; that your personality is poisoned and that a broken relationship exists in your life that causes small-mindedness and unhappiness.

Merciful Lord, cleanse me, through Your indwelling Holy Spirit, of all hatred and an unforgiving disposition. Amen.

1 John 2:1-11

Do not withhold good from those who deserve it, when it is in your
power to act.

~ PROVERBS 3:27 ~

Sincere Christian kind-heartedness must be a spontaneous and true
reflection of the love of Jesus Christ. His life demonstrates that
He acted everywhere where there was distress. He did not put people
off or tell them to come back later; He also did not take long to consider
their requests or first discuss them with His disciples. Christ's entire
life was a demonstration of His own words, *"... Just as the Son of Man
did not come to be served, but to serve, and to give his life as a ransom
for many"* (Mt. 20:28). And when the time came for Him to lay down
His life, He demonstrated His greatest deed of love without a moment's
hesitation.

That is the example Jesus set for His followers and the example that
we must follow if we want to live a life conforming to that of Christ. So
often people hesitate when there is a need. Their unwillingness might
be born out of embarrassment or out of fear of becoming too involved
in other people's affairs. They may be willing to offer assistance of a
temporary nature, but the prospect of any form of permanent
involvement deters them from making themselves available if and when
necessary.

A person with a problem needs your help *now*; tomorrow other
issues may arise which will make it too late. Jesus never hesitated to
help others; dare you do differently?

Holy Spirit, lead me onto paths of service in the Name of Jesus and
equip me to share in the distress of others. Amen.

Proverbs 3:21-35

"'Look after him,' he said, 'and when I return, I will reimburse you for any extra expense you may have.'"

~ LUKE 10:35 ~

True sympathy is a heart-warming experience. When it is offered to others, it could console a sorrowful heart and comfort those who are discouraged. To be deeply touched by the misfortunes of others enriches your spirit, because true sympathy stirs the most profound emotions and enables you to understand the sadness and pain of others.

The Good Samaritan experienced such emotions when he "took pity on" the victim of the robbers at the roadside. However, he did not merely sympathize, but actively did something practical to ease the suffering of the unfortunate man. Sympathy is a splendid sentiment, but it is enriched when practically applied.

How practical sympathy could be applied, however, is not initially clear. Sometimes it would seem as though all you can do is to say, "I feel with you." However, that is better than saying nothing. If you know the person with whom you sympathize, or if he lives in your neighborhood, a short visit will have helping and healing results. Never hesitate to visit people who have experienced sorrow or disaster. Just showing that you care is already a consolation.

There is something which you can do that has healing qualities, and that is to pray for the person. To know that they are receiving support in prayer can be of great consolation to people. And the one who prays is enriched by the knowledge that he is a channel of God's healing grace and comfort.

Make me an instrument of Your healing grace, oh Master, so that I may be a blessing to all who are in distress. Amen.

Luke 10:25-37

SPARE A MOMENT FOR OTHERS

(Joseph) reassured them and spoke kindly to them.

~ GENESIS 50:21 ~

In the merciless world in which we live, friendliness is a priceless quality. All too often we find that people are too busy with their own interests to even, for a moment, think about someone in distress. The pressure and demands of the world of commerce change people from normal beings to fiery and impatient tyrants. They constantly pursue better results and, in the process, drive their subordinates to the edge of despair. They might become very wealthy, but at the expense of their peace of mind. They may have great authority, but they lose the respect of the people with whom they work and with whom they come into contact.

If you want to live a life of fulfilment, you must start by caring about the feelings of others. Show interest in the welfare of your employer, fellow workers and colleagues. Spare a moment to listen to their problems. Be tolerant and leave room for their mistakes, because no man is perfect.

Follow the example of the living Christ who showed sympathy and understanding towards all people. It will give you great satisfaction and peace of mind to know that you are supporting someone on the difficult path of life. There can be no greater reward than to know that you are continuing with the work of the Master.

Holy and merciful Master, in Your strength I will strive to assist my fellow man in need. Amen.

Genesis 50:15-26

When he saw the crowds, he had compassion on them, because they were harassed and helpless, like sheep without a shepherd.

~ MATTHEW 9:36 ~

Compassion was an outstanding characteristic of Jesus' personality. It was a sign of His greatness, not an indication of weakness. It resided in the center of His heart and His doctrines. The Scriptures inform us that ordinary people liked to listen to Him and that they undertook long journeys to hear Him. The short notes that we have on what He did and taught in three years, reveal the depth of His wisdom and the uniqueness of His revelation of God the Father.

The spirit and disposition in which He taught not only touched people's minds, but their hearts as well. They sensed His love for them and responded by opening their hearts in love to Him. Because the eternal Christ still lives today, His compassion and sympathy are just as much a reality today as when He walked this earth. If we read the Gospels, we rejoice in the truths that He preached and our hearts are warmed by the reality of His love for us.

If life has disappointed you, or if you have failed and you are filled with despair, with no idea where to turn for inspiration and strength, remember then the compassion of Jesus. In the power of His love He encourages you to persevere and to rebuild your life.

Compassionate Master, let Your love renew my life, so that I may rejoice in Your love. Amen.

Matthew 9:32-38

"God opposes the proud but gives grace to the humble."

~ 1 PETER 5:5 ~

When you serve the Lord, humbleness is indispensable. If you believe that you are self-sufficient and do not need the strength and guidance of God, you will become spiritually ineffective. No servant of God can be used effectively if he is more aware of his own abilities than what God can do through him.

If you are humble in the presence of God, your spirit is open to instruction by the Holy Spirit of God. Such humbleness does not imply a fawning disposition, because God does not expect anybody to grovel before Him. However, it presupposes the truth of the omnipresence and omnipotence of God. He is waiting to fill the lives of those who want to welcome Him into their lives and who want to bear testimony to Him in their everyday lives.

It is a fact, however, that many disciples are unwilling to sacrifice their own thoughts and ideas and to allow God's wisdom and guidance to control their lives. They revel in their own thoughts, which could often be of a superior quality, and they refuse to allow the influence of the Holy Spirit to fill their thoughts.

When you humble yourself before God and are obedient to Him, you become His partner, and the service that you render to Him and your fellow man carries the mark of true Christlikeness. However, you know all along that it is not you who are working, but Christ that is working through you.

Good Master, grant me sincere humility so that I may truly be Your servant amongst my fellow men. Amen.

1 Peter 5:1-11

THE CHRISTIAN'S TRUST IN GOD

But as for me, I watch in hope for the LORD, I wait for God my Savior; my God will hear me.

~ MICAH 7:7 ~

The world is filled with superstitions in which people place their trust when they plan their future. Some people believe absolutely that their lives are determined by the stars, others ask the guidance of fortune-tellers and others do not do business on Friday the thirteenth. These people come from all levels of society: the poor and the rich; the uneducated and the learned.

These methods, however trustworthy they may appear at face value, are not trustworthy enough to allow us to handle the unknown. There is always the fear of uncertainty or failure, as well as the possibility that you will develop such an obsession with these things that, in the end, failure is all that you have left.

There is only one way in which you can go through life with self-confidence, and that is by believing in God. You will face problems, and when they arrive, doubt will certainly take hold of you sometimes. This is when Jesus comes to say to you, ... *"Take courage! It is I. Don't be afraid"* (Mt. 14:27). In their superstitious minds, the disciples thought that they had seen a ghost, but Christ brought them peace of mind. It is the selfsame peace that He wishes to bring to you and that He wants you to communicate to your fellow man.

Loving Savior, I place myself completely under Your control, for I know that You alone can guarantee me peace of mind. Amen.

Micah 7:1-10

November

God is Love! Our hearts rejoice,
and celebrate the power of love:
that He sent His only Son
our sins to redeem above.

~ Hymn 74:1 ~

$\mathcal{P}$rayer

LOVE FOR GOD AND YOUR FELLOW MAN

This month we worship You as the Source of all true love: from the cradle to the grave, we are carried by Your love; You encircle us, Your love takes possession of us.

More than a mother loves her children, You love us. Your love makes us strong when we are weak; gives us hope when we threaten to despair; gives us peace when our hearts are in turmoil; gives us consolation when we sorrow and are broken.

Loving God, Your love is unfathomable, undeserved and constant; it does not depend on who we are and what happens to us.

As children feel secure in their parental homes, so we feel when we are with You, Lord. When this life is over and I live in eternity with You I will cherish Your perfect love forever.

Help me Powerful Savior, to share Your love with my life's companion, my family and my neighbor.

As You give to me abundantly, let me give to others also.

I pray this for the sake of love and in the Name of Jesus.

Amen

THE SONG OF LOVE

If I speak in the tongues of men and of angels, but have not love, I am only a resounding gong or a clanging cymbal.

~ 1 CORINTHIANS 13:1 ~

This chapter unlocks all the noble qualities of love. In the preceding chapter, Paul spoke about spiritual gifts, but now he points to an even more excellent path: the path of love. He begins by saying that one can possess any spiritual gift, but if it does not bear the stamp of love, it is useless. Even the sought-after speaking in tongues was as useless as the noise of resounding gongs and clanging cymbals when unaccompanied by love. The gift of prophecy or preaching has two kinds of practitioners. There are those who attempt to save souls through hell-fire and damnation. They preach as though they would rejoice as much in the redemption as in the damnation of the sinner. Then there are those who attempt to save sinners for eternity with love and tact.

If love is not part of miracles, of sacrifice, or of our spoken and intellectual gifts, then these are useless.

The gift of intellectual excellence, without love, leads to intellectual snobbery. Knowledge lit by the fire of love, is the only kind of knowledge that can save people. Even faith without love can become a heartless and cruel thing that cuts people up and hurts them. None of these, including the gift to perform miracles, or to live ascetically, is worth anything if it does not go hand in hand with true love. There is virtually no section of the Bible that requires so much introspection as this chapter.

Lord, my God and Father, I thank You that all the love in my life is but mere stepping stones to You. Amen.

1 Corinthians 13:1-13

ᑭATIENCE, OH LONG-SUFFERING PATIENCE!

Love is patient ...

~ I Corinthians 13:4 ~

ᕮhe Greek word for "patience" as used in the New Testament, describes patience with people and not patience with circumstances. It is a word which refers to a man who has suffered an injustice and has it in his power to seek revenge, but refrains from doing so. It is patience with people that you have difficulty in loving. It describes a man who is slow to anger. It is used with regard to God Himself in His dealings with people. We must practice the same patience with people that God practices with us.

This patience is not a sign of weakness, but of strength; it is not defeat, but the only road to victory. Patience is a means to love someone you struggle to love. It is the patience of love that always conquers. Initially, nobody regarded President Lincoln with more contempt than General Stanton. He called him a "cunning clown" and a "gorilla". Lincoln never reacted, but appointed Stanton as head of the defence force because he was the best man for the job. Then came the night of the assassin's bullet in a theatre. In the small room where the president's body lay, Stanton stood with tears rolling down his cheeks, and said, "There lies one of the greatest rulers of people that the world has ever seen." Lincoln's patient love conquered him. We must also love with patience, and we will share in the victory of love.

> Lord Jesus, You were patient towards all people and I plead that, through the Holy Spirit, You will grant me that patience as well. Amen.

1 Corinthians 13:4-8

LOVE THAT IS KIND

And the Lord's servant must not quarrel; instead, he must be kind to everyone.

~ 2 TIMOTHY 2:24 ~

Interpreters of the Scriptures are in agreement that "kindness", as it is used here, means to be kind-hearted. It is the good-naturedness of love. There are so many Christians who are good people, but who are rather unkind. There are those who believe passionately in God, but would like to burn people who differ from them, at the stake. Then there are many good people who have a critical disposition. Many good Christians would have sided with the Pharisees and the Teachers of the Law against Jesus, regarding His conduct towards the woman who was caught for adultery.

The kindness of love strives for justice to prevail – towards God and towards your fellow man. In essence, faith means loyalty and reliability, and both are born from the love of God. This kindness seeks only the best for your fellow men, regardless of what they may do to you. It places all bitterness and thoughts of revenge behind you, and lives in peace with everyone. After all, this is what God expects of us.

Kind love must be the sign of Christ's followers. If we want to bear testimony to Him in this world, we will only succeed if we do so through kind Christian love. Our kindness must be known to all people; they will then start asking after the source of our kindness and, in so doing, they will find Jesus.

Lord Jesus, let my love always be accompanied by kind-heartedness, so that I may spread Your image in this world. Amen.

2 Timothy 2:14-26

The acts of the sinful nature are obvious ... hatred, discord, jealousy fits of rage.

~ GALATIANS 5:19-20 ~

Love ... does not envy.

~ 1 CORINTHIANS 13:4 ~

It is clear that spite, envy and jealousy quarrel about each other's talents and cause discord in the congregation (cf. 1 Cor. 3:3). This is still prevalent in the church of Christ today, to our shame and disgrace.

It is often said that there are only two kinds of people in this world: those that are millionaires and those who would like to be. There are two kinds of envy. The one comprises desire for the possessions of others. This envy is difficult to control because it is such a typical human weakness. The other kind is much worse: it resents the fact that other people have that which you do not have, and would dearly like to have. This jealousy does not so much imply that we would like other people's possessions, but rather that we begrudge those who possess something. Meanness of the soul cannot sink much lower than that.

If the believer succumbs to his sinful nature and does not allow himself to be guided by the Holy Spirit, all kinds of practices of this sinful nature will come to the fore: hostility, hatred, jealousy, rage, discord, disagreement, rifts and envy. It does not only happen to the ungodly, but to children of the Lord as well. The only remedy for this is love that "does not envy", but that accepts things as God has planned them for this life.

Free me, Holy Jesus, from all envy and jealousy so that I may love with impartiality as You did. Amen.

Galatians 5:13-26

LOVE FORGETS ABOUT SELF-LOVE

Knowledge puffs up, but love builds up.

~ 1 CORINTHIANS 8:1 ~

Love ... does not boast.

~ 1 CORINTHIANS 13:4 ~

Paul accuses the Corinthians of falling in with one specific teacher and then boasting about it. Time and again Paul reminds them that their knowledge drives them to boasting. That is a negative form of love which we call self-love.

True love is selfless. It would rather confess unworthiness than boast of its own achievements. Some people give their love as though they were bestowing an honor on the receiver. That is not love; that is conceit. The one who truly loves, cannot stop marveling at the fact that there is someone who loves him. Love is kept humble in the knowledge that it could never make a sufficiently worthy sacrifice for the one he loves.

This also applies to our spiritual life. We dare not accept God's love as a matter of course as though we deserved it. Such pride robs us of the blessing and spiritual growth that God has in mind for us. If people's knowledge of the Scriptures drives them to arrogance, then they are studying the Bible in vain. If we pray to be seen and heard by people, the petticoat of our arrogance is showing. If we go to church for any other personal motive than to glorify God, our church-attendance will bring us no blessing.

False modesty is another form of boasting. Langenhoven justifiably said, "I am so modest that I have become arrogant about my modesty."

Spirit of Love, keep me humble in my love, so that it does not become the cause of pride and arrogance. Amen.

1 Corinthians 8:1-13

PRIDE COMES BEFORE A FALL

"God opposes the proud but gives grace to the humble."

~ 1 PETER 5:5 ~

Love is ... not proud.

~ 1 CORINTHIANS 13:4 ~

True love is always more impressed with its own unworthiness than with its own achievement or excellence. In our text for the day, Peter is calling on younger and older members of the church to be humble towards God and towards each other. People of all ages have been called, after the example of Jesus Christ, to be washers of feet. We want to go for each other's throats, while Christ teaches us to wash each other's feet. We are called upon to help each other and to act towards one another without arrogance.

Pride is often the reason why older people refuse to listen to younger people, and why older people's advice is so easily disregarded by the younger. You must respect older people and listen to those younger than yourself. Because you are but human, you do not have a monopoly of wisdom. At all times, show that you are humble, especially towards God. Always be ready to learn from experienced, as well as less experienced, people; that is wisdom.

We must concern ourselves less with our status and position, and be less concerned about receiving acknowledgement for what we do. God's approval is worth far more than the praise of people. He will bring acknowledgement at a time destined by Him. If obedience to God requires you to be denigrated, you must accept it. In His own time God will pick you up with His powerful hand. All we need to do is to walk the path of God in humility, because there is sincere love in our hearts for Him and our neighbor.

Shield me from pride, Humble Jesus, so that I can become a washer of feet following Your example. Amen.

1 Peter 5:1-11

TRUE LOVE IS PRACTICED WITH GRACE

Love ... is not rude.

~ 1 CORINTHIANS 13:4-5 ~

Here, Paul is probably thinking about incest (5:1) that occurred in the congregation, visits to brothels (6:16) and women who worshiped without covering their heads (11:13). Other connotations can also be ascribed to the word "rude". However, the opposite of that is love that is positive, gracious, courteous and charming. This is what we must concentrate on, and not the negative.

The Greeks use the same word for "grace" and "charm". There is a kind of Christianity that takes pleasure in being abrupt and brutal. It contains power, but no charm; and love is charming. Professor Greyvenstein said to a fellow student in our final year class, who suffered sharp criticism about his probation sermon, "Wherever you go, your face will always be a sermon about love!"

There is grace, charm and elegance in Christian love which never forgets that, while courtesy and tact may be counted as lesser virtues, they are lovely byproducts of love. We must focus on practicing them when we are in the world, delivering our testimony of Christ. This kind of love will shine like a beacon in a loveless and divided world.

Lord, my God, grant that I will always practice my love with grace and that it will never offend anyone. Amen.

1 Corinthians 13:1-13

SELF-INTEREST IS THE DEATH-KNELL OF LOVE

"Whoever finds his life will lose it, and whoever loses his life for my sake will find it."

~ MATTHEW 10:39 ~

Love ... is not self-seeking.

~ 1 CORINTHIANS 13:4-5 ~

True and sincere Christian love does not insist on its rights. In the final analysis, there are only two kinds of people in this world: those who lay claim to their rights and those who think about their duties; those who always lay claim to their privileges and those who always think about their responsibilities; those who think that life owes them something and those who think that they owe life something.

People can be divided into "grabbers" and "givers". The grabbers are those who, with clenched fists and white knuckles, constantly cling to what they regard as theirs. They are dirt poor, bankrupt in love. Mercifully, we also get the givers. Those who are like the myrtle-tree on the plains that gives its lovely fragrance to the heavens, without expecting something in return.

If people were to think less about their rights and more about their obligations, it would be the key to the remedy for much of the evil in this world. Every time I think about my own interests, I drift further away from Christian love. To work behind the scenes without receiving acknowledgement for what you do, is a revelation of true Christian love.

Holy Spirit of God, help me never to show love out of own interest or selfishness, but in the way in which Christ practiced it. Amen.

Matthew 10:32-39

ℒOVE ENSURES A CONTROLLED TEMPER

Love ... is not easily angered.

~ I CORINTHIANS 13:4-5 ~

𝒫 eople who anger easily, explode easily in fury. That is not the path of true love. Love never despairs about people and does not get impatient with them. When we lose our temper, we lose everything. If all around you people lose their heads and burst out in anger, love will enable you to remain calm, to judge things properly and to make the right decision. Anger and logical, just thoughts do not go hand in hand. This is where Christian love is of immeasurable value in human relations.

The even-tempered person is not inclined to hatred and bitterness. He who is master of his temper can reach heights, enabling him to be master of anything. Our temper is an innate human characteristic and a fact to be reckoned with. However, we can channel the nature of our temper. Through the Holy Spirit, we can use it in our favor, depending on how we wish to use it. It is an important part of spiritual growth to have your temper working for you instead of against you, and here love is of immeasurable value. It calms your emotions and helps you not to be easily angered.

Lord, my God, I am so quick to anger. I plead for grace to be calm and loving, even under provocation. Amen.

1 Corinthians 13:1-13

"Therefore, if you are offering your gift at the altar and there remember that your brother has something against you, leave the gift there in front of the altar. First go and be reconciled to your brother; then come and offer your gift.

~ MATTHEW 5:23-24 ~

Love ... keeps no record of wrongs.

~ I CORINTHIANS 13:4-5 ~

ℒ ove does not hold on to every bad memory of people who transgress against it. This is a term borrowed from bookkeeping where everything is written down scrupulously for future use, especially to take revenge. That is exactly what many people do. It is one of life's great arts to know what to forget and what to remember. People often do not want to allow their hatred and thoughts of revenge to be forgotten. They become collectors of grievances and this process poisons their souls and drives the love from their hearts.

Many people cherish their anger to keep it glowing; they brood on the mistakes made against them. Then the grievance begets a whole string of little ones. Later, it becomes impossible for them to forget. Christian love taught the great lesson of forgetting *and* forgiving. If you keep record of the wrongs committed against you, you are inclined to miss the noble, good and beautiful things in life.

This takes us back to the point of departure for all of this: the ability to forgive. If you cannot forgive, you keep record of the wrongs; if you keep record of the wrongs, you gradually lose Christian love from your heart.

Holy Spirit, grant me the heavenly gift of forgiving and forgetting. Amen.

Matthew 5:21-26

LOVE AVOIDS EVIL PLEASURES

So I find this law at work: When I want to do good, evil is right there with me.

~ ROMANS 7:21 ~

Love does not delight in evil.

~ 1 CORINTHIANS 13:6 ~

Love finds no pleasure in something that is wrong or evil. The reference here is not really to pleasure which is derived from doing the wrong thing, but the vicious pleasure people derive when they hear something destructive about somebody else, whether it is true or not. This is unloving. It is one of the peculiar characteristics of human nature that we would rather hear something disastrous about others, than to hear about the good that they do.

It is possible that it is easier for us to weep with those who weep, than it is to rejoice with those who are rejoicing. We are much more interested in a disparaging story that discredits somebody, than in a story where someone is honored. Christian love possesses nothing of that true-to-type human viciousness that derives pleasure from evil rumors about our fellow men.

In Romans 7, Paul complains that this reversal of good intentions also takes place in his own life. He confesses his sorrow and spiritual struggle to out of love avoid evil and to do good. Paul's, "What a wretched man I am!" puts into words the frustration and sorrow of many believers because they do not delight in evil (cf. Rom. 7:24). But we can live in peace with God when love triumphs in our lives. Therefore, we must inextricably hold onto the salvation in Jesus Christ and His untold love that does not delight in evil.

Let me never derive pleasure from evil rumors or somebody's downfall, oh Lord. Let love triumph in my life. Amen.

Romans 7:13-25

REJOICING IN THE TRUTH

A truthful witness gives honest testimony.

~ PROVERBS 12:17 ~

Love ... rejoices with the truth.

~ 1 CORINTHIANS 13:6 ~

Without love you make many mistakes. You end up in the wrong company and start making errors of judgment. Eventually you cannot distinguish between right and wrong. The only defence against this is to allow love to discipline you. You must seek the company of loving people and learn from them. You must be willing to give love a fair chance.

Lies cause loveless rifts between people, but truthful words build bridges between them. When you care about others, you are enfolded by their love. But when you tell lies about them because you do not like them, everything starts to collapse. If your relationship with the God of love is not sound, your entire life becomes meaningless.

To rejoice in the truth is not always that easy. There are times when we really do not want the truth to triumph. Then there are also times when the truth is the last thing we want to hear. Christian love has no need for concealing the truth: it is courageous enough to listen to the truth and to deal with it. It has nothing to hide and finds happiness in the fact that truth *will* prevail. Without love, however, it is impossible to be untouched by truth and not to become panic-stricken.

Loving Lord Jesus, love and truth are inseparable. Let me always remain faithful to both. Amen.

Proverbs 12:14-28

$\mathcal{L}$OVE PROTECTS

This is love: not that we loved God, but that he loved us and sent his Son as an atoning sacrifice for our sins.

~ 1 JOHN 4:10 ~

Love ... always protects.

~ 1 CORINTHIANS 13:4, 7 ~

$\mathcal{J}$ ust as the love of God covers our sins under the mantle of His Son's suffering and death, our love should cover the mistakes of our fellow men; not because we are naïve or condone sin, but because we believe that love is the key to the sinner's salvation.

Love will never drag the mistakes of others into the open, unlovingly exposing them to public contempt. It would rather continue quietly to try to rectify things. Loving people want to make it easier for the transgressor to repent and to confess. They do not want to admonish or reprimand, because they believe that it is God's sole right to pass judgment.

It also implies that love has the ability to carry any insult, sorrow or disappointment, because we know that it is covered by the love of Christ and that His grace is abundant. It describes the kind of love that was in the heart of Jesus Himself: regardless of the hatred, insults, unfaithfulness and suffering, He did not tire of forgiving and His heart could only love. He covers our sins and beholds us in love. That is the example that we must follow in our relationships with our fellow men.

Holy Master, we so much like to expose other people's weaknesses. Let the love of Christ help us to refrain from that. Amen.

1 John 4:7-20

ℒove is the Foundation of Faith

It always protects, always trusts, always hopes, always perseveres.

~ 1 CORINTHIANS 13:7 ~

𝒯his characteristic of love has a dual meaning. In the first place, it concerns our relationship with God. Love takes God at His word and believes absolutely that I can make each of His promises my own, knowing that they are steadfast and true. This is a love born from the certainty that God exists and you can risk your life on it.

Secondly, it concerns our relationships with our fellow men. This implies a love that is always willing to believe the best about other people. It is completely true that we want people to be the way we believe that they should be. If we act as though we do not trust people and regard them with suspicion, we make them unreliable. If we act in such a way that people feel that we trust them completely, unless they are irreversibly corrupt, we turn them into reliable people through our loving protection.

We must protect our children with our love especially as we bring them to maturity and a sense of responsibility. Even when they make mistakes, we must teach them that they can become responsible adults if they use their freedom correctly. Through our loving trust in them, it will become increasingly difficult for them to lie, swear or avoid their responsibilities. They will know that, through our faith in them, they will become stronger people and, in turn, it will be easier for them to believe. In this way the spiral of faith will ripple increasingly outwards to the glory of God's love.

Holy Father and God, help me to use my freedom with love and to use the powerful qualities thereof to Your glory. Amen.

1 Corinthians 13:1-13

LOVE FILLS THE HEART WITH HOPE

Brothers, we do not want you to ... grieve like the rest of men who have no hope.

~ I THESSALONIANS 4:13 ~

Love ... always hopes.

~ I CORINTHIANS 13:6, 7 ~

Jesus believed that no man was hopeless, which is why He loved all people. Hope or despair is found in the hearts of people and not in circumstances. That is why love is so important, because love is the triumph of hope. When things are at their darkest and worst, hope appears in the shape of love to light up the dark of night. There is no room in the economy of God for despair, because He has enough love to avert despair. Hope is woven into the nature of man so that we may trust in the future.

Martin Luther maintained that everything that is done in the world, is done in hope. If the farmer does not sow in hope, he will not have hoped for a harvest. No person enters into marriage if he does not hope for a happy family life. No businessman works hard if he does not hope for fruit on his labors.

No man is able to visualize eternity, therefore God granted us hope out of love. What oxygen does for the lungs, hope does for the soul: without it we would die inwardly. When all is hopeless, then hope keeps us going. Hope is the battle of the soul to enable us to hold onto eternity and onto the love of God. If it were not for hope, we would all have had broken hearts. Praise the Lord, for He is good. His love is infinite. He gives us hope out of love.

Let me never believe that someone is hopelessly lost, because You sent Your Son out of love to save the lost, oh Lord. Amen.

1 Thessalonians 4:13-18

ꕷRIUMPHANT RESIGNATION

I have learned to be content whatever the circumstances.

~ PHILIPPIANS 4:11 ~

Love ... always perseveres.

~ I CORINTHIANS 13:4, 7 ~

ꕷ he Greek word that is used here can be translated as "endure" or "bear". The spirit does not remain passive and endure things without being moved. It is the characteristic of a great spirit to endure adversity and conquer. Your only support in this victory is love.

George Matheson, the author of a number of famous hymns, lost his sight and also experienced disappointment in love. In one of his prayers, he writes that he prays to accept God's will, not only in silent surrender, but with holy joy; not only with the absence of a complaint, but with a song of praise. Love can endure anything, not with passive sullenness, but with triumphant tolerance because he *knows* that God is Love and that the Father's hand will never be responsible for a single tear that falls from the eye of His child.

Paul accepts the Philippians' contribution to support him financially because they gave in the spirit of love and because he sees God's care in it. However, he has learnt to be content whatever the circumstances. That was because he experienced God's love in his life and that enabled him to endure all things. We must trust in God's love, wisdom and promises. He will provide for all your needs in a way that He knows is best. We only need to learn to persevere in love, regardless of what may cross our path.

Holy God, let me accept Your will in joyous obedience and not with muttering dissatisfaction. Amen.

Philippians 4:10-20

Love is Immortal

Love is as strong as death ... Many waters cannot quench love; rivers cannot wash it away.

~ Song of Songs 8:6-7 ~

Love never fails.

~ 1 Corinthians 13:8 ~

Here Paul is emphasising the eternal permanence of love. When all the things that people pride themselves in have passed, love will still be constant. The author of Song of Songs emphasises it in poetic fashion, "Love is as strong as death." Love is powerful. There is nothing that man is more certain of than death, because it ends all. It seems as though it reigns above all, and yet, death can be conquered by love. He is not talking about erotic love here, but love as devotion to the loved one. Such love frees one from the fear of death. Therefore, we are even willing to sacrifice our lives for our loved ones.

Love conquers the pain of death. In our case, God's love will also conquer death. By comparing love to a blazing fire that cannot be quenched by many waters, it is contrasted with the power of chaos. Love also conquers chaos. It is priceless, because one cannot buy it. The highest point of our worldly existence is when we discover the love that wards off the fear of death.

Love is the one great thing that allows us to believe in immortality. When love has entered a life, you begin a relationship against which the onslaughts of time are powerless and that rises above death. God is immortal and God is love; therefore love is immortal.

Thank You Lord God, that love is immortal because You are Love. Let me share in that immortality through the ability to love. Amen.

Songs of Songs 8:5-13

LOVE IS COMPLETE AND PERFECT

When I became a man, I put childish ways behind me.

~ I CORINTHIANS 13:11 ~

Paul says that the things we see now, are but a reflection in a mirror. The Corinthians would have liked this image, because they were famous for the manufacturing of mirrors. However, the modern mirror, with its perfect image, only made its appearance during the thirteenth century. The Corinthians made mirrors out of highly polished steel that, at best, reflected a very poor image.

Paul says that our lives are but a mere reflection of God and we struggle with many things that feel to us like mysteries and riddles. We see that reflection in the work of God's creation, because the work of someone's hands tells us something about the worker. We see that reflection in the Gospel and we see it in Jesus Christ. Even though we see the perfect revelation of God in Christ, our searching mind can only understand it in part because the temporal can never understand the eternal. Our knowledge is still like that of a child. But the road of love will lead us to the day when we will see God face to face and we will know Him as He knows us. We cannot reach that day without love; only those who truly love will see God.

However, we must keep in mind that God already knows *us* in full. He knows whether there is love for Him and for our fellow man in our hearts. To discover that love is complete, revealing and perfect, is one of the highlights of our spiritual growth.

May the world behold in me the reflection of Your Love every day. Amen.

1 Corinthians 13:8-13

ℒOVE IS THE GREATEST OF ALL

These three remain: faith, hope and love. But the greatest of these is love.

~ 1 CORINTHIANS 13:13 ~

ℐn the last verse of this chapter, Paul calls love the greatest of the three things that we must pursue in this life. That is because love is the only one that crosses over into the time that begins with Jesus' return: eternity. Then we will receive the prize for our love, because we will see God face to face. We will no longer have to hope, because the best for which we can hope will then be a glorious reality: *"No eye has seen, no ear has heard, no mind has conceived what God has prepared for those who love him"* (1 Cor. 2:9).

Parents teach their children to talk because they "believe" that their children have this ability. Because they "hope" that their children will speak well one day, they persevere in the instruction process. They do it because they "love" their children. When their children have reached these ideals, faith and hope fall away, but love remains.

Paul emphasizes the absolute supremacy of love. As important as hope and faith may be; love is the greatest. Faith without love is a cold, merciless thing; hope without love is unrelenting. Love is the fire that ignites faith and the light that transforms hope into certainty. Praise the Lord, because He is good! His Love is without end.

"God who is Love, we acknowledge the supremacy of love because we acknowledge You." Amen.

1 Corinthians 13:1-13

The LORD is my rock, my fortress and my deliverer; my God is my rock, in whom I take refuge. He is my shield and the horn of my salvation, my stronghold.

~ PSALM 18:2 ~

A ll people need a shelter at some time. It may be the security of your own home, or a shelter against the wind and rain. In times of war, shelter is sought against falling bombs. But a bomb-attack, rough weather and other forms of attack are not limited to our physical being. Our spiritual and intellectual faculties are often attacked by the storms of life. In order to seek shelter against these and to prevent devastating emotional consequences, we all need a haven in life that will be constant and safe and where we can shelter in complete faith.

Regardless of what may happen to you, and the seriousness of the situation in which you may find yourself, place your trust and faith in God at all times. Even when it seems as though everything is lost and your world collapses around you like a stack of cards, entrust yourself to the love of Jesus Christ. God has promised never to fail you nor forsake you. With this certainty in your heart, you can face the future with confidence. With the newly-found self-confidence that the Holy Spirit grants you, you will know that, regardless of how dark the road ahead may seem, Christ, with His love, is your shelter and safe haven. Where, in this whole wide world, could one feel safer?

Thank You, my Lord and my God, that I may take shelter in You and that I may be safe for time and eternity. Amen.

Psalm 18:1-16

⊘HE CRUCIAL POWER OF LOVE

"You have let go of the commands of God and are holding on to the traditions of men."

~ MARK 7:8 ~

℟ ituals and traditions have always played an important role in the affairs of men. This is especially true in the church, where congregational life and practices are to a large extent controlled by the church ordinance and liturgy, the existence of which is attributable to human reasoning. While it is essential, for the sake of order, that any group of people must adhere to rules so that everything can be run fairly, it is of the utmost importance that these things do not become a dominating factor in any Christian community.

The foundation of any denomination or congregation must be absolute surrender, devotion and obedience to God. It must be born from pure love for Him. Jesus Christ must be the central figure in all things and His will and wishes must get preference, as opposed to the will of people, regardless of how well meaning the latter may be.

In order to be a channel of the love of God, you must surrender yourself unconditionally to the influence and guidance of the Holy Spirit. If you surrender yourself to Christ, you will also be able to identify man-made rules with the wisdom of the Holy Spirit and to implement them in the love of God. In this way, you will be able to serve yourself and your community according to God's will, and in love.

Holy Spirit, bring me to total surrender, devotion and obedience to the God of Love. Amen.

Mark 7:1-13

GOD LOVES YOU DEARLY

"I have loved you," says the LORD. But you ask, "How have you loved us?"

~ MALACHI 1:2 ~

People who have been hurt or broken by life, have a problem in acknowledging that God is a God of love. This is especially true when they have suffered a tragic loss or received devastatingly bad news; especially about someone they love. In such circumstances they have serious doubts about the all-embracing love of God. If these doubts are not allayed, they could have a serious and negative influence on their faith.

You must remember that the love of God is boundless and infinite. It is a love that knows no limits and that is unconditional. It is an eternal love, in comparison to our love that is of a passing nature. His love and care for us is based on that which is good for us, not only now, but in the future as well.

If you do an honest analysis of the setbacks of life, you will discover that these always happen as a result of man's foolishness and that no blame can be attached to the Lord. Nevertheless, the extent of His love is so infinite that the living Christ is by your side in every situation of life, and He waits to support and help you; to console you; to help you overcome stumbling blocks and to be your Shepherd until you sit down at the feast of the Lamb in the House of the Lord. His love is infinite.

Thank You, God of love, that I will sit down one day at the feast of the Lamb, because I love You and You love me. Amen.

Malachi 1:1-9

LOVE IS THE KEY

"If anyone loves me, he will obey my teaching. My Father will love him, and we will come to him and make our home with him."

~ JOHN 14:23 ~

There are people who prefer lingering on the fringes of Christianity, instead of becoming surrendered Christians. They refer to apparent contradictions in the Word of God, or to the failure of a stumbling Christian. They then declare out loud that, unless all Christians become saints, and unless they get acceptable answers to their questions, they are not willing to embrace the Christian faith. Because the conditions that they set are unattainable, such people never become Christians.

Christians are sinners who are becoming saints in the New Testament meaning of the Word. They do not maintain that they are perfect, but they follow Christ and attempt to become like Him. They are not alone in this pursuit, because the Savior is with them, constantly inspiring and comforting them. His love for His fallible disciples transcends human understanding, but it does engender in them a spirit of love for Him that broadens their vision and gives them a better understanding of His ways.

The works of God can, to a slight degree, be analysed by scientists; the beauty of His creation can inspire artists; theologians can attempt to fathom the profundity and mystery surrounding Him. But only a great and passionate love for Him can understand His holy character. Love is the key that unlocks the door to the Most High who reveals Himself to the worshiping souls of His loving disciples.

Lord, You know everything. You know that I love You. Amen.

John 14:15-31

"As the Father has loved me, so I loved you. Now remain in my love."

~ JOHN 15:9 ~

It is a disturbing thought that you could lose your awareness of the love the Master has for you. It is a Scriptural truth that the Master loves His disciples, but how often do you wake up in the morning and thank Him for that love by telling Him how much you love Him? It is an inspiration for the day to wake up and profess, "I sincerely love You, oh Lord!"

The living Christ promised that when you realize your dependence on Him, you would be able to do things that are simply beyond your ability. You can never realize your full potential before you are united with Him in love. He reminds you that, without Him, you can do nothing, but by remaining in Him, your horizons are broadened and your strength increased.

It is a serious tragedy that many Christians attempt to serve the Lord without the indispensable love that they should have for Him. They are active in Christian service, but the inspiration of the love for God and their fellow men is still lacking. The Master has harsh words for these people. He says that anyone that does not remain in Him, will be separated from Him. He does not bring about the separation; they do so themselves through their lack of love.

Develop an ever-increasing love for Jesus Christ so that you will be drawn closer to Him and become aware of His living presence.

Savior and Master, let me never lose the awareness of Your love, but may it always remain fresh and sparkling. Amen.

John 15:9-17

DO NOT BE AFRAID TO DEMONSTRATE LOVE

Now about brotherly love we do not need to write to you, for you
yourselves have been taught by God to love each other.

~ 1 THESSALONIANS 4:9 ~

There are many people who are reluctant to reveal their deepest
feelings. They appear to be cold and introverted. They are afraid
of being misunderstood and revealing an aspect of their nature that
they would rather keep hidden. This is sad, because so many unex-
pressed emotions, that could have enriched the world, remain
slumbering in their personalities.

The greatest constructive emotion is love, but it is often hidden in
the human spirit. There are many married couples who, since their
days of courting, have never affirmed their love for another. There are
more broken and aching hearts than we realize because the short phrase,
"I love you," is never or seldom expressed.

One of the characteristics of true love is expressing appreciation
through your love. It takes so little to say it out loud, and yet, it brings
so much joy to both giver and receiver. Love can be demonstrated in a
variety of practical ways. It can rise above mere sentimental emotion
and enable you to make a way of life out of it that can enrich the lives
of your loved ones. It is the experience of many people that a life that
is filled with declared love can be fulfilling and practical. Why don't
you start today?

> Holy God, I thank You that You have taught me what brotherly love
> is. Help me to demonstrate it every day of my life. Amen.

1 Thessalonians 4:1-12

DEVELOP THE POTENTIAL OF LOVE

No one has ever seen God; but if we love one another, God lives in us and his love is made complete in us.

~ 1 JOHN 4:12 ~

The challenges of Christian love are often so big that we erect stumbling blocks before they progress too far into our lives. It is true that you, as a Christian, are willing to love up to a certain point, but then excuses are made that to love is too demanding and impractical. Sometimes we reach the point where we say, "This is where I stop practicing Christian love." Whether or not you concede that there is such a point in your life, the majority of Christians will acknowledge that they have at some time reached that point.

That is when you find yourself in a situation where you have to acknowledge with honesty, "Here I cannot give love." That is when the true test of your faith begins. This test may occur in any facet of your complex life. You may move in social circles where you meet difficult people, and in your religious world there may be people from whom you differ. Even in issues of color and race your love may not always be sufficiently far-reaching. In many other aspects of life, your love may disappoint in important matters.

It is when you feel that you can no longer give unconditional love, that you need a more profound concept of God's love. The Holy Spirit will guide you past pride, prejudice and small-mindedness to a place where you can enter into a deeper relationship with the living Christ, and where you can love freely and without restriction.

Holy Spirit, thank You that You enable me to love, even when I think it to be impossible. Continue Your work in my life to the glory of God. Amen.

1 John 4:7-21

ℒOVE CAN ACCOMPLISH A BREAKTHROUGH

How great is the love the Father has lavished on us, that we should be called children of God! And that is what we are!

~ 1 JOHN 3:1 ~

In spite of appearances, the majority of people want to receive love. They may be abrupt to a point of rudeness; they may state that they are not interested in the opinion of others and reject all signs of close relationships and love, friendship and assistance. But it is exactly this disposition that conceals the great need to receive love. The majority of people will turn away, reluctant to offer loving advice because of rebuffs and rudeness from such people. They do not want to be involved in a relationship where they could get hurt.

As a Christian, you may hesitate when encountering stumbling blocks that are erected by a difficult person. You may be tempted to ignore that person, but the fact that you have been created in the image of God and that God loves him, bars you from doing so. The ability to appreciate the good in others is the first step towards understanding them. To approach them in a condemning and an I-am-holier-than-thou disposition, only worsens the problem and you will never understand them.

The Eternal Father requires of you to demonstrate your love for Him by loving others. Every disposition of love towards others results in a free flowing of love to you. By offering your love, you will find a path to the heart and life of the most difficult of people. Allow God to love people through you. Tolerance and understanding create the right relationships and you will grow together in Christ.

Lord Jesus, let no stumbling block make me unable to give love. Stand by me in this through Your Holy Spirit. Amen.

1 John 3:1-10

"I have made you known to them, and will continue to make you known in order that the love you have for me may be in them and that I myself may be in them."

~ JOHN 17:26 ~

T he fact that Jesus requests His disciples to practice the ministry of love amongst all people, may cause a feeling of uneasiness in you. It is not that you differ from Jesus; on the contrary, you are in full agreement with Him because you know how great the need for love in this world really is. However, you doubt your own ability to meet the demands that Jesus makes on your love. You would be only too glad to have the depth and quality of the love that the Master requires of you, so that you can represent Him in joy and gratitude. But you are aware that you lack such a love and therefore you turn away from His challenge in sorrow and secretly feel that He asks more than you can give.

Christ never asks the impossible; the difficult yes, but never the impossible. If He asks you to love, He expects you to start loving wherever you may find yourself. You may feel that your love is of an inferior quality and hopelessly insufficient, but devote it to Him and implement it in practice. At first you may feel like a hypocrite, but persevere in sharing the little bit of love that you do have. Before long you will realize that, through the power of the Holy Spirit, His Divine love overshadows and increases your small and insufficient love and you will feel the love of God flowing through you.

Dear Lord Jesus, thank You that You came to make known the love of God to us. Enable us to communicate it to others so that the world may come to know You. Amen.

John 17:13-26

ℒOVE CAN RULE THE WORLD

All of you, live in harmony with one another; be sympathetic, love as brothers, be compassionate and humble.

~ 1 PETER 3:8 ~

The world is filled with the noise of accusations and counter-accusations. Nation against nation; organization against organization; person against person. The turbulent noise of the music of war hangs heavily over virtually all countries. Aggressive dispositions come to the fore and become the rule rather than the exception.

There is not much that ordinary people can do to suddenly calm down the world. However, it is the duty of every Christian to start somewhere. You must start in the neighborhood where you live and work. It costs nothing to be courteous and friendly, obliging and kindly. It is not difficult to offer sympathy to someone who is heavily burdened with problems. That is what Christian love is all about: to care about others.

If you are willing to allow Jesus to use you in the service of your fellow men, you can make an enormous impact on your environment. If everyone would be willing to do this, love can rule the world. All things are possible with God. Open your life to His Holy Spirit and start serving others with love. *You* could be the beginning of a flood of love that will submerge the world.

Lord God, let Your love submerge the world and rule it by conquering the hearts of people. Amen.

1 Peter 3:1-12

Do you show contempt for the riches of his kindness, tolerance and patience, not realizing that God's kindness leads you towards repentance?

~ ROMANS 2:4 ~

It is only when you take note of all the evil in the world and take into consideration the changing disposition of man, that you become aware of the full extent of God's love. People ignore Him, they forget His manifestations of grace, they are disobedient to Him, they rebel against Him and they blame Him when things go wrong in their lives. Nevertheless, in His love, God sent Christ to live amongst people and to die for them so that they could rest assured of salvation and eternal life.

It is highly improbable that any human being would have tolerated the attitude that mankind displays towards God, and still persevere in infinite love as God does towards His people. That is what one starts to appreciate as the true meaning of the Christian faith. Christianity is the only religion rooted in the great love of God that transcends our understanding.

Acknowledge His gracious acceptance of you as His child. Surrender yourself unconditionally to His Son. Follow Him and live life to the full as He offers it to you (cf. Jn. 10:10).

Praise the Lord, because He is good. His love is infinite.

God of Love, thank You that Your love and grace enabled me to find You. I surrender myself in renewed mutual love to You. Amen.

Romans 2:1-11

December

"Glory to God in the highest, and on earth peace to men on whom his favor rests."

~ Luke 2:14 ~

Prayer

Emmanuel! We worship You in Jesus Christ as "God with us!" Therefore we rejoice and celebrate Christmas.

Help us to approach this Feast with the right attitude:

Purify our spirit of all hatred and bitterness;

Cleanse us of all sin through the blood of the Lamb;

Let every gift be accompanied by sincere love, as You gave Yourself as a gift to the unsaved world.

Let every greeting card be a statement of our sincere faith in You.

Let us listen to the old, nostalgic Christmas melodies with new ears, and let Your eternal Word of the Gospel touch our hearts in benevolence.

Grant that Christmas will once again bring reconciliation between God and man, so that every man will call You "Father!"

Grant reconciliation among men as well, so that true peace may come to this world. Let the peace of which the angels sang not merely remain an idle dream or impossible ideal, but let it become a glorious reality through our faith. Thank You for happiness in the family, for the strengthening of bonds between friends, for goodwill amongst people.

Let the miracle of Christmas live on in our hearts when we return to our everyday life, to our everyday duties, our anxieties and responsibilities.

We pray this in the Name of Him of Whom the angels sang: "Glory to God in the highest, and on earth peace to men on whom his favor rests" (Lk. 2:14).

Amen

ℱEAST FOR THE WORLD!

"Do not be afraid. I bring you good news of great joy that will be for all the people."

~ LUKE 2:10 ~

ℱor many people, the mere thought of embracing Jesus and allowing Him into their lives, fills them with an overwhelming feeling of incompetence and unworthiness. The understanding which they link to Christlikeness, results in such fear and anxiety, that many turn away from Jesus. They simply cannot accept the consequences of complete surrender to Him.

Conditions today do not differ in the least from those on the night of Jesus' birth. Just as the angels brought the disciples *"good news of great joy that will be for all the people"*, the presence of the living Christ will bring the greatest joy that you have ever experienced to your life.

The advent of Jesus Christ in your life is the good news of Christmas. Remember that, when appearing to the shepherds, the angels announced the birth as good news of great joy "that will be for all the people". As Christ sacrificed Himself out of love and grace for you, you should not allow fear or anxiety to rob you of the opportunity to make an offer in return. Then you will get to know Him as Savior, Redeemer, Master and Friend. Embrace Christ as the Lord of your life and experience the joy that the angels announced for all people. Then your life will become a feast, the Feast of Christ!

Lord Jesus, Your advent in our divided world is the steadfast proof that God loves us and cares for us. We praise and thank You for that. Amen.

Luke 2:8-20

$\mathcal{F}$EAST OF PEACE

"Peace I leave with you; my peace I give you. I do not give to you as the world gives. Do not let your hearts be troubled and do not be afraid."

~ JOHN 14:27 ~

$\mathcal{I}$n a world where we seem to teeter on the brink of war, where scientific progress and man's abuse of it seem to lead to destruction, it seems naively idealistic to talk about peace. But peace is one of the gifts that God offers us, through Jesus Christ, with every Feast of Christ. It is an eternal truth that all who love and serve God will experience that peace in their personal lives.

The peace of God is a precious treasure in this transitory world. Those to whom it belongs do not escape the problems and sorrows of life, but they know that they possess something more precious than the spirit of the times in which we live. Possessing the Holy Spirit of Jesus of Bethlehem, enables them to keep their balance in all circumstances.

Christ's peace is not a passive quality that shuts your eyes to harsh reality, but it creates a positive approach to life, based on the belief in the trustworthiness of God. If you possess this peace, Advent is a time of festivity!

Praise the Lord! Jesus, You came to bring peace. Thank You for the peace of this glorious truth ruling in my own heart. Amen.

John 14:15-31

⊘HE HUMBLE HOST OF THE FEAST

And there were shepherds living out in the fields nearby, keeping watch over their flocks at night.

~ Luke 2:8 ~

⊘he emperor or governor did not know about it; King Herod and the chief priests did not know about it; but through His angels, God sent the message of the birth of His Son to simple shepherds: the Prince of Peace has been born in a stable in Bethlehem! There was no fanfare of trumpets or beating of drums to acknowledge that the Son of God had been born. This occasion received no publicity, even though it was the greatest event in the history of mankind.

In a way that typified His life here on earth, the arrival in the world of the Host of the eternal feast was quiet and simple. The first to know about it were the poor, the illiterate, the shepherds who lived in the fields and watched over their flock in the cold of the winter night. The events surrounding that night of the birth of Christ speak volumes about the humbleness and simplicity of Jesus Christ. These were characteristics that would distinguish Him throughout His life here on earth.

During Advent, allow God to transform you into the image of Christ, so that, in this festive season, and throughout the year, you will reflect His character and, in so doing, contribute to peace and stability in a torn world.

Preserve me from pride Lord, otherwise I might deny You a home. Amen.

Luke 2:8-20

Always be prepared to give an answer to everyone who asks you to give the reason for the hope that you have.

~ 1 Peter 3:15 ~

Since the birth of Christ, ages have passed and, regardless of a stubborn, disobedient and loveless mankind, He is still the same Savior. God who became man, was born in a humble stable in Bethlehem. The world today is the same as it was in the time before His birth. Man still tramples on the truth in order to achieve his own selfish objectives.

Under different circumstances, we would have threatened to lose hope altogether, but as the year hurtles to a close, the blessed Feast of Christ comes to remind us that Jesus came to this world to save sinners. Regardless of the despondency and despair surrounding us, a beacon of love is shining – the Light of the world – who invites us to leave the darkness behind, put our hope in Him and face the future with hope in our hearts.

Advent should remind us, time and again, that, notwithstanding that which we have to suffer, and regardless of what is threatening us, Christ is our hope for the future, as He has been for His children through the ages. We have the assurance in our hearts that nothing can separate us from the love of God in Christ Jesus. In this hope we celebrate.

Lord Jesus of Bethlehem, thank You that You came to place hope in our hearts and our lives. Amen.

1 Peter 3:13-22

$\mathcal{O}$HE FEAST IS ANNOUNCED WITH A STAR

When they saw the star, they were overjoyed.

~ MATTHEW 2:10 ~

$\mathcal{O}$ here is a very special quality about Christmas that creates a feeling of joy, goodwill and peace in our hearts. The miracle lies in the fact that, since the day of Christ's birth, people of all races have experienced this joy, regardless of all the changes that have taken place in the world.

Jesus came as a light to a dark world. The light of the star guided people to the manger so that they could behold their Savior with joy. In spite of continuous attacks by the forces of evil, who tried to extinguish the light and lead His followers into darkness, the Star of Bethlehem is still shining to lighten your path through the darkness of temptation and enticement, and to bring you to the path that leads to God. There, in a stable in a little bed of straw, you see how God, through the hand of a baby, invites people to return to Him.

On entering the festive season and continuing your journey through life, determine your course by fastening your eyes upon the Savior of the world, your Guiding Star to peace and goodwill, the shining Morning Star, *This is the message we have heard from him and declare to you: God is light; in him there is no darkness at all* (1 Jn. 1:5).

Star of Bethlehem, thank You that you also led me to the Little Child. Amen.

Matthew 2:1-12

LET JESUS TRANSFORM YOUR LIFE INTO A FEAST

Noah was a righteous man, blameless among the people of his time, and he walked with God.

~ GENESIS 6:9 ~

The quality of your life depends largely upon the company in which you feel at home. The large majority of people, unless they have a very strong willpower, are influenced to a greater or lesser extent by the people with whom they associate. Children follow the example of their parents; teachers shape the lives and opinions of their learners; friends and business associates have a major influence on you and your approach to life.

Psychologists often trace the cause of a particular characteristic or behavior to somebody who, through a strong personality, has a dominating influence on a person. The results of these influences could be either detrimental or beneficial, should they be allowed to dominate the life of that person.

However, there is one influence that will only bring the good in your life to the fore, and that is the influence of the Holy Spirit of Christ when you embrace Him as the role-model in your life. Because Jesus is the personification of God's love, it is self-evident that we will find in Him everything that is praiseworthy, true, noble, right, pure, lovely and virtuous: all the components to start the festive season in your life. Take Him as your example and your life will be blessed with a quality that could only come from God.

Thank You, Lord Jesus, that You came to give me quality of life when You were born in Bethlehem. Amen.

Genesis 6:5-22

THE SECRET OF A FESTIVE LIFE

Always give thanks to God the Father for everything, in the name of our Lord Jesus Christ.

~ EPHESIANS 5:20 ~

It is not simply a superficial, poetic thought when we maintain that, in every life, there is hidden something special and Divine, if only we had eyes to see it. It is a fact that, if Christ abides in you through faith, you develop a keener appreciation of the beauty and depth that are hidden in the life of your fellow men, as well as in the world around you.

If you, as far as you are able, live in the Spirit of Jesus Christ, then inspired observation is one of the results. Then there will be no room for lamentations in your life; and the greater your appreciation, the more life will reveal its hidden treasures to you. As the prophet says, ... *To comfort all who mourn, and provide for those who grieve in Zion – to bestow on them a crown of beauty instead of ashes, the oil of gladness instead of mourning, and a garment of praise instead of a spirit of despair ...* (Is. 61:2, 3).

The example of the ten lepers of whom only one came back to thank Jesus, is proof that Jesus regards appreciation as important. When you read the Scriptures, you cannot miss the fact that there is a continuous resounding, triumphant note of gratitude. It is simply an expression of appreciation towards God for all His blessings. God is your Father and you must love Him for His own sake and not for His blessings. He is infinitely patient and His dealings with us are so merciful. How can you withhold your appreciation for all the good things that He gives you?

You come closest to God when you praise and glorify Him, showing your appreciation; then He becomes a reality in your life and your life becomes a feast.

Thank You, Lord Jesus, that Christmas reminds me every year that You have granted me a grateful heart for Your love and gifts. Amen.

Ephesians 5:6-20

ℋOW WILL YOU PREPARE FOR THE FEAST?

For to us a child is born, to us a son is given, and the government will be on his shoulders. And he will be called Wonderful Counselor, Mighty God, Everlasting Father, Prince of Peace.

~ ISAIAH 9:6 ~

During this time of the year, especially in the Western world, people are preparing for the "holiday season". It is a time when things in the academic and business world are gradually coming to a standstill. Christmas is approaching. Families get involved in spending sprees and there is the prospect of pleasure, joy and merry-making on a large scale.

We do not want to condemn such activities at all. We just must not forget that it is also the blessed time of Advent. It is a time in which to prepare ourselves, not for parties or panicky shopping expeditions, but to celebrate, because the Savior of the world was born and we want to celebrate it with joy, and with holy zeal. We must reflect on the reason of His coming to this sin-drenched world. We must once again examine our spiritual life, humbly standing before God, asking Him to make us worthy, through the work of His Holy Spirit, to celebrate this feast.

It is an overwhelming thought that God bent down and took it upon Himself to come and live amongst us as a Man. May it be the foremost thought in your heart and in your celebrations during the days of Advent.

Holy Jesus, prepare our hearts so that we may celebrate Christmas in a worthy manner. Amen.

Isaiah 9:1-6

⟋HERE WAS NO ROOM FOR
THEM, BUT THE FEAST CONTINUED

She gave birth to her firstborn, a son. She wrapped him in cloths and placed him in a manger, because there was no room for them in the inn.

~ LUKE 2:7 ~

⟋he foundation of a healthy family life is the secure knowledge of commitment to one another. A lack of security of this nature could result in discord, instability, and probably even broken relationships.

One would have expected a similar uncertainty developing in the lives of Joseph and Mary during the birth of Jesus Christ. However, it did not, for the simple reason that their faith in God was strong and they knew that, regardless of how difficult things may become, He was always with them and He would never forsake them.

During Advent there are, without a doubt, many people who feel lonely, insecure, unloved and abandoned. Things may not be going well in their lives and they may be living in difficult conditions. There may be those who feel rejected because of guilt that isolates them from the warmth of a friendship circle.

While preparing yourself for Christmas, remember that He was called Emmanuel: God with us! Whatever problems you may have and whatever circumstances you may be experiencing, never forget that God is with you. In these days, cling to His promise that He will never leave you nor forsake you. Strengthened by this promise, open your heart to receive the blessing of Christmas.

Father God, help me to be hospitable and accessible to those who feel lonely, insecure and unloved. Amen.

Luke 2:1-7

But the angel said to her, "Do not be afraid, Mary, you have found favor with God."

~ LUKE 1:30 ~

The Scriptures teach us repeatedly that God is no respecter of persons and therefore all people are equal before God. He shares His love equally with all who acknowledge Christ's sovereignty in their lives and who have embraced Him as their Savior. They may all enjoy the joy and privilege of His abiding Holy Spirit. God shares His love with all people.

There were some great Biblical characters who found favor with God and it would seem that God was partial towards them and that they were elevated above their fellow men. However, God has no favorites. He is indeed selective, and when He lays His hand upon someone for a special task or service, He also gives the accompanying responsibility. He expects loyalty which is revealed in humble love and devotion.

Through the responsibility placed on her, Mary revealed the quality of her life and her devotion to the heavenly Father. As far as it is known, she led a quiet life somewhere in the hills of Judea, unknown, except to her family. And yet, she was chosen above all women as God's instrument through which He would reveal Himself to the world.

Your love for and devotion to God may seem unimportant, but if you offer Him your very best, He will use you in His own unique way. Then you will experience the feast of God's grace.

I praise and thank You, Father, that You reveal yourself time and again to me during this festive season. Use me as an instrument to spread Your love through the world. Amen.

Luke 1:26-38

FESTIVE SEASON OF THE SOUL

"Today in the town of David a Savior has been born to you; he is Christ the Lord."

~ LUKE 2:11 ~

During Advent the world is filled with all sorts of divergent sounds. If you listen with your outer ear, you will hear festive songs, bells, laughter and, now and again, a sob of sorrow and loneliness. If you listen with your inner ear, you will hear the angels, the quiet of inner expectation and the sanctified sound of profound silence. You will hear the pulsating whisper of the Eternal Word that became Flesh in Jesus Christ. Through His boundless grace, the Word also becomes flesh in you in these times.

The world is filled with symbols of Christmas. If you look with your outer eye, you will see gift-laden trees telling a story which they probably would not understand themselves, of gilded stars, burning candles and a manger. If you look with your inner eye, you will see the Star of Bethlehem in your own heart; you will see the manger in your own soul, surrounded by the radiant glory of Christ's presence, newly born, and always reborn in you when you radiate His love.

Bethlehem is here and now and always; it is a region of the soul. Advent is here and now and always; it is the season of the soul. You will certainly look at the external things that you see and listen to the external things that you hear, but through His grace, you will also see with the inner eye and hear with the inner ear, and listen with festive joy to the silent Word that became flesh.

Savior and Friend of sinners, thank You for this season of the soul when we may listen to the soundless Word that became flesh. Amen.

Luke 2:8-20

SLOW DOWN – IT IS THE FESTIVE SEASON!

He leads me beside quiet waters, he restores my soul.

~ Psalm 23:2-3 ~

Ageing people often feel that they no longer understand the world. Their grandchildren talk computer language and use confusing abbreviations. Time passes with breathtaking speed and it seems as though everyone is in a panicky haste. Heavy demands are made on the average person to keep up and demands are made on his time from all sides.

Unfortunately, the speed with which we live causes our spiritual life to go to rack and ruin. We struggle to meet the demands of life, to balance the household books, to maintain a social life, and a number of items of a personal nature demand our attention with a speed that does not allow us to slow down and pay attention to spiritual matters.

To be living in continuous haste, is to live under pressure. This is not beneficial to you, nor to those who live with you. With this realization, comes the knowledge of the important role of your spiritual life. If your Christianity does not help you to slow down, and enable you to have a positive and living faith in God, the time has come to take stock of your faith once again in this time of Advent.

The Master often took His disciples to one side in order to take them away from the pressure of the masses and to spend time in prayer. Learn to slow down and, in doing so, allow God the time to reveal His will to you through the Holy Spirit.

Good Shepherd of my life, help me to slow down in this festive season so that I may become quiet in You. Amen.

Psalm 23:1-6

FAITH TRANSFORMS DEPRESSION INTO A FEAST

"But for you who revere my name, the sun of righteousness will rise with healing in its wings."

~ MALACHI 4:2 ~

Depression and pessimism are soul-destroying conditions of the spirit. Apart from the fact that they are conditions of the mind, they could also influence your physical and spiritual welbeing. They limit your vision of the future and your general disposition towards life is negatively influenced. The causes are too manifold to name, but they include fear, anxiety, financial instability and loneliness.

You may attempt to ward off this condition through manmade plans or temporary solutions, but they will not last. Sooner or later the value of these aids will decline and the condition will return, but in a more severe form.

The only way of combating such emotional disturbance is to open your life to Christ's love and positive influence. Acknowledge Him as the Lord of your life and place yourself in His healing care. This will require you to show faith, but if Jesus has taken control of your life and is showing you the path that He wants you to follow, you will discover that, through your obedience to Him, you will be filled with a spirit of self-confidence and well-being that only the Christ Child can provide. Then you are transformed to form part of the Feast in Christ!

Lord Jesus Christ, thank You that I can unload my tension and stress on You. Thank You that You heal all my diseases. Amen.

Malachi 4:1-6

YOUR HOST AT THE FEAST

Let us run with perseverance the race marked out for us. Let us fix our eyes on Jesus, the author and perfecter of our faith.

~ HEBREWS 12:1-2 ~

There are few people who caused more discussion and discord than Jesus Christ, and yet there is no man who generated more sacrificial love than He did. People preferred to die rather than to deny His Sovereignty in their lives. Others, yet again, took His simple though profound message of love and used it to create theories that confuse ordinary people and cloud their vision of the reality of the Savior in their lives.

Regardless of what denomination of Jesus Christ you may adhere to, it is wise to remember His holy simplicity. When He spoke to ordinary people, He used images with which they could identify. If He spoke about a rebellious son who returned to his father, they understood what He meant, and thus came to a new relationship of love with God. He took the simple things in life, using them to reveal the various characteristics of God.

If, at this moment, you are confused about the large number of different denominations that are propagated by people in the Name of Jesus, compare what they say to the way that they live. Is it based on sacrificial love? Do they respect the doctrine and persons of fellow believers who embrace other theological interpretations of His words? Does your doctrine represent a life of challenging changes, or are you caught up in tunnel vision about matters of faith that leave no room for change?

True Christianity, based on the life and love of our Host at Christmas, does not differentiate between theory and practice. Love must manifest itself in practice, otherwise it is hypocrisy.

Jesus Christ, thank You that You enable us to run the race of life successfully and to receive from You the crown of life. Amen.

Hebrews 12:1-12

ꞇRUST IN GOD

Let us hold unswervingly to the hope we profess, for he who promised is faithful.

~ Hebrews 10:23 ~

ꞇhere are times in our lives when everything looks hopeless and bleak. Circumstances develop in which you feel lost and your dreams are in shreds; hope has died and it feels as though nothing works out right for you. Under these circumstances we are greatly tempted to look for something or someone to blame. You can also succumb to the impulse to throw in the towel and stop hoping. This causes immeasurable damage to your mental and spiritual welfare. In this state of dejection, we become easy prey to the tempter whose main aim is to drive a wedge between our Heavenly Father and us. He usually acts when we are at our most vulnerable.

When you feel dejected, it is important to remember that Jesus has undertaken to be by your side throughout your life. He invites you to cast your problems upon Him and to trust in Him when in distress. That is why He came into this world. Study the Gospels and see how compassionate and loving He was towards people, and draw hope and comfort from that. If you open your heart and life to the Holy Spirit, He will be by your side and guide you onto the path of God. You will know that you are guided by the hand of God and that you can overcome all adversity.

Thank You, Lord Jesus, that even when I feel dejected, You are always by my side. Lift me from the deep well of dejection and let me sing a song of praise once more. Amen.

Hebrews 10:11-25

"Come with me by yourselves to a quiet place and get some rest."

~ MARK 6:31 ~

There are people who fail in their Christianity because they try to find a substitute for the time that they have to spend alone with God. They could even be extremely busy working for God and pride themselves in their humanity and their ability to help the less privileged. They will become involved with any good cause, rather than be alone with God behind a closed door spending time at His feet.

People find that being alone with God can be a disturbing experience. You become aware of your weaknesses and imperfections and see only a condemning Father. It is a Scriptural fact that God is a Just Judge. In your quiet time alone with Him, you not only discover who you are, but also who you could become through His abiding Presence known in solitude. God is the Great Inspirer and to meet Him in quiet is to triumph over your self-centeredness, spiritual failures and defeats.

If you want to live a life of triumph through Jesus Christ, you will have to learn to become quiet in the presence of God and allow His Holy Spirit to bring serenity to your mind and spirit. Then you become receptive to His will for your life. In the bustling time of Advent it is a matter of urgency to be alone with God.

It is wonderful to seclude myself and to be quiet with You in these busy times, my Lord and my God. Amen.

Mark 6:30-34

ALLAY ANXIETY

Therefore do not worry about tomorrow, for tomorrow will worry about itself. Each day has enough trouble of its own.

~ MATTHEW 6:34 ~

*P*erhaps you are one of those unfortunate people who always walks around with anxiety in your heart. Perhaps life is making tremendously high demands on you; responsibilities are ever-increasing and you lose the ability to prioritize. And then it seems as though the hope in your heart is dying. It is in such chaotic conditions that anxiety takes root and flourishes. Anxiety is the product of a confused mind and an inadequate faith.

One way of overcoming anxiety is to determine its cause. For many people, their anxiety is vague and indefinable, but it continues to erode their spirit and their mind, with disastrous consequences. Take hold of your anxiety by writing it down, clearly and simply. Look at it calmly, pray about it, and put it in the right perspective in relation to your whole life. Affirm with conviction that, through Jesus Christ, you are master of the situation and that anxiety is no longer going to bedevil your calm approach to life.

If you do this creative deed today, you will prevent your anxiety from spilling over into tomorrow. The secret is to affirm your intentions in prayer. Christ must become a greater reality to you than your anxiety: He has the ability to transform your life into a feast – today and forever.

Holy Spirit of God, help me not to be anxious about tomorrow, because You have every day in Your eternal and loving hands. Amen.

Matthew 6:25-34

ℰXPERIENCE THE FULLNESS OF CHRIST

For God was pleased to have all his fullness dwell in him, and through him to reconcile to himself all things.

~ COLOSSIANS 1:19-20 ~

According to the doctrines of the Bible, it is not sufficient to maintain that Jesus was "a good person". That this is so, is an irrefutable fact, accepted by all who have made a thorough study of His life. But He was more than "good": He was the personification of perfection. Paul attempts to define the person of Christ by saying that *"God was pleased to have all His fullness dwell in Him"*.

This breathtaking truth is so overwhelming that we could hesitate to approach the Lord. But, if He is your Savior, there is no barrier that can separate you from Him. Then John 10:10 becomes true in your life: *"... I have come that they may have life, and have it to the full."* Then life becomes filled with fullness and festivity, like the Christmas season!

As food for Advent, read Ephesians 3:17-18 again on this day.

So that Christ may dwell in your hearts through faith. And I pray that you, being rooted and established in love, may have power, together with all the saints, to grasp how wide and long and high and deep is the love of Christ ...

How privileged we are, as His children, to be part of this festival of love.

I praise and glorify You, oh Child of Bethlehem, that, through faith, You want to abide in my heart as well. Make it a worthy abode. Amen.

Colossians 1:15-20

"In the desert prepare the way for the LORD, make straight in the wilderness a highway for our God."

~ ISAIAH 40:3 ~

At the time of the birth of Christ, the world was unprepared for His coming and the people were not ready to receive Him. This has been the case throughout history. Centuries before the birth of Christ, through the prophet Isaiah, God had warned mankind to prepare for the greatest event in the history of mankind. The unpreparedness of the world was noticeable in the way in which the Christ Child was born in a stable, because there was no room for Him. The way in which He was rejected in later years, because people could not find room for Him in their hearts. It was only after His rejection on the cross that people realized the sin and foolishness of turning their backs on the fountain of life.

Once again, God grants us the privilege to experience Advent, as we prepare for Christmas. As tradition has developed over the years, much emphasis will be placed on merriment and this time will be filled with a panicky haste in the business world. In the midst of the excitement of the season, we must not forget about the central Figure of the Feast: God who became man in Jesus Christ. Make time to prepare yourself spiritually for the celebration of the birth of Jesus of Bethlehem, who brought light and love, God's gifts to a dark and loveless world. Prepare yourself to receive Christ anew in your life and experience in this way the full meaning of the Feast of Christ: Emmanuel! God with us!

Prepare me for the great feast of Your birth, but also for Your second coming. Let me experience the true meaning of Emmanuel. Amen.

Isaiah 40:1-11

ᗫIVINITY IN THE SIMPLICITY OF A BABY

Jesus was born in Bethlehem in Judea, during the time of King Herod.
~ MATTHEW 2:1 ~

ᗩhis simple text reveals a breathtaking truth: the Eternal God came into history to the benefit of mankind. For generations people had waited for the coming of the Messiah and, in their expectations, they had created images of what He would look like when He eventually appeared. The splendor of an Eastern palace would have paled before His glory. So the people then waited with great expectation in their hearts for a splendid revelation of the Divine arrival.

A baby was born in Bethlehem, but only a few wise men and a group of shepherds beheld the miracle of the Christ Child in the manger. Their thoughts and views regarding the arrival of the Christ Child were not limited to the popular concept of all the trimmings that are usually associated with kingship, because they believed God's promise of the coming Messiah. They looked past the obvious and saw Deity in the simplicity of a Baby.

Many sincere Christians are looking for a revelation of the Holy Father in that which is breathtaking and wondrous. It is unwise to base a faith on the miraculous, because it is an unreliable foundation. True faith is founded on Christ and who He is, not necessarily on what He does. God works in silence and it is only when we reflect upon it, that we realize that God was at work in this event.

Holy Child Jesus, thank You that You always reveal Yourself unexpectedly to those who believe in You. Strengthen my faith in these days. Amen.

Matthew 2:1-12

⊘HE GLORY OF GOD

The Word became flesh and made his dwelling among us. We have seen his glory, the glory of the One and Only, who came from the Father, full of grace and truth.

~ JOHN 1:14 ~

W hile preparations to celebrate Christmas are in full swing across the whole word, we are reminded of the fact that Jesus took on the form of man. Through this, God revealed the highest meaning of love to mankind. In a cruel world, where there was so little compassion, so much indifference and contempt for human rights and truth, God realized that the only way to bring His message to mankind was by doing it personally. The Son of God was thus born and came to live amongst us.

The world in which we live desperately needs love, compassion and caring. There is overwhelming evidence of violence, lack of involvement, cases of unconcealed cruelty. In many areas moral standards have declined, with the result that there is a fierce battle for survival, while people show little respect for Christian principles.

In this time of Advent, you have the opportunity to help and restore love, peace and stability in an unsettled world. You may wonder what you could do, but in the power of the Holy Spirit you can reflect the glory of God by allowing His love to flow through you, helping to lighten the burden of others. Do this and you will know the true meaning of Christmas.

Incarnate Word, help me to spread love, caring and compassion, such as You demonstrated to me. Amen.

John 1:1-18

FIND GOD IN ORDINARY THINGS

"This will be a sign to you: You will find a baby wrapped in cloths and lying in a manger."

~ LUKE 2:12 ~

There are many modern-day disciples of the Master who have to journey through the wilderness in their spiritual pilgrimage. There are those who experience moments when God appears to be distant and they lament the fact that their lives have become empty and that they have lost contact with God. Regardless of all their efforts through worship, meditation, Bible study and prayer, they still suffer from spiritual frustration and disappointment where they find themselves in a spiritual wasteland.

While you reflect upon the events surrounding the birth of Christ, think of the following: who would ever have thought that the Son of God, the long-expected Messiah, would come into the world in the form of a baby, from a working-class family, in a humble stable? But God took on the simplest and most humble form to come and live amongst men.

Circumstances today are not any different. You will find God in ordinary things: a friendly smile; a deed of love; a comforting gesture. Where a need is filled with love, you can rest assured that God will be present. Seek the Christ of Bethlehem in the circumstances surrounding you and you will without a doubt find Him.

Lord my God, help me to find You in ordinary, everyday things. May I find Jesus in the things that surround me day after day. Amen.

Luke 2:8-20

◯HE BLESSING OF GRATITUDE

Always give thanks to God the Father for everything, in the name of our Lord Jesus Christ.

~ EPHESIANS 5:20 ~

ℐn the hustle and bustle of everyday life, it is so easy to forget about ordinary courtesy. During Advent, we are very busy and involved in many things; people do nice things for us; shop assistants serve us with courtesy and a smile. But, because people are being paid for the service that they render, we forget that a word of appreciation could change their routine into a blessing.

The habit of saying "Thank you" undoubtedly enriches every aspect of our lives. It costs nothing, but creates so much joy for both the giver and the receiver. If you doubt this statement, just be on the lookout for those opportunities where courtesy and friendliness are shown towards you. Do you accept it as self-evident? Always be ready to express thanks. If this were to become your general attitude, you will discover how much joy you can bring to others. Apart from the fact that you enrich and bless the lives of others, your own life will be enriched. The power of gratitude must never be underestimated.

If this is true on an ordinary human level, how much more effective would it be if we were to express gratitude towards our Heavenly Father. All that we have, He gave to us, and we so seldom say thank You to Him. When we indeed do it, our spirit is set free and we experience a joy and blessing that could only come from God. When you thank God in these days for His immeasurable love and all His blessings, you will experience true festive joy.

Give me a grateful heart, oh God, for all the wondrous things that You have done for us, but above all, for the birth of Jesus, our Savior. Amen.

Ephesians 5:6-20

ℰMMANUEL! GOD IS WITH US!

I rejoice in your promise like one who finds great spoil.
~ PSALM 119:162 ~

When the outlook is bleak, people become disheartened. Especially in the uncertain times in which we live. The world is experiencing major problems and difficulties, and this causes people to be scared, anxious and uncertain. This creates a feeling of instability that could have far-reaching consequences for your emotional, mental and physical welfare. Some people fight the good fight to remove obstacles in their own strength, but to no avail. Others fold and crack under the burden.

One of the great joys of the Christian faith is the assurance given to us by God Himself: He is with us. Jesus confirmed this by promising that He would be with us till the end. He will not forsake us, and never fail us. Such a gracious assurance from the almighty God Himself must undoubtedly fill you with new hope. Jesus triumphed over the worst of what man and life could do to Him, and now the triumphant Christ gives you His promise that He will be with you in every situation and under all circumstances in life.

In order to enable you to deal with life under difficult circumstances, it is vital that you will invite Christ to take control of your life. Subject yourself to His Sovereignty and faithfully follow His commands. Be sensitive to the guidance of the Holy Spirit, who will transform your despair into hope, your depression into a Christmas celebration!

Emmanuel – God with us! Let it be the motto of my life throughout the year. Thank You that You are always with us in Christ! Amen.

Psalm 119:161-176

ℱEAST OF CHRIST!

Today in the town of David a Savior has been born to you; he is Christ the Lord.

~ LUKE 2:11 ~

ℱor all who are tired and burdened; all who are despairing and aggrieved and under the shadow of sorrow and pain; all who are trapped in sin and unrighteousness; all who find neither joy nor faith in life ...

For all who are victims of injustice and oppression; all who have been hurt and seek revenge; all who fear death and hate life; all whose children have abandoned them and who mourn throughout the night but can find no peace ...

For all who build in vain and labor in futility and who find no satisfaction, no meaning in any of it; all who will die tomorrow or the next day and who are calling but to no avail, seeking an answer from men ...

For all who are without friends, without a home; all who hate and who experience hatred, jealousy and blind anger; for all who are without love because they have never known true love ...

To you a Savior has been born today! He will heal your wounds in love and grace; He will touch your unseeing eyes with tenderness so that you may see; He will take away your hatred, pain and sorrow, and will console you gently. He is coming to you: Incarnate Word. He is coming to you in love and grace, great beyond description. All He asks of you is to embrace Him, love Him and follow Him faithfully. That is the Feast of Christ!

Holy God, we praise and thank You for Your visit to us, Your children, through Jesus Christ. Grant that it may be a blessed visit. Amen.

Luke 2:8-20

The shepherds returned, glorifying and praising God for all the things they had heard and seen.

~ LUKE 2:20 ~

The festivities are over: the wilted festive tree is out the backdoor; the glossy paper is crumpled; party hats lie neglected in a corner; the decorations and balloons look pitiful as they flap in the breeze. The excitement and joy that most people associate with Christmas, are now something of the past and everybody returns to the everyday routine of life.

But this should not be the case! The joyous event that we celebrate on Christ's birthday does not begin and end there. This event symbolizes the unfathomable love of God for His children, not only with the birth of Christ, but to eternity. The Christ Child in the stable of Bethlehem is the Savior of the world. Through His Holy Spirit He offers you true life. He wants to guide you in love on His path of righteousness every hour of the day.

Certainly, Christmas is a day of exuberant celebrations when we attempt to thank God for the gift of His Son. Notwithstanding, today and every day should be reason enough for you to praise and thank God for the presence of the living Christ who is with you, every day of your life.

We praise and thank You, Lord Jesus, for yet another Christmas. May every day of our lives be a Feast of Christ. Amen.

Luke 2:8-20

CHEERFUL GIVERS

God loves a cheerful giver.

~ 2 CORINTHIANS 9:7 ~

As God gave us the great gift of His Son, we give each other gifts during these days. A gift that is given with reluctance infinitely reduces the value of the gift. When given freely and with joy, it increases and elevates the value of the gift. It is the duty and privilege of every Christian to be a giver. When the Holy Spirit of the living Christ flows through you, He teaches you to love and withhold nothing that will bless and enrich your neighbor. Your purpose in life is to be a blessing to others.

Let your gift always be accompanied by a prayer of thanksgiving and a desire that God will bless the gift, and then thank Him that you are able to give. However, giving money or possessions is not the most important gift that you can offer. God has equipped you with a personality and, as a Christian, you must do your very best to develop it to His glory and to the service of others. To show the world a cheerful personality, in the Name of Jesus, is to be like a ray of light that breaks through a dark bank of clouds. The world urgently needs sincere, cheerful Christians. That is something that every Christian can offer their fellow men – regardless of their financial position or social standing.

Irrespective of the form your gift may take, do not calculate whether you will profit from it. If this is the case, then your gift is no longer a gift, but an investment that places the receiver under an obligation to you. God gives freely, without any obligations, and you and I should do the same.

You gave us Your Son, oh Father. Grant that we will give ourselves unconditionally to You. Amen.

2 Corinthians 9:1-15

Are you seeking the Lord?

"If only I knew where to find him; if only I could go to his dwelling! I would state my case before him and fill my mouth with arguments."
~ Job 23:3-4 ~

Throughout the Christian world today we find people who are seeking the Lord so that they could get to know Him better. You find them in care groups, revival campaigns, seminars, study groups, and those who meditate in solitude. Their desire for God is so great that they strive endlessly to find Him.

Many such people maintain that they have a relationship with God that originates from a dramatic form of worship where emotions reach a high and where much emphasis is placed on excitement. Others again, maintain that they have found Him in the solitude of meditation.

If you truly want to find Christ, look at the world around you – where you live and work. When you help a beggar, or show compassion to somebody in distress, where you offer friendship to the lonely, when you dedicate your time to converse with the aged or to play with young people, when you visit the sick and console the mournful, where you attempt to comfort the dispirited. If you do any of these things and be of service to your fellow man: look deep into the eyes of the person that you minister to and there you will find Jesus who said, "' ... *Whatever you did for one of the least of these brothers of mine, you did for me'*" (Mt. 25:40).

Lord God, let me find You in the world around me and amongst the people who need me. Amen.

Job 23:1-12

DEAL WITH YOUR FEELINGS OF GUILT

You crown the year with your bounty, and your carts overflow with abundance.

~ PSALM 65:12 ~

W e are inclined to think that, because the year is almost over, its hold on our lives has lessened. The discouragement, failures and frustration suddenly do not seem so formidable when we look in expectation to the new year. The coming days are vivid with promises waiting to be fulfilled. In spite of that, however, the influence of the past is still with us. The habits that we acquired during the past year will still be part of our personality and they will become an integral part of our character in the year to come. Regardless of how noble our hopes for the coming year may be, we basically remain that which we have been over the past year and no amount of wishful thinking can change this truth.

It could be discouraging were it not for the fact that Jesus demonstrated to His disciples how to deal with the past. In reviewing the past year under the guidance of the Holy Spirit, you will see the dark valleys of disappointment and dejection, but also the summits of inspiration. You can learn from both these experiences.

When you have evaluated the past year, rejoice in it and find further inspiration in everything that is Christian, true and noble. When the ghosts of your failures and sins torment you, ask God's forgiveness for the times when you were disobedient to Him. And know that, because you have asked, He *will* forgive you through Jesus' sacrifice of atonement. Then you must forgive yourself and not enter the new year with feelings of guilt. Do not allow thoughts of the past to cast a shadow over the beauty and happiness of the present and the future.

Holy Spirit of God, let me review the past year with equilibrium, and let me take the good from it and build on it in the new year. Amen.

Psalm 65:1-14

So do not fear, for I am with you; do not be dismayed, for I am your God. I will strengthen you and help you, I will uphold you with my righteous right hand.

~ Isaiah 41:10 ~

When the year draws to a close, there is always the temptation to look back. Unfortunately, for many people this means concentrating on failures, disappointments and other setbacks. This causes them to face the future with fear and hesitation.

Meditating on the past definitely has its place in your life, but it must be done constructively. You should develop the ability to learn from your mistakes, without groaning under their burden when you open up feelings of guilt. Similarly, when you think about the successes of the past, it is no excuse to rest on your laurels. It should serve as inspiration to take you to greater heights.

After you have reviewed the events of the past year, it is essential for you to decide to meet the new year in the intimate company of the living Christ. Allow Him to be your Counselor and Guide. Let your mind be sensitive to the whisperings of the Holy Spirit and resolve to be unconditionally obedient to Him.

In so doing, you can rest assured that, regardless of what happens in your life, you can face the future with confidence, assured of the peace that comes from God alone.

Eternal God, thank You for the assurance at the end of this year, that You are always with us and that You will hold us in Your hand. Amen.

Isaiah 41:1-12

GOD IS ALWAYS THERE FOR YOU

"And surely I am with you always, to the very end of the age."

~ MATTHEW 28:20 ~

The availability of God, through the living Christ, to all who need Him, is one of the fundamental truths of the Gospel. Even so, many people struggle to enter His presence. Some spend anxious moments in prayer trying to achieve this objective.

The Scriptural truth is that the Lord is right where you are. He is with you in your efforts to get to know Him and in your struggle to break through your doubts and uncertainties to the realization of His holy presence. It seems as though He says to you, "Stop struggling with your self-created fear and doubt and come to Me. I am with you wherever you may be; even in your moments of doubt."

Christian disciples know that to accept such a gracious invitation, means discarding the besetting sins that have become part of their daily lifestyle. They want to enjoy the presence of the Savior, but on their own terms. This can never happen, because to experience and enjoy His presence, you must subject yourself to His commands.

Embracing the living Savior as your Savior and Redeemer is the foundation of your Christian experience. It is the basis of your faith and, without it, you will never experience His presence in your life. With Jesus, you also embrace the Holy Spirit, and in so doing, you become aware of His presence from day to joyous day. Praise the Lord, as He is Good! His love is infinite!

May Christ and the Holy Spirit abide in me. Praise the Lord, for He is good! Amen.

Matthew 28:16-20

ᴛEXT REGISTER

$\mathcal{T}$HEMATIC INDEX

HEALING
28 Apr

HEARING GOD
7 Jan

HOPE
24 Aug; 15 Nov; 4 Dec; 9 Dec; 24 Dec; 29 Dec

HUMBLENESS
4 May; 3 Jul; 12 Jul; 13 Jul; 14 Jul; 15 Jul; 30 Oct; 6 Nov

INTERCESSION
16 Apr; 22 Apr

INTIMACY WITH GOD
17 Feb; 27 Feb; 26 Apr; 27 Apr; 27 May; 12 Jun; 20 Jun; 23 Jun; 3 Sept; 4 Sept; 25 Sept; 24 Nov; 16 Dec; 30 Dec

JOY
19 Feb; 2 Jul; 15 Aug; 30 Aug

JUDGMENT
5 May; 23 Oct

KINDNESS
9 May; 3 Nov

LEADERSHIP
30 May

LIFE'S CALLING
3 May

LONELINESS
17 May

LOVE
3 Jan; 19 Jan; 10 Feb; 25 Mar; 2 May; 14 Jun; 28 Jun; 20 Sept; 24 Sept; 10 Oct; 19 Oct; 1 Nov; 5 Nov; 8 Nov; 17 Nov; 19 Nov; 22 Nov; 23 Nov; 25 Nov; 27 Nov; 28 Nov

MERCY
18 Jul; 19 Jul

OBEDIENCE
8 Sept

OPPORTUNITIES
5 Jan

OVERCOMING DIFFICULTY
18 Jun

PATIENCE
9 Jan; 8 Apr; 23 Apr; 2 Nov

PEACE

10 Apr; 11 May; 23 Jul; 24 Jul; 13 Aug; 2 Dec; 12 Dec

PERSEVERANCE

24 Apr; 6 May; 6 Aug; 12 Oct; 16 Nov

PRAISE

7 Mar

PRAYER

2 Jan; 8 Jan; 25 Jan; 2 Feb; 14 Feb; 23 Feb; 28 Feb; 1 Apr; 2 Apr; 3 Apr; 4 Apr; 7 Apr; 9 Apr; 11 Apr; 12 Apr; 13 Apr; 14 Apr; 17 Apr; 18 Apr; 20 Apr; 21 Apr; 29 Apr; 30 Apr; 24 May; 22 Oct

PROTECTION

22 Aug; 20 Nov

PURITY

20 Jul; 21 Jul; 22 Jul

PURPOSE

12 Sept; 16 Sept; 22 Sept

REFRESHING

4 Jun; 22 Jun.

RESPONSIBILITY

16 Jun

RESURRECTION

2 Jun

SACRIFICE

6 Mar; 8 Mar; 9 Mar

SALVATION

15 Jan; 3 Mar; 5 Mar; 14 Mar; 15 Mar; 16 Mar; 20 Mar; 21 Mar; 28 Mar; 18 Sept; 1 Dec

SEEKING GOD

4 Jul

SERVING GOD

25 Jun; 26 Jun; 29 Sept; 13 Oct; 28 Dec

SERVING OTHERS

5 Oct; 6 Oct; 7 Oct; 8 Oct; 11 Oct; 17 Oct; 26 Oct; 21 Nov; 29 Nov

SILENCE

12 Mar; 13 Mar

SIN

10 Jul; 11 Nov

SORROW

6 Jul; 7 Jul; 8 Jul; 9 Jul